"What an excellent boo[k] _____ *as a Pastor's Wife* is so t___ _____ _____, _____ _____ con-sideration to the many challenges pastors' wives face in their unique roles. You won't find cliches or pat answers here! It is theologically sound and spiritually mature while also being very practical. Thank you, Christine, for this gift to ministry wives!"

Susie Hawkins, wife of O. S. Hawkins and author of
From One Ministry Wife to Another

"I read this book on a Saturday, between preparations for all my 'pastor's wife' responsibilities on Sunday morning. Oh, how this book kept me joyful and true as I was being tempted by pressures to perform. Christine Hoover's wise and compassionate voice speaks into the lies in which I am often entangled and shows me a way out of the deadly labyrinth of self-trust. Her words must have come at a great cost. Her counsel is not some general encouragement but points to specific, blood-bought promises of God, written in the ink and tears of a pastor's wife who knows."

Irene Sun, author of the picture books *Taste and See: All About
God's Goodness* and *God Counts: Numbers
in His Word and His World*

"In *How to Thrive as a Pastor's Wife*, Christine Hoover lovingly frees us from the trap of trying to live up to a title. She understands our specific calling as pastors' wives and speaks directly to our significant role in kingdom work. She writes with authentic vulnerability about the distinctive temptations faced in ministry marriages—from bitterness to blaming to burnout—always pointing back to our kind King who will faithfully provide for each of our needs. Read her biblical advice and, for the sake of our marriages and ministries, learn to thrive as pastor wives!"

Jani Ortlund, executive vice president of Renewal Ministries

"The role of pastor's wife can seem lonely and enigmatic. We are not all alike, but we are all hoping to fulfill a similar calling. Christine writes as one who has been there and is still there. From my tendency toward the savior complex to the complexity of parenting pastor's kids, I found kinship, courage, and wisdom in her words. I encourage every pastor's wife to read this book."

Lauren Chandler, pastor's wife, author, and worship leader

"Christine helps us navigate the complex role to which we have been called. I, too, am not the 'typical' pastor's wife and never fit the stereotype. She is the friend I wish I had in my early years to help me avoid unhealthy pitfalls and embrace the unique gifts God gave me to serve the body of Christ out of joy and passion instead of duty. Let this book from a seasoned pastor's wife encourage you as she gives words to your insecurities and struggles and guides you through to full engagement with God's Word and purpose. In Christ, you are uniquely gifted and equipped—embrace the call, celebrate the privilege!"

Donna Gaines, pastor's wife, author, and Bible teacher

"Christine Hoover is a rich, trusted source for any pastor's wife. Whatever she writes on the subject should be read. Her words are honest, vulnerable, and imminently helpful. She speaks to the most critically important compartments of our worlds with a freeing reality and helpful life-giving truth. This book will generously nourish the soul of any pastor's wife. Don't miss it!"

Kathy Litton, pastor's wife and director of Planter Spouse Development at the North American Mission Board

"Christine Hoover honestly and effectively voices the challenges and rewards of life as a pastor's wife. Her vulnerability and grace will encourage your heart, while her practical wisdom offers guidance to navigate the unique challenges pastors' wives face. Whether you've been living the ministry wife life for minutes or decades, this is a must-read, reference, and keep resource."

Heather Creekmore, pastor's wife, podcast host, and author of *Compared to Who?* and *The Burden of Better*

"As a pastor's wife of over twelve years, I found Christine's book to be an intricate mosaic capturing the beauty, pain, and tension of being a pastor's wife all in one place. Like an intimate chat in the home of a seasoned pastor's wife—honest, vulnerable, and deeply encouraging—*How to Thrive as a Pastor's Wife* paints an authentic picture of what it looks like to not just survive but truly thrive in this beautiful calling."

Amber Williams, pastor's wife, Sojourn Church
Midtown, Louisville, KY

"Christine Hoover has given pastors' wives a true gift in *How to Thrive as a Pastor's Wife*. She explores our place in ministry, faithfully reminding us of our identity as believers in Jesus first and foremost. She helps us see how to guard our marriages and families practically while still serving Christ in our local churches. This was the book I needed twenty years ago, and I commend it to pastors' wives everywhere."

Glenna Marshall, pastor's wife and author of *The Promise is His Presence* and *Everyday Faithfulness*

"*How to Thrive as a Pastor's Wife* is a welcome compass for navigating church ministry and a beautiful offering for the sisterhood of pastors' wives who gracefully serve Christ's precious body. Even after twenty-six years of leadership, I soaked up this reminder from Christine that my role is the gift by which I serve the church, but 'pastor's wife' is not my identity. Through seasons filled with growth, harmony, and great joy and seasons of heartache, disappointment, and discouragement when people mischaracterize your church and leave, she lovingly calls us to rhythms of rest and renewal with the God who sees and knows us, and she helps us move untangled by performance and free to flourish in our uniqueness."

Dorena Williamson, first lady of Strong Tower Bible Church, bridgebuilder, and bestselling author of *ColorFull* and *The Celebration Place*

"The pains and pressures of ministry can be daunting for a pastor's wife. Expectations from yourself and others can feel inescapable. But what matters most is this: What does Jesus want from you? In *How to Thrive as a Pastor's Wife*, Christine Hoover serves as a trusted friend to help sisters steward their unique calling. Whether you've always dreamed of being a pastor's wife or never expected to be one, I trust this resource will help you faithfully walk on the path Jesus has called you to."

Garrett Kell, pastor of Del Ray Baptist Church and author of *Pure in Heart: Sexual Sin and the Promises of God*

How to THRIVE AS A PASTOR'S WIFE

Practical Tools to Embrace Your Influence
and Navigate Your Unique Role

CHRISTINE HOOVER

BakerBooks
a division of Baker Publishing Group
Grand Rapids, Michigan

© 2022 by Christine Hoover

Published by Baker Books
a division of Baker Publishing Group
PO Box 6287, Grand Rapids, MI 49516-6287
www.bakerbooks.com

Printed in the United States of America

Library of Congress Cataloging-in-Publication Data
Names: Hoover, Christine, author.
Title: How to thrive as a pastor's wife : practical tools to embrace your influence and navigate your unique role / Christine Hoover.
Description: Grand Rapids, MI : Baker Books, a division of Baker Publishing Group, [2022]
Identifiers: LCCN 2021035425 | ISBN 9780801094491 (paperback) | ISBN 9781540902016 (casebound) | ISBN 9781493434039 (ebook)
Subjects: LCSH: Spouses of clergy.
Classification: LCC BV4395 .H57 2022 | DDC 253/.22—dc23
LC record available at https://lccn.loc.gov/2021035425

The author is represented by the literary agency of Wolgemuth & Associates, Inc.

Baker Publishing Group publications use paper produced from sustainable forestry practices and post-consumer waste whenever possible.

22   23   24   25   26   27   28   7   6   5   4   3   2

To my colaborers in the gospel,
women in ministry all across the globe.

Contents

Dear Pastor's Wife

My husband, Kyle, accepted his first church staff position within our first year of marriage. Having sensed since high school that I was called to vocational ministry, I wholeheartedly linked arms with my husband in this new adventure and, with great anticipation for the days ahead, packed the moving boxes.

We'd be moving three hours south from our tiny seminary house and joining the team of the church we'd attended in college—a large church led by a pastor whose preaching had transformed the way we viewed Scripture. Kyle would be tasked with leading the very university ministry we'd loved in our halcyon college days. It was a dream job and would be our first taste together of all that vocational ministry entails.

Together is an intentional word, because you and I both know just how much of a team sport ministry is. When I speak of Kyle's work to church members, I catch and correct myself when I use *we* or *our*—"When *we* were on staff at that church"—because it's not officially my job, and I also want to seize a small teaching moment, drawing for them a delineation between Kyle and me. *This is not my job. This is his job.*

And yet, we are one; his calling spills over onto me and mine onto him. For this I'm thankful, even if it confounds me at times, for we share in a unique calling that carries with it significant meaning and eternal impact.

These are things I learned later, however, long after those boxes were unpacked, when the brightness of our new adventure wore off, and I realized I didn't have a clue what I was doing as a pastor's wife.

We moved into a rental house in that college town a week before our first anniversary, and, because of my instant uncertainty, I was relieved and excited to learn that another of the church's staff members and his family lived down the street from us. He and his wife had years of ministry experience under their belts, so I was eager to learn from her. Certain she was aware of my need, I waited for her to come down the street and check on me. I waited and waited, and one day, to my great delight, she showed up at the door to say hello. We sat on my couch, nervousness emanating from my end, and engaged in small talk. I specifically remember that neither of us sank into the cushions of the couch but rather we remained at the edge, formal with one another.

I waited for her to broach deeper topics, but she never did. And while many pressing questions about ministry were burning in my mind and heart, *I did not ask her a single one.* Looking back, I see that I'd already taken on the posture of self-protection that has never served me well in ministry. I'd also taken on the equally unhelpful posture of waiting on others to go first rather than initiating and asking for help. So, after some small talk, she left, and, not long after, she and her family moved away from our church and our street.

As soon as I closed the door behind her, I regretted all that I had not asked. *How do you support your husband when he's discouraged? How do you and your husband draw relational boundaries? How do you know what God wants you to be involved in within the church? Why do some women stop talking when I come near? Will I ever find friends? How do you kill the sins of resentment, pride, and the desire for self-glory? How do you forgive hurts that no one else sees or knows about? And who can I talk to about all of these things?*

What had held me back? I didn't ask because I believed I was the only pastor's wife at our church (and quite possibly everywhere) who didn't know what she was doing, and I couldn't admit my insecurities.

From Where I Write

Kyle and I spent almost eight years in that church—a large, multi-staff and multi-ministry church in the American Bible Belt. He led the college ministry and eventually took on missions as well. We grew in marriage, expanded our family through the births of our three boys, and internalized ministry lessons we learned both through trial and error and through the example of other pastors (and their spouses) on staff.

Around the time our third baby was born, God put an inescapable and holy discontent in our hearts. We sensed he was calling us to something beyond college and missions and, after much prayer and seeking wise counsel, the holy discontent finally subsided into peace when we alighted on the idea that God was calling us to plant a church.

Six months later, we moved into a new home in a small city I hadn't known existed a year prior: Charlottesville, Virginia. This new place was liberal leaning, intellectually driven, and just outside the Bible Belt, and we found ourselves facing newfound ministry challenges. For one, we didn't know a soul, so there was that. But also we were church planting, which we quickly discovered was a totally different creature than serving at an established church.

We started our church with ten people in our living room, five of whom carried the Hoover last name. I spent the entire first gathering chasing a crawling baby and keeping a toddler and preschooler snacked and entertained while my husband taught from Philippians. I missed most of the teaching time because I was off wiping bottoms in the bathroom.

There were tears—the first of many to come—when the five non-Hoovers left. And there were new questions and uncertainties nagging at me. *How am I supposed to manage all of this? How will I engage people when I'm always wrangling my kids in a different room? How do I help my husband take breaks from the constant demands of ministry? What do I do with my own spiritual and emotional needs when I'm always pouring out for others? How can I ensure my kids grow up to love God and his church? Will ministry always be this exhausting? Am I going to make it?*

I thought I'd left all my questions, insecurities, and uncertainties behind me at our previous church, but this new ministry opportunity opened up many more that serving in an established church had never revealed.

I write this from Charlottesville, over a decade removed from those first Bible studies in our living room. God grew our church slowly but surely, one relationship at a time. We've since added elders and a few staff members. I've had my hands in literally every ministry of the church except men's ministry. And we've raised our boys—now teenagers—as pastor's kids within this faith family we've planted.

In other words, we've made it this far, and only by the grace of God. Although the tint of church planting remains—our church meets in an elementary school gym—God has established us in this community we've grown to call home.

I tell you this, dear pastor's wife, to give my writing context for you. As you read, you may find I don't completely understand your context for ministry. Aside from short-term trips, we've never served outside of the United States. My husband has not been bivocational, and we've not lived in an urban center. However, although we've served in both large churches and small, inside and outside the American Bible Belt, in both church and parachurch settings (in our first year of marriage, my husband led a parachurch ministry), and in both established churches and a church plant, my experience and context are not ultimately what I rely on as I offer you these pages. "For what [I] proclaim is not [myself], but Jesus Christ as Lord, with [myself] as your [servant] for Jesus' sake" (2 Cor. 4:5).

In other words, I've written this book to you as that veteran pastor's wife, purposefully coming down the street to see you, sinking into the cushions on the other end of your couch, and digging deeply with you into the challenges we all face at some point in our ministry. Those insecurities and uncertainties you have? You're not the only one.

Imagine my demeanor with you like this as you read my words: I'm leaning forward, listening. I'm willing to hear and address the things you're afraid to say and ask because you think you should be further along by now. I'll tell you stories of my own foibles and fumbles and the tangled webs I've been caught up in, because I know exactly what it's like and can empathize with you. I'll be brutally honest about what's gone on in my heart, hoping you'll see yourself in me and, if needed, be pricked and poked by the Holy Spirit. I'll share some tips and tricks I've learned along the way that can be applied to any ministry context. And then, with urgent passion, I'll remind you of the ancient truths: God is with you, he loves you, he sees you, he is helping you, and he is worth pursuing and serving. There are challenges, yes, but there is also abundant joy and reward to be had living beside—and *being*—a minister of the gospel.

Envisioning Life as a Pastor's Wife

Throughout this book I'll use a landscape architect's drawing to illustrate life as a ministry wife in order to emphasize boundaries, relational proximity, and priorities. I'll explain in future chapters why, as a visual learner, this has become a valuable tool for me as I navigate life and make decisions regarding my time and relational energy. In fact, God gave me this picture at a time in my life when I felt hurt, overwhelmed, and unsure I could persevere in ministry. I'll invite you into my story in future chapters, but for now, I simply want to note that this is *my* visual picture for *my* life. Your life likely looks different from mine, as you may work full-time outside the home, have no children, have grandchildren scattered across the globe rather than children still in your nest, or perhaps may work for the church your husband pastors or work alongside him in parachurch ministry. I don't want you to follow my plan as you might a formula or a job description or condemn yourself (or me!) for having a different God-given context. Rather, think of this drawing as a tool you can edit according to your circumstances that may help you envision a properly ordered life and help you flourish as a pastor's wife.

What you'll notice in this visual aid is an emphasis on boundaries—delineations that preserve and help cultivate sacred relationships. You'll also notice an emphasis on distance. Some parts of our lives involve more intimacy, accessibility, accountability, and priority than others. When relationships are in their proper place, there is vitality, life, blessing, and thriving, and threats to our spiritual, emotional, and relational well-being are kept out.

God himself sets boundaries for his people. In Isaiah 5, through the prophet Isaiah, God tells his people how he planted them as a vineyard in a perfect location to produce choice grapes. To protect the vineyard and its fruitfulness, he surrounded his people with hedges and walls. But because they defied his borders, rotten grapes grew on the vines and God withdrew his protection, allowing them to become a decaying wasteland. This word picture of the trampled vineyard reminds us that boundaries enable us to remain within God's will and protection and to enjoy a fruitful ministry.

Dear pastor's wife, may you find *love* in my words. I love pastors' wives and have a passion for helping them thrive. I wholeheartedly believe you are one of the unsung heroes of the global church: often (but not always) serving behind the scenes in unseen ways, a buttress to your pastor-husband, a discipler of your children, a pillar in the community, and a passionate lover of both God and others.

May you also find *truth* in my words. Scripture doesn't offer ministry wives a job description, and this should come to us as great news. There is no mold we must fit into and no formula to which we must adhere, but, thankfully, all of Scripture speaks to this life we live—no matter our experience, age, context, or role. I take great delight in sharing with you what God has shown me in his Word that has carried me through the years and made my weary heart sing.

Finally, may my words also remind you that *you aren't alone*. In the global church, God's servants are abundant and are steadily plowing, planting, and reaping. You, I, and the many women like us are counted among them.

> Therefore, since we are surrounded by so great a cloud of witnesses, let us also lay aside every weight, and sin which clings so closely, and let us run with endurance the race that is set before us, looking to Jesus, the founder and perfecter of our faith. (Heb. 12:1–2)

You are dear, dear pastor's wife.
Let's run on together.

PART 1

You

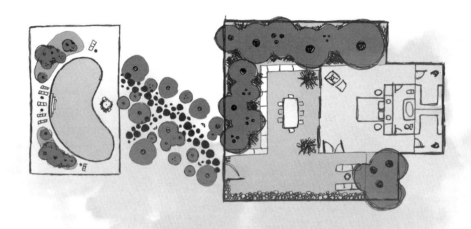

one

Locating You

Our wedding anniversary is March 11, 2000, so of course on March 11, 2020, my husband and I planned a nice evening out at our favorite restaurant in Charlottesville to celebrate twenty years of marriage. We were looking forward to a long-awaited (and long saved for) trip two months later, but we couldn't let the date itself go by without reflecting on our twenty years together.

Just before we left for dinner, my husband received a phone call: the school where our church meets on Sundays had temporarily closed its doors to both students and outsiders. Earlier that day, we'd marveled that March Madness and the NBA were canceling their games, that the local university had informed their students not to return from spring break—and now this too? All because of this strange new virus no one knew much about called COVID-19.

March 11, 2020—our wedding anniversary—was the day the world started shutting down, and it was also the day Kyle stepped into crisis leadership that we thought might last a few weeks but that, as of this writing a year later, continues even now. For most church congregations and ministries, the year 2020 mixed a perilous cocktail of a pandemic, racial strife and nationwide protests, a contentious political environment, and many financial and mental health needs among congregants. For everyone, but especially pastors, 2020 was a year unlike any other.

We didn't get to go on our anniversary trip in 2020, but in early 2021 we slipped away to a warm tropical location at what felt like God's perfect timing. In other words, we were running on fumes, Kyle was close to burnout after a year of crisis leadership, and, frankly, our marriage was suffering. For the few months prior to our trip, God had been bringing what was in our hearts to the surface, and it wasn't pretty.

But in some ways, I also felt vindicated, defended, and seen. I'd felt lost for a while, or rather as if I'd been in a snow globe and someone had been shaking it endlessly. I'd held hurts close to my chest. I'd sensed a loss of connection to others and to myself. It had seemed as if nothing in my life or in our marriage was in its proper and peaceful place but rather that we were running at top speed and getting nowhere.

In the ways God was working, however, I knew he saw me. I couldn't locate myself in the swirl, but he'd never lost me. Over and over, he reminded me that he was shepherding me and coaxed me to trust and follow him.

One of the areas I most felt lost was in relation to church and ministry. I knew my relationship to the church was off somehow, and I knew Kyle's relationship to his work was similarly off, so we spent endless hours on our trip dissecting what that "off" was and asking God to help us put the areas of our life together in their proper places.

The visual picture I'm sharing with you developed out of one of our conversations. Toward end of the trip, I told Kyle I was apprehensive about returning home, primarily because we'd had such a wonderful and restorative time away together—truly like a second honeymoon. I wasn't ready to return and share him with others.

When we had this conversation, we were sitting in a gated patio outside our room, a beautiful area complete with palm trees waving in the breeze, a hammock, an outdoor breakfast nook, and a tiny private pool. In other words, paradise. Outside the gate, a serpentine sidewalk surrounded by more palm trees and tropical plants led toward the resort's main pool and restaurant.

Attempting to explain my apprehension to Kyle, I pointed to the gate and said, "I feel as if returning home is like walking outside that gate together. The church staff, elders, and congregants are waiting for you just outside the gate with questions and needs, ready for your attention and time. I have your undivided attention on vacation, and then when we return home, we walk out that gate, and I wave goodbye and release you to everyone else."

That may have been how we'd done things previously, but we needed a new, healthier way of remaining *together* while also parenting, working, and fulfilling God's call on our life.

For both of us, the analogy of the gate and our surrounding environs was like a light bulb flickering on in a dark room. Using the layout of our cabana—a place of joy and restoration—we mapped out where things *should* be, moving forward, in order to protect proper boundaries, thrive in marriage, be engaged with our kids, and also be purposeful in ministry.

Like a mall directory, it was as if God said to me through the visual picture, "You are here." *I see you. I've got you. I have you where I want you. I'll lead you. You're not alone. There is a better way forward for you and Kyle together.*

God was asking me to release fear, self-agenda, and self-protection. He was identifying and locating me, whispering into my heart, *Let me remind you who you are.*

He took me back and reoriented me around the lessons I'd been learning all along, lessons I now share with you.

Two

You Are Anchored

oping to meet new people soon after we settled in Charlottesville, I volunteered for a women's committee at our local hospital and was required to attend a volunteer training meeting. New to the city and without a friend to my name, I headed into the meeting with eagerness and earnestness, ready to strike up a conversation with anyone who even glanced my way.

I sat down at a table next to a woman who also happened to be new to town, which gave us immediate common ground and fueled great conversation. We volleyed the usual questions back and forth: *How old are your kids? What do you do? Where are you from originally?*

In my mind, I'd already considered the potential outcome of this conversation: a new friend!

And then I asked it. As soon as the question fell off my lips, my stomach clinched with regret, because I knew she'd politely extend the same question back to me, and then we'd step together into dangerous territory.

"What does your husband do?"

She answered and then returned it, but slightly off-script: "What brought you to town?"

My mind went on high alert. How was I going to answer her question without losing my new friend? I wasn't ashamed of Christ, why we moved to Charlottesville, or that my husband was a pastor. I simply knew the answer would turn the conversation either really awesome or really awkward in a matter of seconds, and I wouldn't know which way it would go until I put it out there.

"My husband is a pastor."

(Pause.)

"We moved here to start a church."

(Pause.)

"In our living room."

(Extended pause.)

"Would you like to come?"

By the look on her face, she was apparently conjuring images in her mind of a group of misfits gathering in an eerily darkened room, possibly lit by candles, all of us drinking Kool-Aid and wearing weird clothing. Either that or she was replaying our conversation, trying to remember if she'd let loose any cuss words.

But all she said was a flat, "Oh."

I attempted to lightheartedly continue the conversation, but it was obviously over.

I wanted to say to her, "I'm not *that* kind of pastor's wife."

Almost every ministry wife I encounter repeats some version of this sentiment: *I'm not the typical pastor's wife.* I think what we're trying to convey is that we're not a stereotype or some sort of trophy, perfectly put together but having no ministry or mind of our own.

But the stereotype seems to loom largest in our own minds.

We each enter ministry with an idea of what it means to be a pastor's wife—what we should do and how we should act—and if we were to dissect each of our individual ideas, there'd be some variance, but I imagine we'd find most of them soaked in high standards and expectations we'd hoisted onto our own shoulders.

We bristle against the stereotype, certain God's not calling us to squeeze ourselves into some predetermined mold. But if not that, then what? What *does* it mean to be a pastor's wife?

How must we think of ourselves?

"Pastor's Wife" Is Not Your Identity

I spent many years trying to figure out who I am and what I'm to do as a pastor's wife. It was as if I had been handed some sort of heavy mantle when we entered ministry, and I couldn't figure out how to wear it properly. So I copied the women around me whom I admired: the pastor's wife at the church down the street, the pastor's wife at my childhood church, and my fellow ministry wives at the church where we served. I jumped into ministry spots and opportunities I thought I *should* be doing, and I said yes to everything and everyone who came my way. I also tried to appear very spiritual and have all the right answers, because isn't that what pastors' wives do?

In attempting to figure it all out, I finally realized I was trying to make "pastor's wife" my identity. I'd traded in "disciple" and "dependent child of God" and even "wife" and "friend" for a nebulous label of "pastor's wife." I spent years willing myself to rise to the challenge of the persona, unaware I'd been the very one who'd put the ill-fitting mantle on myself. The mantle felt outsized and unmanageable because it was not my true, God-given identity. "Pastor's wife" is a title, yes, but it's not an identity that defines who I am at the very core of my being.

And it's not yours, either.

In saying this, I'm not trying to throw off a role God has given me, and I'm not trying to incite your defensiveness or apathy. I embrace and enjoy being a pastor's wife. Being married to a minister is an honor, sanctification on steroids, and a rewarding opportunity to love God by loving others, *but it's not an identity by which I can live.* It's simply the *means* by which I can serve others.

In fact, I've discovered over the years that thinking of myself first as the pastor's wife, rather than seeing it as the means or opportunity by which I can serve, actually holds temptations that have tripped me up, caused me to sin, and inflicted pain on myself and others. There is overwhelming pressure in attempting to live up to a title.

In contrast to a title, a true, God-given identity is a weight not that we hold but rather that holds us—an anchor for our souls. An anchor is any device for holding fast and securing firmly—think of a boat resisting a current by dropping an anchor into the water. Do we in ministry not need something to secure us firmly and hold us fast as we navigate the rough waters of criticism, discouragement, blurred relational lines, and uncertainty? Do we not need a permanent core identity that calls to mind God's righteousness and provision rather than a reliance on our own abilities? Do we not need an identity that can never be stripped away no matter the circumstances or context we're in?

Knowing Who You Are Begins with Knowing Who You Aren't

When I've tried to live up to the title of "pastor's wife," I've been driven to perform rather than serve God. I've been driven to say yes to every need presented to me. I've felt as if I had to be involved in everything at our church. I've felt responsible to help my husband fix systems and people's hearts when they're broken. It's been my self-appointed job to make sure people are connected and connecting, both to the Lord and to one another.

Did you notice my word choices? I *have to* say yes to every need. I'm *responsible* to fix hearts. It's *my job*.

These word choices betray the belief that I should be able to do everything and be everything that is needed for the people around me. If I don't, I'm failing as the pastor's wife. I am not to have my own needs or weaknesses or limits. I'm to have *all* the gifts and *all* the abilities, without fail.

Can you relate? Do you feel the pressures bearing down on you to be all and do all for all?

We must see these thoughts and pressures for what they are: a belief that we can be a type of Christ. I think this is a very common temptation for men and women in ministry, because there are innate rewards in saving, rescuing, delivering, and being the one others look to and depend upon.

We would never say that we are the Christ, but we push ourselves to attempt to imitate the incommunicable attributes of God—all-powerful, all-present, self-sufficient, without limits, self-existent, all-knowing, and in control of all things—rather than imitating the communicable attributes of God we can and are told to imitate, such as his truth-telling, love, mercy, grace, and compassion.

The very real truth is that we are not able to ease the sufferings of others, we are entirely unable to produce spiritual change in others, and we cannot be the Spirit of God to them. *We are not the Christ.* Any attempt to be Christ to others is a weight we aren't made to handle, but this is what we attempt to do when we live according to a title rather than a God-given identity.

I take this wording—*we are not the Christ*—from John the Baptist. The crowds were coming to him, trying to identify and categorize him at the point in time when Jesus's ministry began to take shape. They wanted, in other words, to "title" him. They asked, "Who are you?" (John 1:19), attempting to locate him according to what they knew of God's story.

His place in the kingdom story is one we know well. John the Baptist began his ministry after four hundred years of God's silence, a time barren of his prophets and his visible activity. John's birth was heralded by the angel Gabriel, he was tasked with calling God's people to repentance, and he developed a large following in a short time. In other words, John the Baptist was important. He was a strong leader with an impressive résumé, the cool megachurch pastor of his time.

That's how we think of him, and the crowds had developed certain ideas about him, but how did he think of himself? What identity anchored him?

> He confessed, and did not deny, but confessed, "I am not the Christ." And they asked him, "What then? Are you Elijah?" He said, "I am not." "Are you the Prophet?" And he answered, "No." So they said to him, "Who are you? We need to give an answer to those who sent us. What do you say about yourself?" He said, "I am the voice of one crying out in the wilderness, 'Make straight the way of the Lord,' as the prophet Isaiah said." (vv. 20–23)

John rejected any title or identity not clearly given to him by God. In essence he said, "I am not Elijah and I am not the Prophet. Those roles, those identities, those responsibilities aren't mine." He recognized he had a very specific calling from God. This calling was to a specific people, at a specific time, in a specific place, for a specific purpose. It was not to be a savior or a rescuer, or to fulfill the entire mission all by himself. He was only called to be faithful with his specific task: to make straight the way of the Lord.

We'll talk about calling in the next chapter, but for now consider how silly it would have been for John to say, "Why, yes, I am the Christ," and inflate his own importance and calling! What a weight and burden he would have taken on that he was not capable of carrying.

Yet how often do I think of myself as a type of Christ to those I am serving? How often do you?

We know we're not the actual Christ, but we're tempted to believe that we have to *act* as if we were. We put so much pressure and expectations on ourselves: *If I say the exact right thing in a difficult situation, I can save a person from going down a path of destruction. If I respond to an unbeliever in the exact right way, they'll be saved. With the right words and actions, I can somehow remove a church member's grief and pain.*

We must reject inflated self-importance.

We are not the Christ.

The Anchor of Identity That Holds Us

Did you notice that the priests and Levites kept asking John the Baptist to identify himself? They wanted to know his title, and they repeatedly offered him suggestions of who they wanted him to be.

This is the same battle we fight. As ministry wives, not only do we struggle internally to think of ourselves rightly but there are many who want to identify us according to *their* ideas and categories. Everyone we serve has an idea of what their leaders should be and do. Some will express disappointment that we're not what they hoped, and some will want to elevate us beyond what we actually are. The temptation for every ministry leader is to endlessly spin our wheels, trying to win over the disappointed while maintaining our elevated status in the eyes of the pedestal-builders.

What more, then, can we learn from John the Baptist? John 3 records a new group coming to him with a concern:

> Now a discussion arose between some of John's disciples and a Jew over purification. And they came to John and said to him, "Rabbi, he who was with you across the Jordan, to whom you bore witness—look, he is baptizing, and all are going to him." (vv. 25–26)

John had obviously communicated who he was and who he wasn't, because they regurgitated his words back to him, calling him a witness-bearer. However, he'd evidently been such a good witness-bearer that he'd gathered a following. In fact, this passage tells us he had his own disciples but many of them were now leaving the umbrella of John's teaching and leadership and transferring their allegiance to Jesus. Apparently, the disciples who remained with John the Baptist wanted to protect his numbers, platform, reputation, and ministry. They wanted to make much of him.

The same pitfall awaits us in ministry. We will be tempted not only to inflate our importance and abilities but also to let others do so. People seek wise counsel and godly leadership from us, which is well and good and not the issue. The issue is how we respond to their seeking. Will we point them to the real Christ, or will we allow them to believe we have capabilities beyond our capabilities or to attribute the power displayed in our life and words to us and not to the Christ?

What was John's response to this temptation of letting others exalt him?

> A man can receive nothing unless it has been given to him from heaven. You yourselves bear me witness, that I said, "I am not the Christ," but, "I have been sent before him." He who has the bride is the bridegroom; but the friend of the bridegroom, who stands and hears him, rejoices greatly because of the bridegroom's voice. Therefore this joy of mine is fulfilled. He must increase, but I must decrease. (vv. 27–30 NKJV)

John would not let others attribute qualities to him that solely belonged to Christ. And in speaking of his identity, he gives us an anchoring identity as well.

First and foremost, John said there is a Christ, and his name is Jesus. He is the Light of the World, the Groom who came for his bride, and our Savior and Messiah. And he is the reason John's ministry existed. The Bible describes his ministry as bearing witness about Christ (John 1:6–8), standing as a friend of the Groom as he vows his love to the bride, and rejoicing in Christ himself. This ministry, John said, was *received*, given to him from heaven.

In other words, heaven had written his identity—not the religious leaders, not his followers, and not even John himself. He served on heaven's orders alone.

The same is true for each of us. We are not the Christ, but we bear witness of the Christ, we rejoice in the Christ we proclaim, we point to the Christ, and we exalt the Christ.

This is great freedom for us in ministry! Like John the Baptist, we're called to a specific people in a specific place with specific gifts for a specific purpose. We take our cues from heaven, not from our own or anyone else's ideas of what we should be or what our title means. We're simply called to be faithful to shine a light toward the Light of the World, using whatever gifts we've been given, as well as to stand as witnesses to the union of Christ with those we love and serve.

We are not marrying others to ourselves; we're inviting them to be married to Christ. We're not the center of attention. How awkward it would be if all the attention were to turn toward a bridesmaid at a wedding! How inappropriate if one of the groomsmen started making eyes at the bride! We would call it not only inappropriate but adulterous.

The fact that we are not the center of attention is, in John's words, something to rejoice in. Why? Because it speaks to our true identity: like those we serve, we're also married to the bridegroom, which means we're secure in the love of Christ and don't need the approval or validation of those around us.

Paul Tripp says it like this:

> The most important encounter in ministry is not the person's encounter with us, but his encounter with Christ. Our job is simply to set up that encounter, so that God would help people seek his forgiveness, comfort, restoration, strength, and wisdom.[1]

It's not our title of pastor's wife that anchors us but rather our identity that does. And what is our identity? We are servants of God for the benefit of others (2 Cor. 4:5). We may be introduced by a church member as their pastor's wife or to the sending church as the missionary on furlough, but that is not who we are at the core. *Those titles just tell others in what capacity we serve God.*

Our identity as "servant of God" is the foundation of all we do. Christ died for us; therefore, we are alive to God, not to ourselves (2 Cor. 5:14–15). We're not our own but rather belong to him. We pour out our life for God's pleasure.

A Servant to a Servant

When we first entered ministry, I thought, to be very honest, that it would be a position of honor—that it would in some ways be glamorous. I had no concept in my mind that I'd have to get my hands dirty, that I would in many ways feel invisible, and that the core and goal of ministry is laying down one's life for the sake of others. I was in for a rude awakening—a good rude awakening, I might add.

In my ongoing struggle to lay myself down and serve, I find it helpful to return to passages that describe Jesus and his ministry on earth. When we consider him in Philippians 2:6–7, we read that Christ, "who, though he was in the form of God, did not count equality with God a thing to be grasped, but emptied himself, by taking the form of a servant."

He took the form—the *identity*—of a servant. That is who Jesus is and that is who I am to be. Not someone seeking honor, respect, admiration, and approval, not someone looking for a way into the spotlight, not someone looking for appreciation or letting others do the grunt work.

I'm prone to thinking more about who is doing what for me, how that person at church responded to me in a hurtful way, or who will engage me on Sunday morning or invite me into their social circle. But Jesus not only said he came to serve rather than be served (Matt. 20:28), he also said it is more blessed to give to others than to receive (Acts 20:35). He said life and ministry will be better, more satisfying, and more joyful for us if we focus not on what people are doing for us but rather what we can do for them in his name and for his glory.

Why would it be better? Proverbs 11:25 says, "Whoever brings blessing will be enriched, and one who waters will himself be watered." Isn't there a satisfaction we feel when the Lord leads us to meet a need or give an encouraging word? That's the watering Proverbs talks about—the joy of being used by God as his servant.

This verse doesn't mean we get exactly what we give. It means we enjoy the specific happiness that comes from obeying God's command and showing love to others. This is the specific happiness Jesus himself experienced (Heb. 12:2). I think it also puts us in a position of trusting God to meet our needs and looking at him with eager anticipation of how he will give us what we need. Loving others, Jesus says, is for our joy. Thinking of ourselves, then, is not going to serve us well in ministry. It will only make us bitter and unable to receive with thanksgiving what *is* offered us.

When we live according to a false identity—anything other than a beloved servant of God—we're weighed down with tremendous burdens rather than held by an anchor. It's the difference between ministry resting upon our abilities or upon God's, and reliance on self is a draining business, because self is innately weak. There are high highs when things are going well, but when we face criticism, obstacles, or discouragement, we fall into very low lows.

Are you currently weighed down under a heavy mantle you've put on yourself or under the lofty expectations of others? The expectations may be real, but the gospel of Jesus Christ lifts those burdens from you. In his mercy, he has removed your sin. In his grace, he has given you everything you need for life and godliness (2 Pet. 1:3). You don't have to complete any checklist or meet the expectations of others in order to receive or maintain what he lovingly gives. You are loved, so much so that his love identifies and characterizes who you are.

When you live and serve as the beloved woman you are, you find yourself able to constantly pour out but never be truly emptied.

THRee

You Are Called and Gifted

P eople often ask me what it's like to be a pastor's wife, and I tell them I don't know what it's like to *not* be one. My husband's calling colors every part of my life in a way that's difficult to explain and, in a sense, is difficult even for me to understand. His calling is my calling is his calling; we are individuals, yet we're one.

Some people approach me with the underlying idea that being a pastor's wife makes me wholly "other." I experience life, they imply, much differently from those around me. And in some ways, they're right.

On the other hand, some well-meaning people, wanting to ease whatever pressure they imagine I feel, have cheerily explained to me how I am no different from other women in the church and should not imagine I'm required to do anything aside from following God and loving people—just like everyone else. And in some ways, they're right too.

During one such recent conversation at church, the well-meaning person was interrupted twice as they were speaking: once by a volunteer who asked me to pass along the visitor cards to my husband, and the second time by a new visitor who "Just had to meet the pastor's wife" and had been pointed in my direction.

So which is it? Am I to embrace or reject my "otherness"?

The truth is "pastor's wife" is not a biblically assigned role, nor is it a job, but on a weekly and even daily basis every pastor's wife must navigate social scenarios and ministry situations that arise *only* because she's married to the minister. I've mostly learned to embrace this, because I see how God has given me influence and how I can use it to honor him and bless others. And while I formerly found the lack of scriptural instruction regarding my role discouraging, I now find it *encouraging*, because the silence implies three things. One, we're called to greater (and better) commands than simply fulfilling a role. Two, we're called to cultivate godly character more than we're called to fulfill specific tasks or activities. And, finally, there is freedom and variance given by God in how we each can serve him in ministry.

Our Common Calling

Let's start with the first implication: we're called to greater and better commands than simply fulfilling a role. They are given to all disciples of Jesus, and we share these commands—and therefore a calling—with all those to whom we seek to minister. What are those commands?

We're called by God to love and obey him. This is the first and greatest commandment. All of our life and ministry is founded upon and flows from this command. Within it lies the reason we do what we do: we love because he first loved us (1 John 4:19). His calling is an invitation to secure, steadfast love, one that offers forgiveness for our sin and can handle our daily needs, concerns, cares, and joys.

The way we demonstrate love to God is by obeying the commands he gives in Scripture. This seems obvious, but I emphasize it because sometimes I want to excuse myself from basic biblical commands that are challenging in the ministry context: forgiving wrongs, confessing sin, bearing burdens, and loving enemies. Being the pastor's wife never excuses us from obedience. In fact, our obedience flows directly from our greatest calling, which is to love God with all of our heart (Matt. 22:37).

In the Gospel of Matthew, Jesus used parables—concrete, tangible examples from everyday life—to help his disciples grasp intangible realities of his kingdom and what it meant to fulfill their calling to love God with all their heart. The parables were often agricultural in nature, which made sense given the time and region within he and his audience lived. Jesus often described himself as a farmer sowing the seed of the gospel. The seed is implanted in the soil of hearts, grows as we submit to and obey the Word, and eventually shows itself fruitful in our life, making us people of refuge and peace.

In later parables, the characters start to shift. Often, an owner or master of a property has gone away and left his property in the hands of his servants. So Jesus moved from stories in which we're the recipients of his message to stories that describe us as servants who are stewarding plots of land God has given us.

Our Master, Jesus, has ascended to heaven with the promise that he will return for us. In the meantime, according to Jesus's parables, we are left in charge of his property and affairs as managers and stewards. Within that land, we've found buried treasure and have sold all to buy what we've found (Matt. 13:44).

Each of us who are in Christ have the exact same treasure buried in our plot of land—the seed of the gospel in our hearts, received, taken root, and growing. The treasure is Christ himself and all of the riches he's given us by faith: we've put on Christ; we're heirs of the promise; we've been saved; we've each been given good works to do; we have one Spirit, one hope, one Lord, one faith, one baptism, and one God over all and in all. So this treasure or seed is what is unseen, tucked away, and yet producing fruit in and through us.

Jesus makes it clear through the Parable of the Talents that the man who finds the buried treasure isn't just to buy the land and squat on it, waiting. He's to multiply what he's been given. He's to cultivate that plot of land. He's to do what he can with what he has in order to give it as a gift to the Master when he returns (25:14–30).

This is the calling of every believer.

So we, as pastors' wives, are not "other." Like all believers, we're stewards of the gospel.

A Specific Stewardship

As pastors' wives we've been called to a *specific* stewardship. That stewardship is the reason you picked up this book: you're married to a pastor. This is what God has given you as the specific way he wants you to know his character, experience his sanctification, and honor and serve him.

In other words, being a pastor's wife is the particular plot of land you're called to cultivate.

Sometimes it feels less like a plot and more like a burdensome lot in life; sometimes people look at us with pity, as if we've been handed a diagnosis for a terminal illness. Sometimes we look at *ourselves* that way. But our good God has deemed this specific stewardship as our opportunity for worshiping him. A plot of land indicates cultivation, creativity, beauty, fruit, and, yes, hard work. It is our plot to manage nonetheless, so that we may lay our crop at the feet of the Master when he returns to gather his saints.

Our specific stewardship is what makes us often stand out in the church or group in which we're serving. While we are like the other women around us in that we're disciples of Christ, our stewardship is not shared by all, and this is the occasional otherness we feel. Other women aren't intimately connected to the one carrying the church's burdens. Other women may not love and yearn for the growth of God's people as we do, knowing their struggles and stories in detail.

I love how Titus 2:10 speaks of specific stewardship. Writing to bondservants, Paul encourages them to use their lowly position to "in everything . . . adorn the doctrine of God our Savior."

In some ways we're also in a lowly position—much of our stewardship happens behind the scenes, such as when we're giving requested input on the sermon or carrying a burden others may not know about. But we're also in an influential position simply because we're married to a minister. Whether in a "lowly" or "influential" moment of service, we're to make it our aim to adorn the gospel. We're to highlight its beauty and make it irresistible to others, and at the same time remind ourselves of its application and relevance to our own lives.

Godly character is our primary adornment. Of course, our good works are to make others marvel at God (Matt. 5:16), but the one thing Scripture is *not* silent about regarding the wife of a church leader is what type of character she should exhibit: "Their wives likewise must be dignified, not slanderers, but sober-minded, faithful in all things" (1 Tim. 3:11).

> We're to be dignified: reverent, worthy of respect, and handling our influence thoughtfully, with careful intention.
>
> We're not to be slanderers: exhibiting discretion in what we say and share and not being malicious gossips.
>
> We're to be sober-minded: self-controlled and disciplined, not given to extremes.
>
> We're to be faithful: thoroughly trustworthy and dependable.

In addition, the pastor's wife should encourage and value in her husband the godly character that maintains his qualification for leadership: that he be above reproach, sober-minded, self-controlled, respectable, hospitable, gentle, not quarrelsome, not a lover of money, a good leader of his family, disciplined, humble, and a lover of good (1 Tim. 3:2–7; Titus 1:6–8).

These verses tell us *what* our specific stewardship is but not *why* we're to wholeheartedly embrace what our husband's role means for us or *how* we're to cultivate such virtuous character.

Returning to the idea of master and servant, we recognize as stewards that all belongs to God. Nothing about our life is actually ours—not our bodies, money, skills, jobs, or influence. Everything we have is a good gift from God. And God makes perfect judgments.

This is such an important truth to meditate on and return to over and over again, for when our "otherness" feels too weighty or isolating, we can remember that our good and gracious God has chosen for us this specific plot of land where we're not only to serve but also to flourish and grow.

He himself meets us in our specific stewardship.

Our Common Gifting

Whatever God has called you to do in ministry, he has also gifted you to do it. "Him we proclaim, warning everyone and teaching everyone with all wisdom, that we may present everyone mature in Christ. For this I toil, *struggling with all his energy that he powerfully works within me*" (Col. 1:28–29, emphasis mine).

In these verses, Paul expresses the focus of ministry and the hard work it entails, but he also reminds us that God's power undergirds, fuels, and livens all we do. He comes alongside each of us in our calling through his Spirit.

Speaking to his disciples, the name Jesus used for the Holy Spirit in John 16:7 is *Helper*: "I tell you the truth: it is to your advantage that I go away, for if I do not go away, the Helper will not come to you."

The Greek word translated "Helper" is *paraclete*, *para* meaning "alongside" and *kletos* meaning "to call." In other words, the Holy Spirit is also called; his calling is to stand alongside the believer. In Greek culture, the word *paraclete* was usually applied to an attorney, but not just any attorney. Paraclete gives the image of a family's attorney who is kept on permanent retainer.

Thankfully, I've never stood accused before a judge, but if I ever am, my first call will be to a good attorney. An attorney advocates for their client, helps them understand the law and navigate the court system, tells them when and what to speak in court, and fights for their best interest. The client puts their total trust in their attorney and follows their lead.

The Holy Spirit is called to come alongside a believer to spotlight Jesus and the words he spoke (v. 14), reminding us of truth in moments we're swirling in confusion or hurt. He empowers us to speak the gospel to unbelievers (Matt. 10:19–20) and to benefit and edify the church (1 Cor. 12:7).

Some versions translate *paraclete* in John 16:7 as "Comforter," which in this context doesn't primarily mean consoling someone but rather giving them strength. As R. C. Sproul says, "The Holy Spirit comes to the people of Christ not to heal their wounds after a battle but to strengthen them before and during a struggle."[1]

And so, we are daily strengthened for this life of ministry to which God has called us. It's quite often a struggle or laborious toil, but we struggle not according to our own strength but according to the Spirit's strength within us.

A Together Calling

When Kyle and I got married, I was months away from finishing my seminary degree, so after we returned from our honeymoon, I began looking for jobs. I knew I felt called to vocational ministry, and I'd worked at a large church as a children's intern for a year leading up to our engagement, so I naturally assumed that meant I was called to children's ministry.

Kyle and I met with the pastor who married us to discuss how we should proceed forward.

I'll never forget his response.

He said, "You are one flesh, so you have one calling. You can't pull in two different directions. The best way ministry and marriage works together is if you pull in the same direction."

He didn't mean only one of us could get a ministry job. He didn't mean only one of us could work outside the home. He didn't mean we weren't individuals, with individual desires and passions. He simply meant the way we'd discern God's leading is that when he called one, he'd call the other. Ministry is a together calling.

I know some of you can't relate to my story because you never had a sense of being "called" to ministry. Some of you were surprised in middle age when your husband left a successful career in order to become a pastor. Some of you were fine with your husband pursuing a ministerial job but were reluctant to embrace what it meant for you.

And that's okay. There is no one right path in. But one thing is certain: if God has called your husband, he has also called you. He hasn't called you to the same *role* as your husband, but God has called you to love, respect, and help him as he follows, obeys, and serves the Lord.

Your husband's obedience belongs to the Lord, but his covenant promise is to you—not to the church. This is an important distinction that protects the health of the church, the pastor, and the pastor's wife and family. The church is Christ's bride, and Christ's commitment is to uphold, protect, and sustain her. In other words, the together calling keeps Christ at the core of the marriage rather than the ministry itself at the center.

The truth that this is a together calling has grounded me over the years, especially during difficult times when I struggle with how Kyle's job affects me and desperately want to escape the pain of people leaving the church, the expectations I sense from others, or the demands of ministry life. The urge to escape was especially high during our early church planting days, when it was all hands on deck and we were exhausted. It felt as if our marriage and family had been swallowed whole by his calling, and I resented him for it. Notice I said *his* calling. That little creeping thought I let in started a crack between us that put my husband in an untenable situation: *choose to obey God or choose to obey me.* That's not to say we hadn't created marital dynamics that needed evaluation, or that my husband was always right, but my rejection of the together calling led to sinful bitterness and anger.

The together calling plays out differently for every ministry couple. Just as we all share in common commands to love God and others and a specific stewardship in which we do so, we ministry wives share in a common together call with our husband but also have a specific marriage in which we carry out that call. In other words, each marriage is unique.

Some marriages may approach ministry together as a "supportive calling," meaning one person feels called to ministry and the other does not, but the person not called is fully supportive of their spouse in the work they do.

Other marriages may experience a "compatible calling," where both feel equally called to ministry but carry out that ministry in different ways. Jeff Iorg, seminary president and former pastor, says,

> My wife and I share this mutuality of call. I preach, teach, write, and lead. She mentors, consults, and enjoys hospitality. We work together

on some projects, apart on others. Our leadership roles fit together and complement one another. We both feel we have answered God's call.[2]

Finally, some marriages may experience a "shared calling," in which both spouses feel equally called by God to do similar work, such as international missions or husband-and-wife team pastoral counseling.

Each couple must choose their own model. If the couple is happy and the church or organization where they serve is happy, they must reject all outside attempts to stereotype or pigeonhole what a "ministry marriage" must be like.

Your Specific Gifting

Have you noticed that we started with the general call and gifting each believer has in common but have moved more and more to specifics and differences? Just as John the Baptist spoke of his specific calling at a specific time to a specific group of people, under the large umbrella of vocational ministry, we will all serve in a variety of ways, in a variety of contexts, and with a variety of gifts. This is what makes the global church dazzlingly beautiful.

You can be confident knowing God has gifted you for the context in which he's placed you. He never calls without also providing the spiritual resources we need to do what he's asked of us. In fact, over many years of church ministry I've seen how he's enhanced certain gifts or abilities for certain times and then pulled to the surface different gifts and abilities at other times. He's never wasted an experience, a lesson, or even pains I've encountered and mistakes I've made. He has resourced me abundantly for the stewardship he's given me.

We often ask, "How do I find my place in this specific ministry?" Pastors tend to fulfill similar duties: preaching, teaching, shepherding, counseling, and leading. However, because being a pastor's wife is not a specific job or role, we have more freedom in deciding how we'll involve ourselves. This is a good thing, but this freedom also leaves things so open-ended and subjective that we often struggle to discern where God wants us or how he could use us. It'd be much easier sometimes if there *were* a job description.

Finding your place in your specific ministry context means knowing your God-given spiritual gifts, passions, season of life, and personality. What are ways the unique combination of these qualities can adorn the gospel among the people you love and serve?

First, consider your spiritual gifts and passions. You can, of course, take a spiritual gifts test online or list what you enjoy doing, but I believe the best approach, especially for young ministry wives, is simply to "try on" different ministry opportunities (just not all at once!). Over time and through experience, you'll soon realize there are some areas of ministry that come naturally to you and, more importantly, delight you. When you serve this way, it feels like worship to you, and it sparks in you an affection for Christ and his church. In addition, others confirm at various points that God is using you. Take note and press further into these opportunities. On the other hand, you'll find some areas of ministry feel to you like carrying a gorilla on your back. It may be a great ministry and perhaps even something you feel like you "should" do as a pastor's wife, but it weighs you down and creates dread in your heart. Take note and, as you can, release this ministry to another.

Second, consider your season of life. Again, the pastor's faithful ministry could be pictured as one long straight line, but the pastor's wife's availability and ability to be involved in the ministry fluctuates much more based upon the couple's season of life. Are you young and new to marriage and ministry? Are you carrying babies and chasing toddlers? Are you homeschooling? Are you working outside the home? Are you middle-aged, keeping a calendar overflowing with teenagers' needs and activities? Are you an empty nester? Are you a grandparent living far from precious grandbabies and wanting to travel often to see them? These and many other factors affect availability—chronic illness, caring for an aging parent, miscarriages and infertility or other private pain, dealing with mental illness, living far from family and not having childcare, or cost of living and financial needs.

Finally, consider your God-designed personality. I am an introvert and simply cannot run at full speed relationally for weeks at a time without stopping to refuel. Sometimes I've wished for a different personality, thinking it would make ministry far easier, but knowing this about myself and knowing my personality is God-given have helped me appreciate my limits and make decisions about my ministry involvement accordingly.

Personality also gives clues, for example, of whether we're more of a behind-the-scenes servant or are more comfortable being "out front," and whether we prefer one-on-one conversations or hosting big parties.

Think of our unique qualities as the accessories to an outfit. We could all wear the same black dress—which symbolizes our specific stewardship—but the accessories at our disposal will vary widely from one another and, as we put them on, will differentiate our look from others, each one as beautiful as the last. In the same way, through our God-given "accessories," we have the opportunity to adorn the gospel.

Our many differences showcase God's wisdom, and we must remember that we're called to unity, not uniformity. The Spirit gives a variety of gifts, a variety of roles, a variety of callings.

We don't give an account to one another or to our church congregants about how we use our gifts and fulfill our callings but rather will give an account to God. Because we answer only to God for how we serve him, we can find our confidence to act according to our passions and gifts from him as well.

> Such confidence we have through Christ before God. Not that we are competent in ourselves to claim anything for ourselves, but our competence comes from God. He has made us competent as ministers of a new covenant. (2 Cor. 3:4–6 NIV)

There is so much freedom and joy in remembering our goal. Success is faithfulness to what God is asking of us, not certain results, and not what he's asking of anyone else.

We're to be faithful to our specific calling.

And the Holy Spirit will be faithful to his.

FOUR

You Are Human

When our three boys were in their early preschool and elementary years, we were running on all cylinders in ministry. My husband was the lead pastor of the church we'd planted; I was helping get our women's and discipleship ministries off the ground; we were regularly opening our home to church visitors, neighbors, and church members; and we were hosting and leading a community group each week in our living room. And somewhere in there we were trying to be married and raise a family.

After years of this, and adding even more to our plates, I found myself deeply resentful of my husband and all the people clamoring for our attention. I wasn't only resentful; I was angry. The anger I felt and that kept spewing out of me surprised and scared me. Where was it coming from? And why wasn't Kyle listening to me when I tried to explain how I felt? He was carrying so many burdens for others that he couldn't seem to add mine to his load.

One day I googled "burnout" and nodded my head as I read the symptoms, feeling both validated and depressed at the same time. Validated, because there was a name for what I was experiencing.

But also depressed, because I couldn't see a way out. My feet were stuck in the hardened concrete of commitments—some might say *over*commitments.

Here's what we learned through experience in those years: ministry can—if we let it—create a certain dynamic. I wanted to support Kyle well, and I also observed all the burdens he was already carrying. I didn't want to add to those burdens by being one more person he needed to counsel, so I swallowed my own needs and pressed on. At some point, however, my needs (and, I would argue, his) became glaring. They couldn't remain buried forever but instead exploded out—which I experienced as anger and resentment but can also exhibit as anxiety, depression, marital conflict, shutting down, avoiding difficult conversations, and full-on burnout. My reaction, of course, didn't invite Kyle's listening ear but rather his defensiveness, frustration, and emotional apathy. In other words, we were both contributing to the dynamic. I wasn't voicing my needs and concerns in a way Kyle could hear me—with specific and thoughtful requests for change—and because he was merely trying to survive an overwhelming sense of responsibility at home and at work, he wasn't emotionally available to me.

We were unhealthy people.

We were living as employees of God and his church, not as nurtured human beings. Everything in our life focused on church—our conversation, our activities, our relationships, our schedule, our minds, *everything*.

If you'd met me in those years and asked me simple questions like, "What do you like to do for fun? What refuels you? Who are your friends? What are you passionate about? What makes you tick?" I couldn't have answered them. I didn't know myself anymore. All I knew was ministry. Rest, rejuvenation, hobbies, friendship—those were for other people. In fact, I felt it was part of my "job" to encourage and even create spiritual and relational opportunities like these for others but couldn't enjoy them myself.

Unhealthy living eventually catches up with you, and it caught up with us.

And when it did, I was scared to death we weren't going to make it in marriage, much less ministry. We'd sacrificed so much for the sake of the church; was this how it was supposed to be? Isn't laying down your life the biblical call of the disciple? If so, why were we experiencing such rotten fruit in our personal lives?

Our shared fear of where we found ourselves led us to seek counseling.[1] We read and discussed helpful books together. We shared our emotions in fits and starts, because we'd started to mistrust them (me) or keep them tightly bottled up (him). We talked about the patterns and rhythms of our ministry, marriage, and family. We fought to find one another again. We fought to find joy in the Lord again.

Through all of this, we realized that we'd tried for far too long to live as superhumans. We'd believed and acted upon the idea that we were the exception to the rule of God's design, that in fact pushing the limits of our humanity was *required* for our calling. It'd become normal to us—but then again, we'd forgotten what normal actually was.

We knew we wouldn't make it for the long haul unless we changed, so together Kyle and I developed new life and marital rhythms that honored God, one another, and the fundamental truth that we are, in fact, human.

Pour Out, Pour In

Perhaps you can relate. Ministry involves so much pouring out, giving, serving, and being available to others. Even when we're not actively doing the work of the ministry, we're often *preparing* to do the work. Pouring out is not a bad thing; healthy people pour themselves out regularly for the benefit of others. They are intentional. They take initiative and meet needs.

But healthy people don't just pour out; they also incorporate rhythms into their lives that allow them to refuel and take in sustenance. Unhealthy people may constantly fill their schedules because they genuinely want to impact the kingdom of God, but they often imagine they do not need (or are not allowed to need) what others need. They think because they are doing "the Lord's work," they would be selfish to say no or take a day off. Inevitably, they flout God-given limits until God purposefully slows them down.

Healthy people, by contrast, embrace their God-given limits and make commitments accordingly.

In our family, Kyle is responsible for car maintenance. At necessary intervals, he takes our cars out of commission and into the shop for oil changes and tire rotations. Without these rhythms, our cars won't run as they're designed to run. For example, if he never changed the oil and we continued driving the cars, we'd eventually ruin the cars' engines. He knows what our cars need based upon experience and knowledge of basic car maintenance, but if he ever is unsure, he checks the owner's manual, which reiterates how the cars are designed to run and how we can care for them to ensure their longevity.

As human beings, we're designed by God to function a certain way. Our "dashboard" incorporates mental health, emotional health, physical health, and spiritual health, and if we don't monitor ourselves and choose healthy rhythms according to God's Word (our owner's manual), we'll see those dashboard warning lights flashing in no time. We must diligently maintain our minds, bodies, and souls so we can ensure our longevity in ministry.

In other words, we have needs, and nothing thrives without vigilance.

As we take on the mindset of a servant in imitation of Jesus (Phil. 2:1–10), as we discussed earlier, we do not then become robots. We are still broken, sinful people in need of the very Savior we give away to others. We have emotions, struggles, concerns, disappointments, discouragements, hurts, and everything else others have who come to us looking for counsel or help. We need the care of others, we need the sanctification of the Spirit, and we need to be in fellowship with others. And yes, I say, "We need," because we're designed to be that way.

Let's distinguish, however, between needs and expectations. Consider: What is God's expectation for you in ministry? God doesn't expect you to be different from those within your church or ministry. He doesn't expect that they are flesh and blood but you are not. He knows you're weak and needy, so he is not impatient and frustrated that you, at times, feel your weakness and neediness greatly.

What is your expectation of yourself? Oftentimes I see in myself and others in ministry this diminishing of ourselves, not in a healthy, servant kind of way but in an unhealthy way. Ministry folks, for example, are prone to emotional unhealth, because to feel or be able to label how we feel and what we need may not be easy to engage in. We also wonder where we can share those feelings, especially if they are about the church and the people with whom we're in community. But even the attempt to shut down our negative emotions because we don't know how to navigate them shows that we often think we're the exception to God's design for humanity and shouldn't have needs or brokenness.

I've seen in my own life that constantly pouring out without letting God pour in means I start running on my own strength. I try to survive my schedule rather than genuinely connecting with people and loving them well. And I become reactive, increasingly acting out of self-protection and self-perseveration because my insecurities—that I'm a failure, that I'm disappointing everyone, that I'm unliked and unloved—start screaming loud. I fall back on natural rhythms I learned in childhood in order to quiet those insecurities, which usually means I just fill my schedule more and run harder.

Receive God's Abundant Care

You may be thinking, *Okay, Christine, yes, I have all these needs, but what do I do with them?* And I know you may also be running through a litany of excuses why you can't stop and rest or can't have fellowship within the church or can't share your needs with anyone else.

I said earlier that we must distinguish between needs and expectations. I referenced God's expectations of us and our expectations of ourselves, but in answering your imagined rebuttal, let's consider your expectations of others. Do you have expectations of how others around you and in your church should meet your needs?

When Kyle and I were going through burnout and its subsequent marriage issues, I had a huge light bulb moment. I realized that the wonderful people in our church wanted us to be healthy and for our marriage and family to thrive, but no one else aside from Kyle and I could make the choices for us to be healthy and thriving.

The same is true for you. No one else can make the choices for you. No one else can set healthy rhythms for you. The lovely people you serve aren't going to realize you need rest and make it happen for you. You have to *choose* it. You cannot *expect* others to meet your needs, as if they are your hope—but you can trust God to meet your needs, and at times he will use others to do so.

If you lay down your expectations, you will find, as I have, that God is continually providing for your needs. You must set up rhythms in your life that allow you to receive his care.

Where is he providing for our care? And how does he want us to receive that care?

God's care for his children is not scarce or doled out according to our merit. His care for us is abundant and accessible, an overflow and an outworking of his very character. He demonstrates kindness, upholds those who feel as if they're falling, raises up the bowed down, gives sustenance, satisfies desires, hears our cries, and comes near to all who call on him (Ps. 145:13–19). He renews and refreshes through his Spirit (Titus 3:5). He provides for our deepest soul needs through Jesus, the bread of life and living water (John 6:35; 7:37–38).

Let's look together at how he tangibly offers this care.

Receive the Care of the Lord through Scripture

The primary way we receive care from the Lord is through his Word. When we present ourselves to the Scripture with open hearts and focused minds, God renews our minds, prepares us for action, and reminds us of his trustworthiness. Scripture proclaims the gospel to us again and again, and God uses his Word to convict, settle, and comfort. If you are not yet in the rhythm of meeting with God each day, decide now how you will incorporate this discipline in your life. What needs to be changed, removed, or added in order for you to receive the care of the Lord through Scripture? There is nothing better you can do for yourself, those you love, and those you serve than to make your daily meeting with God your highest priority.

In regard to Bible reading, one rhythm I'm finding more and more essential in my life, and one I commend to you, is going to Scripture before my phone. Somewhere along the way, I got into the habit of spending the first twenty minutes of my day scrolling through my phone and then opening up my Bible. I found myself consistently distracted and unable to digest what I was reading, often because I was already engaged in my mental task list for the day or, worse, dwelling on a social media post I'd seen. I decided to experiment: Would leaving my phone plugged into the charger and going straight to my Bible better help me engage the Lord? My experience on the very first day of the change convinced me: I was able to focus better and dig deeper into the Word, and what I read stuck with me throughout the day.

Receive the Care of the Lord through Engaging Your Physical Body

We inhabit bodies, and our bodies are designed by God to move, sleep, learn, and exhibit emotion. Our physical health is intimately intertwined with our spiritual, emotional, and mental health, which means we can't neglect any of the components of who we are without experiencing the effects. For example, physical exercise releases endorphins that positively affect our mood. Engaging our minds with stimulating books or using an innate skill to serve others often stirs our wonder and worship, enhancing our spiritual growth. Engaging our emotions in an appropriate way—naming them, acknowledging them to God and those we love, and seeking to reject what doesn't align with truth—can often point us toward the need for physical rest or time with friends. In other words, God cares for us as we engage the body he's given us.

One area ministry leaders must be especially mindful of and careful to cultivate is emotional health. Emotional health involves being able to acknowledge, name, and deal well with negative emotions. Pastors and church leaders, pastors' wives included, are called upon to enter into many harrowing situations with people in their church, whether it be an affair or an addiction or an unexpected death. In addition, pressing national and global issues affect their congregation, decisions, and the pastor's preaching. The result is that leaders learn to shove their own needs, uncertainties, sadness, and weakness aside, sometimes to the point where they can no longer recognize a negative emotion in themselves, much less deal with it appropriately. They don't have time for grief or discouragement or loneliness. And even if they can name it, what do they do with it?

I think this is when we get into trouble—when we go long periods of time without acknowledging our own emotional needs and experiences. We must learn to slow down and name how we're feeling to someone who loves us. One thing my husband and I incorporate in our daily communication is not just rattling off a list of what we did that day but also naming one emotion that encapsulates the day. Being able to name our emotions to one another and support each other in those emotions allows us to process our fast-paced life and remain connected to one another.

What are you neglecting about your physical body? Are you cutting corners on sleep? Do you avoid exercise? What are you neglecting in your emotional life? What needs to change in order for you to receive the care of the Lord through your physical body? What new rhythms need to be established in your life?

Receive the Care of the Lord through Sabbath Rest

At the point in ministry where I googled "burnout," Kyle and I were not taking weekly time to rest. For years, we consistently rejected God's invitation to put work and ministry aside, slow down, and receive refreshment. It's no wonder we were falling apart. When I look back at this time, I'm mortified at our pride in believing we could color outside God's lines without consequence.

And yet, so many pastors and pastors' wives I speak with think they are the exception to the rule when it comes to Sabbath rest. They feel guilty for taking time off, doing something fun, not answering the phone, taking a nap, or going on vacation. Some don't even entertain the idea of time off because they feel (or perhaps want to believe?) they're essential or irreplaceable within their church. Some don't want to face imagined criticism from their congregants. Some wives are waiting for their husbands to take the lead in this area, and some husbands are being pushed by their wives to work harder or to "fix" the problems she sees in the church.

But what does God say? He doesn't simply invite us to rest; he *commands* it. He indicates that life and ministry will go better for us and be more fruitful if we stop work and rest at regular, consistent intervals. There must be no guilt in obeying what God has commanded; guilt only indicates a false belief or idol. And even if someone in the church doesn't fully understand, the example of saying no and observing a Sabbath rest is in itself a powerful sermon about first allegiance and being a biblical and healthy disciple of Jesus.

I'll share with you what we do to receive God's gracious gift of Sabbath rest, but it is in no way prescriptive. The way we rest has shifted according to our season of life, our children's ages, and our work. We've experimented with Kyle taking different days of the week off and with what we do on those days until we've found a rhythm that works for us. Currently, we have three boys in school, so Kyle takes Fridays off. Fridays are sacred days in our home. He and I don't do household chores, check email, answer our phones (although Kyle does check his caller ID, in case it's an emergency), or cook. Instead, we often go out for breakfast, take a long walk together, read, and nap. Sometimes we drive to a nearby town and window shop or play tennis in our neighborhood.

When our children were younger, we'd switch off doing activities to recharge as individuals. He would take the kids for a long walk, giving me time in the house by myself, or I'd keep the kids at home while he'd go to a coffee shop to read a book unrelated to work. We'd also save up our credit card points so that once a year or so, we could send each other off to the nearest big city for a stay in a hotel and a personal retreat.

It's far more important, however, for you to consider how you rest or Sabbath than it is to consider how *we* do it. Your husband may be reluctant to take a day off because of the pressure he feels. How can you encourage him and help him rest?

When we first started making rhythm adjustments in our marriage and family, adding in Sabbath rest was the most uncomfortable change, because it meant letting work and ministry sit unfinished. That's hard to do when you've been running at full speed for years. Common sense pushes us to finish the work and then rest, but in ministry, the work is never finished. We have to purposefully set it aside.

In addition to discomfort, I personally felt guilty on our Sabbath day. When I considered why, I recognized that I tend to idolize productivity and performance. These things aren't bad, but when I take them to the extreme, I am acting from a belief that I know what I need better than God does. I act outside God-designed limits and set myself up for consequences later.

As Sabbath rest has become normal in our life, Friday has become our favorite day of the week. The Lord renews us, and we can see how God's provision of rest has enabled us to endure and persevere in ministry. I no longer wonder if we're going to make it in marriage and ministry, because we've carved out space to connect with God and one another.

Friend, are you receiving the care of the Lord through Sabbath rest? It is absolutely one of the best gifts he gives.

Receive the Care of the Lord through the Body of Christ

Who pours into you? That's a question I get asked quite often. I know what many of these people are really asking: "Do you have an older woman in the church with whom you regularly meet who offers you biblical wisdom and a shoulder to cry on?" I've had that before, but I don't have it currently, and for some reason I feel kind of bad saying that out loud, almost like I'm doing something wrong.

I find the question interesting. I wonder if, in all our talk of discipleship and mentoring and "pouring into," we've created for ourselves a culture of entitlement. Do we believe it's a biblical imperative that there will always be a Paul to our Timothy? Should we *always* have someone "pouring into" us in a linear, hierarchical sort of way?

I don't think so. I think it's more circular than that. And I think to believe we are entitled to have a personal "pourer" is to cripple ourselves from the growth we crave.

But perhaps that makes my point. Do we actually crave growth? Or do we crave a person who is godlike and who can tell us what to do, empathize with our emotions, absolve us of our sins through spoken forgiveness, and guide us through our circumstances? Growth can definitely come from processing our life intimately with another, but if we aren't prioritizing the growth that happens in relating directly with God, we will be spiritually stunted.

The Bible speaks of believers making progress by "eating" the Word. Babes drink milk but then grow to maturity and eat meat. A babe drinking milk is in a receiving posture, but when I think of eating meat, I think of how I purchase it, cook it, and serve it to my children. I am a "pourer" who is also feeding myself on the meat I prepare. Babes in the faith need pourers, but if we aren't babes in the faith, we must be able to feed ourselves (and are *expected* to do so).

Part of growth is actually being the pourer. *All non-babes are meant to be pourers*. If we're getting frustrated and resentful that no one is personally pouring into us, we're missing something. Perhaps it is our turn to be a pourer and, in pouring, we'll find the "filling up" we're looking for.

I'm not saying we aren't to be or shouldn't seek to be poured into. It just often looks different from what we expect, and our problem is that we stick to only one formula—the hierarchical formula. In fact, God has given us the church so that we might be poured into. This elevates the idea of church, because we must be open with our needs, our sins, and our victories if we are to be poured into as we desire. I think we often wait for that one person to open up our heart and life to, but God intended for the mature to open ourselves up in community so that we have a *circular* discipleship in which we serve and are served. This doesn't come easy. We have to fight for it.

So when I am asked, "Who pours into you?" I don't think of one specific person. I think of my pastor-husband who preaches verse by verse through the Bible. I think of the elders who provide for and protect our church. I think of the young women who ask me hard questions and cause me to search the Scriptures for answers. I think of the women I'm discipling who in turn disciple me. I think of the staff and elder wives who serve so faithfully and encourage me to use my gifts. I think of my friends who are willing to say hard things. I think of the people in my community group who pray for me. I think of longtime friends who live at a distance and listen and respond objectively to my struggles. I think of those who use their gifts on Sunday mornings to provide space for my worship. And, yes, I think of several older women who occasionally help me know what to do in parenting and marriage. This is the church, and this is God providing for my needs.

This is God providing for yours as well.

And if God asks you to walk through a season of pouring without much receiving, know this: he will feed you.

Five

Cultivating the Skill of Knowing When to Say Yes and When to Say No (Part 1)

I know what you may be thinking after reading the last few chapters: *How do I know what I'm supposed to do and not do with the myriad opportunities before me? Christine, just tell me what to do!*

In the past I would have picked up this book, skimmed through until I found the pastor's wife job description, and done exactly what was listed.

I *will* get more specific about how I practically make decisions regarding opportunities, but I won't give you an extrabiblical job description. As previously cemented, you are a servant of God. Having the mindset of a servant, however, doesn't mean you must meet every need and serve in every way presented to you. We've already discussed how that is a savior complex, and we are not the Christ.

So, how do we know when we should say yes and when we should say no to a ministry opportunity?

Responding well to requests for our time, gifts, counsel, or input is a competence developed by first cultivating wisdom and discernment. So that's where we'll start.

Wisdom is skill in the art of godly living that begins with the fear of the Lord (Prov. 1:7). Because he is the source of all wisdom (Col. 2:3), as we consistently walk with him and seek him, he grows in us the ability to apply biblical truth in the practical details of everyday situations and relationships.

We know instinctively we need this wisdom, because we're faced with our lack and uncertainty almost every day. We need wisdom for how to handle our time, help our children navigate growing up as pastor's kids, and how to respond to hurting people. We need wisdom for what to do with private hurts and a disheartened husband. And, of course, wisdom for saying yes or no and, if no, how to say it graciously.

In order to develop wisdom and discernment, then, we must develop the muscle memory of *calling upon* the source of wisdom. We know how to call upon stores of knowledge and understanding, because we do it each time a difficult situation arises. I've gone to Google for answers and comfort in the face of a difficult diagnosis. I've gone to the magazine racks at the bookstore looking for mind-numbing escape.

And when faced with difficult ministry situations, I've gone to stores of discernment from myself—what feels right, what common sense says, what my emotions tell me, or what I most want to do. But these are not sources of wisdom and knowledge. They've instead been trapdoors of fear, conflicting solutions, emptiness, sinful actions, and stunted growth.

The only perfect source of wisdom and discernment is God. According to 1 Corinthians 2, godly wisdom is based upon the ideas and power of God. The wisdom of humankind is based upon the power, intellect, and ideas of people. Godly wisdom boasts in Jesus and what he did, while worldly wisdom boasts in self and accomplishments.

The question isn't if we need wisdom or not—that answer is a definitive yes—but rather if we're women who intentionally seek wisdom from the right stores of knowledge and understanding, with the goal of growth and obedience.

Seek and Search

Colossians 2:3 says, "In [Christ] are hidden all the treasures of wisdom and knowledge." When we talk about growing in wisdom, we're talking about seeking the person of Christ and cultivating our relationship with him.

When we're in relationship with someone, we begin to think like them, act like them, take on their mannerisms, and love what they love. For example, I have a friend who loves hot, sunny days. When a day like that hits, I think of her, text her sun emojis, and even go outside and feel the heat of the rays on my skin in her honor. I've started to notice and enjoy what she enjoys, because I love my friend.

Similarly, as we seek Christ and are in relationship with him, we begin to know, by the Holy Spirit, the mind of Christ. We begin to think like him, love what he loves, hate what he hates, and act like he acts. And we begin to hone the skill of knowing how he's leading us to respond in everyday situations—a vital skill for everyone but an absolutely necessary one for us as we pursue longevity in ministry.

A life characterized by wisdom doesn't just happen. It doesn't come merely through aging, life experience, or having wise parents. So how do we grow in godly wisdom?

Our answer is found in Proverbs 2:4–11:

> If you seek [wisdom] like silver
>   and search for it as for hidden treasures,
> then you will understand the fear of the Lord
>   and find the knowledge of God.
> For the Lord gives wisdom;
>   from his mouth come knowledge and understanding;
> he stores up sound wisdom for the upright;
>   he is a shield to those who walk in integrity,

> guarding the paths of justice
>   and watching over the way of his saints.
> Then you will understand righteousness and justice
>   and equity, every good path;
> for wisdom will come into your heart,
>   and knowledge will be pleasant to your soul;
> discretion will watch over you,
>   understanding will guard you.

Notice we're called to only two simultaneous actions: to seek and to search for wisdom.

Notice what God's actions are in response. He pours out stores of wisdom on those he's made righteous. He benefits us through his poured-out wisdom by shielding, guarding, and watching over us. He gives us understanding for every step and grants us peace.

Also notice where wisdom is found: "from his mouth come wisdom and knowledge" (v. 6).

The wisdom we need is located in the words from God's mouth: Scripture.

Putting this all together, we see that if we want to have practical skills in godly living, including how to respond to an opportunity or request, we must consistently seek and search the Scriptures.

Sideways Wisdom

As pastors' wives, we often bemoan that we cannot speak to others about private hurts or conflicts we're navigating within the church. Or we may carry an unfulfilled longing for an older woman or ministry wife to mentor us. Neither of these is a wrong lament or desire, but if we long for such things because we want someone to tell us exactly what to do that will rescue us from said difficulties, we've overlooked the fact that we have constant access to *the* source of wisdom.

Older women, pastors and shepherds, books, loving friends, and counselors are wonderful resources God has given us in the body of Christ, and they may dispense godly wisdom they themselves have received from the Source. But this is what I call sideways wisdom—when we look to others for godly wisdom rather than finding it in God himself. If sideways wisdom is our only source of wisdom, we will experience stunted growth. Here's why.

We'll lack the discernment to distinguish God's voice from others. We instead may be easily swayed, prone to imitating another person's convictions and calling without considering that it may not be what God wants for us.

Our trust muscles won't be exercised. Again, going to an older woman or a friend isn't bad, but it also doesn't require us to actively pray and seek the Lord. In addition, like us, the older woman or friend is limited in knowledge, wisdom, and insight.

We'll miss the experience of finding the treasure ourselves. Discovering a jewel in God's Word yourself rather than someone else discovering and showing it to you is a totally different experience. Their mining may enhance your relationship with them, but it doesn't always strengthen your relationship to God, nor does it give you a growing desire for Scripture.

Wise people in our life are to our growth what commentaries are to Bible study. We go to the source first and then confirm our conclusions with secondary sources.

Gulp Living Water

If I could hammer home one thing to women in ministry, it is that we must learn to study Scripture and develop a devotional life that resembles gulping water. Or as Scripture describes it, "As the deer pants for streams of water, so my soul pants for you, my God. My soul thirsts for God, for the living God" (Ps. 42:1–2 NIV).

I use the word *gulp* because it reminds me of one of my heroes, Corrie ten Boom. Interned in a Nazi concentration camp during World War II, Corrie was starved of freedom, food, and family. What kept her alive was a contraband Bible she miraculously kept hidden throughout her ordeal. Corrie describes "gulping" entire Gospels in one sitting and "living" in the truths of the Word as if they were written for her exact situation. In a flea-ridden bunkhouse, so filthy that no guard would enter it, she and her sister, Betsie, would open the Bible and read aloud, waiting as different voices translated the life-giving words into German, Polish, and French.

> Like waifs clustered around a blazing fire, we gathered about it, holding out our hearts to its warmth and light. The blacker the night around us grew, the brighter and truer and more beautiful burned the word of God. . . . I would look about us as Betsie read, watching the light leap from face to face. More than conquerors. . . . It was not a wish. It was a fact. We knew it, we experienced it minute by minute—poor, hated, hungry. We are more than conquerors. Not "we shall be." We are![1]

If Scripture sustained these women in the darkest of places, surely it can be our sustenance in both the mundane days of ministry and the days that feel too overwhelming and hard.

Confession: for the first five to seven years of serving in vocational ministry, I did not consistently seek the Lord through Bible reading. I'd open my Bible only when I felt inspired, when I felt guilty, or when I was preparing to teach.

But then suffering hit like a gigantic wave, and I became desperate for comfort, answers, and stability. At the same time, I felt constantly rocked by the demands and struggles accompanying ministry and was in overwhelming need of an anchor. I knew my anchor was Christ, and as I searched for hope in the Word and consistently found it, I began craving it like I never had before and devouring God's words because I was so desperate.

The Bible doesn't tell me specifically what to do as a pastor's wife but rather tells me about Jesus. Scripture speaks to me about the One who walks through my suffering with me and how to think about the challenges I face. I need that far more than I need a job description.

This is why Jesus is the source of all wisdom. In knowing him personally through his Word, I can feel him changing me, teaching me how to think, what to value most, how to respond in obedience and calling me to do so, and telling me about the power I can depend on that will help me obey and serve him.

Over time, I've seen the fruit in my life of consistently studying God's Word. Anytime I'm tempted to give up my daily routine, I recall the many benefits knowing God through his Word brings to the believer's life. The fruit of reading Scripture is not immediate, but Psalm 1 tells us that a person who consistently meditates on Scripture will be like a tree planted by rivers of water that brings forth fruit in its season. I don't want to give up. I don't want to neglect what can produce that kind of fruit.

And I don't want you to neglect it either, because if you are to persevere in faith, life, and ministry, it will be because you have tethered yourself in relationship to God and his Word.

Seek and Search Persistently

Think of a woman of faith involved in ministry whom you admire and would say is filled with wisdom. Imagine her at your age or in your stage of life. She too was once exactly where you are, holding the same questions and uncertainties. How did she become wise?

Hebrews 5:12–14 says,

> For though by this time you ought to be teachers, you need someone to teach you again the basic principles of the oracles of God. You need milk, not solid food, for everyone who lives on milk is unskilled in the word of righteousness, since he is a child. But solid food is for the mature, for those who have their powers of discernment *trained by constant practice* to distinguish good from evil. (emphasis mine)

The milk-drinkers have not applied themselves to the discipline needed to gain and grow in wisdom. These are people who are floating along and never meditating on or digesting the truths in a way that changes them. They therefore remain infants—immature and foolish—because they are unskilled in the word of righteousness.

Contrast these infants with how the wise are portrayed. The simple are dull of hearing, but the wise are actively listening to the Word of

God. The wise woman is able to teach others, which doesn't necessitate being a Bible teacher but rather having words of wisdom on her tongue. She herself eats solid food. While the emaciated are drinking from a bottle, she is sitting at a table with a rich feast spread out before her. And it is assuredly a big feast, because the more she seeks wisdom, the more she realizes what she doesn't know and just how much more there is to digest. She is satisfied and strong and healthy. She has enough to share with others. She never goes hungry, even in times of trial and suffering, because she is skilled in righteousness. God has built in her storehouses of wisdom to draw from at all points of her life.

The question is, How did the woman you thought of gain her wisdom? How does she know how God would have her respond to the demands on her time? Her powers of discernment have been trained by constant practice to distinguish good from evil. *Constant practice.*

Pastors' wives face countless situations that require wisdom. As we give ourselves to persistent study of the Word, God will grow us. Wisdom is not instantaneous, because the Bible is not primarily an answer book. It is instead the means by which we know the Source of wisdom and, over time and by the power of the Holy Spirit, begin to think and act like him.

Pastor's wife, out of his storehouses he will grant you the wisdom and understanding you need to know when a yes is appropriate or when a no is best. I can't tell you exactly what you should do and not do in your role, but I can give you a few questions to consider.

Do you have the mindset of a servant? Are you willing to serve as the Lord leads you? "As the Lord leads you" is the key phrase.

Do you trust that as you walk closely with God, he will guide you by his Spirit? Because he will.

Do you seek his answer before you give it to others? And do you seek him before you seek his answer?

The storehouses of wisdom are waiting to be mined.

Six

Cultivating the Skill of Knowing When to Say Yes and When to Say No (Part 2)

uring our decades of ministry, I've learned countless lessons regarding leadership, hospitality, discipleship, evangelism, counseling, and handling setbacks and criticism. But there is one skill I've struggled to learn and implement: saying no.

I definitely know how to say yes. I'm an out-front leader, so I'm not afraid to take on responsibility. I've learned how to say yes in a way that hides my occasional reluctance, and I'm committed to following through with my every yes, sometimes to the detriment of my sanity.

In other words, I often say yes when I should say no. It's not that I struggle to discern whether an opportunity *requires* a yes or a no.

When I'm faced with a decision, I know almost immediately what the answer *should* be according to my God-given priorities. Of course, at times I've had little choice in what I would or wouldn't be involved in. (I'm looking at you, church planting wives and small church pastors' wives.) But apart from the early days of church planting, God has written more distinct lines for me in ministry according to the ages of my children, my capacity, the needs of our church, and the gifts and passions he's given me. That's how I know what my answer should be, because the opportunity either fits in the specific calling God has given me and where he has me in life, or it doesn't.

The truth is that I *could* do many, many good things. I even have an interest in and passion for many, many good things. That's what makes saying no so difficult. However, just because the opportunities are good and noble doesn't mean they come with divine orders on my life. In fact, when I try to do it all, I find myself doing few things well and even keeping other women alongside me in the church from developing and using their gifts.

Knowing and Living according to Your God-Given Priorities

When I'm unclear what God is leading me to do, I consider the relational priorities I know for sure he's given me: I'm a disciple, a wife, a mother, and a professional writer. I'm a pastor's wife, a disciplemaker in community with others, a daughter, a sister, and a friend. If I've made certain commitments, I must also let my yes be yes (Matt. 5:37) until a natural break occurs. For example, if I've committed to teaching Bible study for the school year, I'll reevaluate my commitment after completing the entire year.

All of my relationships and roles are markers, boundaries, and signposts as to where the majority of my time and energy should go. Will there be an occasional yes to something outside of these primary relationships? Of course, but they are rare, because a yes to something outside of what I know I'm to prioritize is most often a no to my husband and children. If I pile up too many consecutive commitments outside of my primary God-given relationships, it costs those closest to me.

As ministry wives bombarded with options and opportunities, our decision-making must be intentional, and our responses to requests must be deliberate. Our hearts must also stay soft and open to people— I try to say yes as much as I can, and I try to communicate love and openness to anyone who approaches me. At the same time, I've learned to never give an immediate answer, especially when a request is made in person, because that's when I'm most tempted to respond how I know the person wants me to respond.

For example, if someone comes up to me after church and requests a coffee date, after thanking them for the invitation I'll ask that they follow up with me through email or text. I do this because (1) with the volume of conversations I have on Sundays, I'll quite likely forget the specifics and (2) it puts the ball in their court. In the early days of ministry, I took every request as my responsibility to follow up on and make happen. I eventually realized that sometimes people just say something in passing—"Let's get together!"—and don't actually intend to follow through with it. I also take this tack because my goal is to bring everything to the Lord in prayer and wait for his direction. I can look at my schedule and see what works for me. The person may have requested an immediate coffee date, but if my schedule screams at me that this will overload the system, I can suggest something further out on the calendar.

As women in ministry, we worship God when we look to please him with our enthusiastic, Holy Spirit–backed yes or our unapologetic, Holy Spirit–backed no. We become disciplined leaders when we consistently and prayerfully reevaluate what our few God-given passions are to be and then align our schedules and decisions accordingly. And as disciplined leaders we're poised to deeply impact the kingdom of God.

If you need to grow in the skill of discernment and saying no, here are some suggested next steps.

First, know that you have permission to say no. The ministry to which God has called you is often difficult, sacrificial work, but he's not calling you to do everything for everyone. It's right to live as a limited person; this very much honors the One who made you.

Second, spend some time praying and thinking about where God is drawing boundary lines for you. Imagine a line down a page. Consider one side of the line as his priorities for you and the other side as those good-but-not-essential opportunities. Write down names, roles, commitments, and ministry areas on either side of the line so you can refer to them again and again and begin to adjust your schedule accordingly. Make sure you're not saying no to the priorities God is giving you by saying yes to too many opportunities on the other side of the line.

Third, prepare yourself to respond well when no is not an option. There are situations in ministry when the schedule or the priorities go out the window—someone shows up at the door in tears, a crisis occurs, or a volunteer quits unexpectedly and your husband asks you to step in for a while to provide stability. We don't want to live simply reacting to life and not making intentional choices about our time, but then again, we don't always have the choice. Interruptions are at times God's way of asking us to set aside our plan for the day so we can listen to and love a hurting person, to joyfully sacrifice time with our husband so he can offer the ministry of presence to a grieving church member, or to serve outside our comfort zone for a season in order to edify the church. Prepare yourself in advance to embrace these times as opportunities to sacrificially serve the Lord.

Finally, consider how you will graciously say no to the opportunities on the nonessential side of the page when they're presented to you. How will you handle Sunday morning requests? Requests through emails and texts? Resolve to always communicate gratefulness for the invitation and honor for the person asking. Communicate how much you wish you could say yes to the opportunity but cannot at this point because your schedule or season of life won't allow it. And consider how you'll prepare yourself to respond to the inevitable discomfort in knowing you may disappoint people with your no.

As I said before, this last step is where I stumble. It's not enough to *know* what needs a yes or a no. I have to actually *say* no, but I get hung up by the fear of disappointing people. The desire to please people instead of God has, at times, caused me to be an undisciplined leader who very rarely said no. This idolatry can easily cause me to become dangerously busy, spreading myself out to anyone who asks. I needed to develop the skill of saying a gracious no.

After repenting of my idolatry, I first asked the Lord to be clear with me about *his* calling and *his* priorities for me. Our yes and no come from his direction, not our own desires. As we walk with him, poised to obey his direction, he hones our discernment and clarity. Psalm 25:12 says, "Who, then, are those who fear the LORD? He will instruct them in the ways they should choose" (NIV).

And then I asked God to help me actually say no when it was necessary.

I quickly learned that saying no when you've been saying yes to most opportunities is extremely uncomfortable. I second-guessed myself constantly. I felt selfish and pretentious. I fretted over what people thought of me after I declined their request. But what I found is that, over time, God's leading in my life came more and more into focus.

God clarified and confirmed what my gifts and calling actually were, something I couldn't see well underneath all my indiscriminate yeses. I also began enjoying relationships again and moving at a healthier pace. God granted me joy in serving him that replaced the misery of spinning plates for the approval of people.

Instead of focusing on what you're saying no to, you will soon discover your focus turning toward the energizing and unique tasks and relationships God has given you. Not only that, but you will have the high capacity and experience the passionate joy of living to please God alone.

Managing the Calendar Together

One Sunday during our second year of church planting, I sat down in my seat at church, looked at the bulletin, and found out for the first time—along with everyone else in the congregation—that a church event was happening at our house that very week, and I was the hostess.

My husband said he thought he'd talked to me about it.

He had not.

As you can imagine, I was none too happy with him, but his fumble led to a fruitful conversation about how we were going to handle communicating about the logistics of our busy ministry life. Up until that point, we'd been winging it, but life and ministry were growing increasingly more complex, so we needed an intentional plan for managing our calendars.

What we started that day has changed somewhat over time according to the ages and needs of both our children and our church, but the need for communication about our schedule has remained constant. Again, what I share is not prescriptive but will hopefully spark good thought and conversation between you and your husband.

Every Sunday evening, we pull out our calendars and discuss the upcoming week. We use Google Calendar so we can share our calendars with one another and I can also see the church's calendar. With our calendars open, we talk about the demands of the week, who is taking care of what, and what ministry or social events are coming up. We also discuss requests involving both of us that we haven't yet answered and make decisions together.

After talking about the week ahead, sometimes we look at the rest of the upcoming month. We schedule family time and date nights every few weeks, and consider potential people we want to invite over or spend time with. We seek to invest intentional time in church staff and elder relationships and people we're discipling, so that's discussed as well.

This may sound rigid and formulaic, but it's become a rhythm of life and communication that helps us stay on the same page and make healthy decisions for ourselves, our marriage, and our family.

You certainly don't have to do it the same way we do, but I do think it's important to consider how you're managing your schedule. You may not be a planner, but if you don't plan in some form, ministry will run your life, and you will be tossed by the wind and waves of everyone else's demands on your time. I think it's also important because the way you schedule yourself and the priority you place on this as a couple communicates your commitment to one another, to your children, and to your church.

What are you communicating by the way you schedule your life?

Managing Yourself

There are many times when I simply feel overwhelmed by it all. I often say I feel like I have a full-time job and two part-time jobs: I'm a pastor's wife, a mom, and a writer. On any given day, I'm not always sure which is the full-time job and which are the part-time jobs. They all require every ounce of my capacity and engagement.

I know you can relate. One of the confounding questions on the mind of every pastor's wife is, *How do I juggle family, work, church, friendships, and community ministry?* There aren't enough hours in the day to fit it all in, which is why an innocent request for a coffee date on Sunday after church can send us into a tailspin.

Just as we must intentionally manage our calendars, we must also intentionally plan and manage our days.

I've found it helpful to think of a typical day in "chunks." It's my goal that these chunks reflect the priorities God has given me. Thinking in terms of chunks or blocks of time also helps me keep certain times open for women in my church or building friendships. Depending on my season of life and work schedule, I typically pick out weekly times I can offer women in our church (a walk on Sunday afternoon, coffee dates before kids come home from school, early morning breakfasts or hanging out on our porch after kids go to bed) so I have chunks to offer when they ask.

Here's an example of the chunks in my typical day:

- Early mornings before kids get up: spending time in the Word and prayer, checking in with my husband about how we can be praying for one another.
- Mornings: exercising and working.
- Early afternoons: meeting up with women from church or friends and running errands.
- Afternoons: helping kids with homework, spending time with my children, shuttling kids to appointments or activities, and making dinner.
- Evenings: enjoying dinner with my family and time with my husband; one to three nights a week typically include ministry-related activities.

That is what works for me. You may be a homeschooling mom, you may work outside the home full-time, or you may live in a different culture from mine in which the flow of social relationships happens differently, so your chunks of time may look different, but the point is to consider how your schedule reflects your priorities.

Ministry *is* a juggling act, but remember: intentionality is important so that whatever you do, you can do it for the glory of God (Col. 3:23).

PART 2

You
AND
God

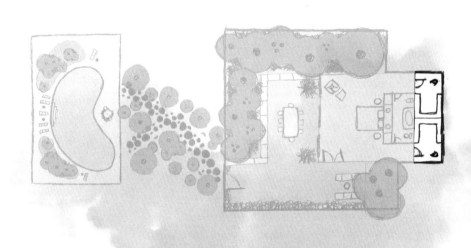

Seven

Locating God

*N*ow that we've located ourselves—remembering we're anchored in identity, giftedness, and humanity—let's turn our attention to the most important relationship in our life. We'll start by returning to the architect's drawing in order to specifically locate God.

Notice on the image, deep in the back crevice of your private room—representing the intimate marriage you share with your husband—is a personal closet. This closet symbolizes the heart of God's plan for your life, because the closet is where he calls you to meet with him: "But when you pray, go into your room and shut the door and pray to your Father who is in secret. And your Father who sees in secret will reward you" (Matt. 6:6).

Daily, God invites you to meet with him there in the quiet space through prayer, Scripture, journaling, tears, and song.

Of course, God goes with you everywhere you go and helps you in everything you do, but it is in your prayer closet that you bow before him in complete vulnerability to commune with him. There you cast your cares upon him, ask him for what you need, and hear through the Scriptures of his love toward you. There he renews your mind and reorients you once again around the gospel.

And then the closet is where you get dressed in preparation for the day ahead.

> Put on then, as God's chosen ones, holy and beloved, compassionate hearts, kindness, humility, meekness, and patience. . . . And above all these put on love, which binds everything together in perfect harmony. (Col. 3:12, 14)

> Put on the whole armor of God, that you may be able to stand against the schemes of the devil . . . [and] withstand in the evil day, and having done all, to stand firm. (Eph. 6:11, 13)

Your daily time with him, tucked away in intimate communion with the Lord, is the foundation and fuel for all the other arenas and relationships in your life. In fact, you will not experience vitality in your marriage or family, nor fruitfulness in ministry, without this intimate communion. "Abide in me, and I in you. As the branch cannot bear fruit by itself, unless it abides in the vine, neither can you, unless you abide in me" (John 15:4).

An impactful life is only an overflow of private devotion to the Lord.

I invite you now to join me in the prayer closet and discover who God is to you in the deepest recesses of your soul and in the deepest needs of ministry life.

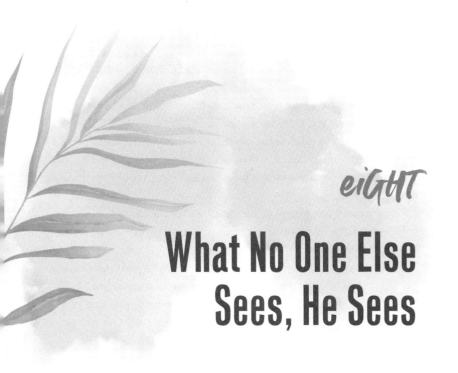

eiGHT

What No One Else Sees, He Sees

Several years ago, I stood at a lectern in a room filled to over-flowing with pastors' wives, teaching with my friend and fellow pastor's wife Shauna. At the conclusion of our talk, we took questions. One young pastor's wife stood up and, with her voice trembling, asked, "What do I do if I feel my husband loves the church more than me?"

A hush and a heaviness fell over us, and as Shauna moved toward her in empathy, every single woman who was sitting, standing, or scrunched in a corner of the room started crying.

We cried because we knew.

We instinctively understood the pain she was feeling, the complexity of church ministry and how the wife of a pastor could come to such a conclusion, and the panic of uncertainty of where to turn or what to do when you are the one people constantly turn to, looking for answers. We knew the isolation of smiling when you want to cry and enduring when you want to escape. We understood the weight of the pastor's burden, so we knew the burden this young woman carried as well. We were crying for her but also for ourselves—not out of self-pity but rather the God-honoring groan of longing for wrongs to be made right and tears to be wiped away forever.

As Shauna responded to her question, I felt a desperation to erase this woman's difficulties or give her a simple solution, but in ministry, as in life, difficulties can't always be deleted and solutions don't come easy, if at all.

This is every Christian's calling: to move through a broken-down world with faith, our eyes set on Jesus and our feet running the race he's set before us. And the specific race he's set before you and me is being a pastor's wife: loving our pastor-husband, serving God's people, and setting out the gospel for others like a lit-up city on a hill.

As you know well, the race he's marked out for us has unique joys and challenges. Now, in this section of the book, we will turn our attention to the challenges and how God meets us in them.

Fellow pastor's wife, I ask that you trust me with your heart and your hurts in this and the following chapters. If you're anything like me, you often don't want to read someone else's take on the difficulties of being a pastor's wife. You *live* them, for goodness' sake, and on the one hand, you don't want more unnecessary tears. You don't want to wallow in how the challenges of ministry have affected you. You've done that before, and you know it's not productive or helpful. Your latent anger doesn't need fuel. Your wounds don't need reopening.

On the other hand, you don't want anyone to paint a rosy picture of ministry that ignores the reality of your experience. You don't want anyone addressing the life you live by glossing over challenges and putting a Bible verse as a bow on them. You want honesty and vulnerability.

That's why I ask for your trust. I promise to give honest voice to the challenges of ministry and also to remind you of truth and your very real hope. We will neither gloss over nor wallow. We will, together, walk the narrow path of faith toward our good God.

That's what we did that day when the young woman stood and asked her brave question with quivering lips. We cried, acknowledging the pain and difficulty. *Sometimes it hurts so much.* And then we said what's true in the midst of this broken-down world we seek to impact: God sees, he is with you, and he will never leave you.

He's worth it all.

Hidden Vulnerabilities

On Sunday afternoons, my husband and I often go for a walk and debrief the church service. We talk about the sermon, and I offer him specific ways God spoke to me through his preaching. We talk about what encouraged us and, sometimes, what discouraged us. Finally, we talk about our various conversations, whether with longtime members or new visitors.

There have been many times in our two decades of ministry—usually those discouraging days—where I've recounted my Sunday morning to Kyle and closed by saying, "I so badly wish I could explain to others exactly how I experience church as the pastor's wife." If only I could voice in detail what's hard or what hurts or why I think they should appreciate my husband more, I'm convinced I'd feel better. I'd feel known and seen, and everything about ministry would become easier.

Usually this is just me complaining, and I'm quickly reminded by the Lord (and, often, my husband, in gentle love) that ministry is not about me and my own comfort.

But sometimes I face legitimate hurts and unmet desires, and in most cases I can't voice those things within the church. For example, it wouldn't be appropriate for me to tell people in the church that I'm struggling to love them or am wearied by their demands on my husband's time. Instead, I must lovingly absorb what's hard or what hurts for their sake, seeking to meet them with God's grace and truth in every conversation and interaction.

This is what it means to be a leader.

You may be a ministry wife who shuns the spotlight, but those you serve still consider you to be one of their leaders. Your position alone grants you influence, and this positional influence can create similar dynamics to what your out-front leader husband experiences.

What we experience in positional leadership is what Andy Crouch, in his book *Strong and Weak*, calls "hidden vulnerability." He defines *vulnerability* not as transparency but as "exposure to meaningful risk" and *authority* as "the capacity for meaningful action."[1] He says,

> Leaders have evident authority—but almost by definition, they also bear vulnerability that no one else can see. . . . This is what it is to be a leader: to bear the risks that only you can see, while continuing to exercise authority that everyone can see.[2]

The difference between the pastor and the pastor's wife is that she often bears invisible vulnerability with only *perceived* authority. In other words, we carry similar emotional risks to those of our husband but, other than influencing our husband, we often have few pathways for meaningful action. For example, if someone is upset at our husband or there is conflict or discord within the church, we often know the details but don't typically have recourse for approaching the person nor the opportunity to produce resolution.

So we carry it all internally.

A pastor's wife could be compared to an iceberg (though hopefully not because we're coldhearted!). What the church sees is only the tip of the iceberg: they observe where you sit on Sundays, they know who your children are and a few details about them, they know whether or not you work outside the home, and they could accurately describe your personality if asked. They see how you relate to people and in what ways you visibly serve. However, just as the majority of an iceberg is beneath the surface of the water, most of what you do and most of the burdens you carry could be considered unseen: the insights you provide for your husband as he prepares the sermon, the way you get the kids to church on your own, the prayers you offer every day for hurting people, the sacrifice of time you make, and the conscious decisions you make to keep quiet rather than defend your husband when he's questioned or slandered.

And they *can't* see these things, not because they are unloving or apathetic toward you but because *this is what leadership entails,* especially leadership in ministry. Leadership in ministry is servant-hood: using our positional authority and influence to help others know Christ and grow in relationship to him and others. So if we're to endure in what God has called us to do, we must learn to bear our hidden vulnerabilities well.

What are some of these vulnerabilities we encounter throughout ministry life? The list is long.

Loving the church in a way others may not relate to or understand.

Experiencing a constant pull on our attention and time.

Wearing multiple hats at church: wife, mom, congregant, and positional leader.

Navigating blurred lines between church community and social relationships or friendships.

Absorbing criticism of the one we love most in the world.

Carrying concern for a disheartened and discouraged husband.

Fearing that church pressures will drive our children to despise God's people.

Having many acquaintances and being known by name and sight in crowds of people but feeling lonely.

Carrying conversations and being asked few personal questions.

Living in the shadow of a gifted and admired husband.

Experiencing financial strain.

Living far from family.

Being warily cautious of friendly overtures because of past betrayal.

Fighting to keep a soft heart while carrying private hurts.

Recognizing the weight of our influence and words and, at the same time, our humanity and weakness.

Sharing our husband with everyone.

Juggling availability and openness to people with family time.

Interacting with someone whom we know is upset with our
   husband.

Loving people who are lukewarm in faith.

Serving in ways we don't necessarily feel passionate about or
   equipped for.

Living with the weight of inescapable responsibility.

Questioning whether or not God is using us.

Wrestling with guilt over not being or doing enough.

Grieving when a friend leaves the church.

The apostle Paul so knowingly summarizes gospel ministry: "And,
apart from other things, there is the daily pressure on me of my anxiety for all the churches" (2 Cor. 11:28).

When pastors' wives confess in survey after survey that they are
lonely, I think more often than not they're expressing the isolation
they feel that is a natural consequence of their hidden vulnerabilities.[3] By "natural consequence," I mean there are many things that
remain under the surface of our relationships because they can't be
explained in words; they can only be experienced by those in our
shoes. In addition, there are some things that *must* remain under
the surface—unsaid and unacknowledged—because this best honors
God, our husband, and people in our church.

How, then, do we bear our hidden vulnerabilities well?

Turn to the God Who Sees

First, a caveat: we are not the only group of people who bear hidden
vulnerabilities. Anyone who seeks to obey Christ must take up their
cross and die to themselves. Because obedience is a type of death,
it can be excruciating, uncomfortable, and raw. It can leave us feeling exposed, fragile, and shaky, like the last leaf swinging on the tree
branch in fall. Often, we must fight terribly hard to resist temptation,
sit in the discomfort of the crucified flesh's last gasps, and do all of it
without promise of immediate benefit. In other words, the wrestling

and self-death obedience requires are rarely seen or fully understood by others.

One way we fight against self-pity or isolation in our hidden vulnerabilities is to remember that the people we minister to have their own vulnerabilities we aren't aware of. They too come to church on Sundays with private hurts and hang-ups. They too wish others could understand their specific experiences. They too make sacrifices for the sake of the gospel. If we remember this, we starve any exceptionalism and isolation we're prone to and instead feed our empathy and faithful perseverance.

Each time I start to pity myself for what my husband's job means for me, I remember Proverbs 14:10: "The heart knows its own bitterness, and no stranger shares its joy." In other words, there are feelings we have, both joyful and sorrowful, that ultimately cannot be understood by another person. Sometimes we can't even express how we feel to others, and sometimes even when we try, when we lay it all out, bare, we still aren't fully understood. There are limits to human love, and if we rely solely on human love for our comfort, we'll grow bitter and hard and distant from others in our disappointment.

Thankfully and incredibly, God loves differently. He is not hindered or limited in his understanding or love. He loves us intimately. All those feelings we have about our life situation? All those thoughts we wrestle with? All our struggles to comprehend and navigate our difficulties? He knows them even more than we can articulate them to ourselves, much less to others.

Because he knows us intimately, he also comforts us intimately by fully entering our pain. Unlike most humans, God can handle its weight, emotion, and complexity in its entirety. We can go to him and be understood. And that is when our pain is eased. From him, we gather strength to face another day. Through him, we see others with his eyes, and we realize that everyone has pain. In him, peace finds a dwelling place in our souls.

He is the God who sees.

The first time in the Bible God is named the God of Seeing (El Roi) is by Hagar in Genesis 16. Because Hagar conceived a child with Abram,

Abram's wife, Sarai, dealt so harshly with Hagar that she fled her home. The situation was rife with sin: Sarai's self-made plans to get a child from God, Abram's willingness to go along with the plan and his passiveness toward Hagar, and Hagar's contempt of Sarai after discovering her pregnancy. Hagar had no recourse to protect or provide for herself and her unborn baby—she was a slave who'd been mistreated. In other words, she was completely vulnerable. In response, she retreated to the wilderness. There, an angel of the Lord appeared to her, telling her that her unborn child was a son she should name Ishmael, meaning "God hears," because God heard her affliction.

Hagar's response? "You are a God of seeing. . . . Truly here I have seen him who looks after me" (Gen. 16:13).

Ministry wife, perhaps you empathize somewhat with Hagar. Maybe you feel stuck in a no-win situation. Perhaps someone has dealt harshly with you, even though you've tried to serve them well.

God sees you. He looks after you. You are not alone.

What a comforting and encouraging thought!

But there's more. God doesn't just see; he also *understands* what it means to bear vulnerability as a result of service. Andy Crouch says,

> His authority was evident to everyone—at every turn of the gospel narratives we see Jesus exercising unparalleled capacity for meaningful action as well as restoring authority to the marginal and the poor. But no one fully grasped Jesus's vulnerability. Those around him comprehended almost nothing of his true purpose and destination. The gospel writers report that even when Jesus began to try to explain to his disciples the fate he knew awaited him in Jerusalem, they resisted and did not understand. As his ministry brought him nearer and nearer to the final confrontation with the forces of idolatry and injustice, only Jesus understood what was truly going to be lost.[4]

How did Jesus endure his hidden vulnerabilities—being misunderstood by his closest friends and slandered by religious leaders, having no home in which to take refuge, and knowing God's will was to lay the wrath for sin upon his shoulders?

He endured because of the joy set before him (Heb. 12:2). He set his sights on pleasing his Father, whose goal was to use him to bring "many sons and daughters to glory" (2:10 NIV).

We're told in Scripture that this is how we bear our own hidden vulnerabilities: by "looking to Jesus, the founder and perfecter of our faith" and "[considering] him who endured from sinners such hostility against himself, so that [we] may not grow weary or faint-hearted" (12:2–3).

When we consider Jesus, we find

> we do not have a high priest who is unable to sympathize with our weaknesses, but one who in every respect has been tempted as we are, yet without sin. Let us then with confidence draw near to the throne of grace, that we may receive mercy and find grace to help in time of need. (4:15–16)

Our sacrifice, though not equal to Christ's, does not go unnoticed by God, nor is it forgotten. Rather, it is greatly rewarded by the God who sees all. He honors those who give away their lives in his honor.

Turn to him, dear sister, with the pain of your hidden vulnerabilities. In the next chapter, we'll look at how Scripture gives us language when we do so. But for now, know that the Lord has borne your sins on the cross; certainly he can bear every thought, question, and emotion you carry as well.

Turn to Those Who Understand

During a difficult period in ministry, I tried voicing a tiny sliver of my pain to others when they sought me out to share their own pain with me. I wanted to empathize with them and communicate that they weren't alone, but I also felt as if I were dipping my toe in the water, testing to see if they'd probe further and seek to minister to me.

None did, and I later realized why: I was attempting to reveal some of my hidden vulnerabilities with people who had little ability to understand them and no meaningful authority to affect my circumstances.

I remember thinking, *Is this my lot in life: going it alone?*

The answer is a resounding no. As I already noted, it wouldn't be appropriate for me to share all of my hidden vulnerabilities with those my husband and I serve. But I *can* share them. As Andy Crouch puts it, "No one survives hidden vulnerability without companions who understand."[5]

Friends are an important component to our spiritual and emotional vitality, which we'll discuss in later chapters, but who are companions who definitely understand? Other ministry wives!

I think again about how it felt to stand in that room of pastors' wives, seeing tears on every face. All it took was one brave woman to voice a struggle we each knew well for a sense of togetherness and unity to fill the room. To conclude our time, Shauna had us all stand and link arms. As she prayed, asking God to help us fulfill what he'd called us to, I thought to myself, *What a picture of who we are to one another.*

Pastors' wives are a gift to one another. We can spend time together and get right to the heart of things, because we don't have to explain. We know.

Enjoying the gift of a companion who understands does require vulnerability, however, and I've been in many a room of pastors' wives where authentic transparency was severely lacking. I can only speak for myself in saying that I often go into those spaces thinking, *I'm the only one struggling. It seems like everyone else knows exactly what they're doing.*

I've found, however, that when I voice an honest struggle combined with an honest desire to honor God, other women meet me in my vulnerability.

I encourage you, ministry wife, to go to the God who sees and find comfort in him, but then consider who are your "companions who understand." Don't wait for others; make the first move. Gather ministry wives in your church or in your community. Join an online network. Call up your long-distance friend who is also in ministry. Attend an event your network or denomination is hosting for pastors' wives. Wherever you can, develop relationships with companions who understand. Link arms with them and bear one another's hidden vulnerabilities with the help of the God who sees.

Nine

Cultivating the Skill of
Lament

I received an email last week that pierced me to the core: a friend told me she was leaving our church.

Over the course of ministry, more people have chosen to leave than I care to count, and it never gets easier, even when a person leaves well. Although many have assured me, as they walked out the door, of their respect for me and for my husband, it's difficult not to take it personally. Being left always hurts, as if a comrade in war has decided to walk away and abandon us in the midst of battle.

Feelings are not always truth, but they definitely take over in the moments when the email arrives in the inbox or, more often, we hear through the grapevine that someone has gone.

One of the most common questions I receive is, "How do you handle it when people leave your church? How do you not take things personally?" One church planting wife voiced to me the confusing predicament we often find ourselves in: "[Since we started our church plant], we've had three or four families move on who were very close to us. We consider them friends and of course want them to worship where they feel called. However, it still really hurts, especially for my husband. How do you navigate this journey? It is awkward and sometimes I don't know whether to reach out to the wife or just let it go. It is a lot to go through as a family when you realize people that you labored with will no longer be there. And then the congregation questions us as to where these people have gone or why they have left."

In situations like this, there is no way around taking it personally—that would require turning off our emotions—but there is a way *through*: bringing our hidden vulnerability to God using the biblical language of lament. Lament is a practical way we turn to our God who sees.

According to Mark Vroegop, lament is "the honest cry of a hurting heart wrestling with the paradox of pain and the promise of God's goodness."[1] Stacey Gleddiesmith elaborates further: "A lament honestly and specifically names a situation or circumstance that is painful, wrong, or unjust—in other words, a circumstance that does not align with God's character and therefore does not make sense within God's kingdom."[2]

A lament expresses emotion: "You hold my eyelids open; I am so troubled that I cannot speak" (Ps. 77:4).

A lament at times holds our questions out to God: "Why, O LORD, do you stand far away? Why do you hide yourself in times of trouble?" (10:1).

A lament can even be a complaint: expressions of sorrow, fear, frustration, and even confusion.[3] "In arrogance the wicked hotly pursue the poor" (v. 2).

Ministry holds many lamentable experiences, but how often do we stop and actually lament them before God?

Most of the time we tell ourselves we're fine and just try to keep moving. Who has time to sit in their feelings? Who wants to dwell on negative experiences and emotions? And isn't it wrong to complain about hard things?

Actually, God invites us to do this very thing.

The Day I Learned to Lament

One summer, as I walked along the beach on a family vacation, God invited me to lament the lamentable parts of my life. I'd just been reading a passage in a book about the practice of lament; I no longer remember its words, nor do I remember the exact book, but I do remember my hesitancy at the idea of thinking too deeply about the unchangeable things, the unfixable things, the *painful* things in and around me.

I walked in silence, thinking and waiting. *Why,* I wondered to myself, *does it feel as if I'd be doing something wrong if I were to voice to God what aches in my heart?* The salty mist clung to my skin; the sun's heat I'd attempted to escape with an early morning walk burned hot on my neck. I felt uncomfortable inside and out.

Suddenly I remembered the simple phrases from the psalmist's pen that had kept me afloat toward the end of the previous spring: *God sees. God hears the cries of the afflicted. God has not overlooked.*

The memory of these words was the invitation again, for if he sees and hears me, then he already knows what pains me. He's simply asking me to voice it to him.

And so I began, tentatively at first but bravely by the end, telling God what he already knew but what I could only just then admit to myself: mainly that there are costs to following and serving him.

There are costs for me in this, I told him, looking up at the sky. By that point of the vacation, we'd been removed from our usual routines long enough that I could see my life back at home with such clarity.

The costs scare me, I continued. *I don't know if I can endure in them.* Then I began to name them out loud, one by one, painful things cascading out of me like the waves breaking on the shore.

I'd known there were costs to following and serving Jesus; the Bible lays it all out, right there in black and white and sometimes red. Perhaps that's why we recoil at the idea of lament, because we tell ourselves we should have known what we were in for and shouldn't do anything that resembles complaining. Or maybe we recoil because we don't think being a Christian allows for grieving parts of what it actually means to be a Christian.

What I discovered that day on the beach is that when we get down to the details and the specifics and the realities of what it means to follow Jesus, when we experience pain because of it, an important part of embracing those costs is mourning them before God himself.

I stopped walking, stood where my toes were washed momentarily in the tide, and watched the ocean liners in the distance. As I spoke my costs out loud to God in prayer, I felt as if he were taking them from my hands in order to intently observe them, much like I'd done the day prior when my children had brought me a hermit crab they'd found. We'd put the crab in a sand bucket, circled up, and bent over to watch its every move as it frantically tried to escape its plastic cage. God also closely and compassionately observed my pains.

God sees. He hears the cries of the afflicted. He has not overlooked.

We discover these truths most intimately when we mourn before God, even if the mourning is about what he's asked of us. Without lament, we don't know the richness and the reality of the truth. Without lament, we feel and emote without also inviting truth to reign in our hearts and our hope to be reset in God.

In the months leading up to that walk, I'd felt the costs much more than I'd known the truths of God's perfect care. I hadn't given him opportunity to reach out his hands and take my concerns. Instead, I'd fostered my own bitterness, feeling the costs but assuming I'd nowhere to throw my pain.

With each care I handed him, he didn't remove its costs or rescue me from the unchangeable. Lament doesn't change our circumstances. The person still leaves the church. The friend doesn't return to her husband or to the Lord. But through lament, God redirects our gaze.

The weight of ministry had grown so heavy because I'd tried to carry it without complaint, without shedding a tear, without acknowledging my own mourning. As a result, I'd daydreamed of a way out. I wanted a different race to run, not the one God had clearly set before me.

Only in gazing at Jesus did I see why God had invited me to mourn. Because the One who sees, who hears the cries of the afflicted, who

90

has not and will not overlook the faithfulness of his followers, is One who knows the truest costs of all. Looking at Jesus, as Hebrews 12 tells me to do, I know what he endured will never be asked of me. Looking at him, I see that the costs are worth it. I can lament them before God, knowing he cares for me—and in the end knowing I'm secure from the worst lament possible.

Following Jesus isn't all about costs. It's also about rewards. Jesus endured the cross in order to have joy. We too know rewards that only come through embracing the costs: peace, purpose, salvation, heaven.

On the beach that day, in the midst of my tears, with all my unfixable things left unfixed, I also began telling God about the rewards of following and serving him. They far outnumbered all that I'd mourned a few moments prior, and I'd only seen them so clearly after my lament.

The Pattern of Lament

How exactly do we lament our hidden vulnerabilities? Numbers 11 gives us a good example to follow.

As the chapter opens, the Israelite camp is overcome with discontented people. They've been caravanning in the wilderness for two long years, and they're dwelling on their "misfortunes" (Num. 11:1). In their frustration, they complain to one another: "Oh that we had meat to eat! . . . [Our] strength is dried up, and there is nothing at all but this manna to look at" (vv. 4, 6). Their words drip with ingratitude, forgetfulness, and entitlement.

They have a legitimate desire—there's nothing inherently wrong with their specific craving for meat. What's wrong is where they have *turned* with their desires. The Israelites turn against Moses and toward one another, echoing and fueling one another's complaints. They don't even consider turning to God, who has led them out of Egypt and provided for them every step of the way.

Angered by their complaints, the Lord disciplines them, eventually naming their location *Kibroth-hattaavah*, which means "graves of craving" (v. 34). In their right desire and need, they've turned away from God and straight into a grave.

Moses models a different way of responding to our vulnerabilities. He experiences everything the Israelites do in the wilderness: the uncertainty, the waiting, and the longing for home. Surely his stomach also growls for something more than manna. But when Moses has a need, he doesn't seek understanding or answers from others; he instead turns to the Lord.

As the contagion of complaints echoes through the camp, Moses takes his discouragement to God: "I am not able to carry all this people alone; the burden is too heavy for me" (v. 14). He asks for relief, and even seems to be complaining. Scripture sees no problem with this, however, because he has turned *to* the Lord rather than *away*, bringing a legitimate complaint and need. He remembers what the Israelites have forgotten: God is the faithful provider, so Moses can and does request God's response based upon God's nature.

When we too are trapped in the pain of our own personal wilderness, it matters where we turn. We can turn toward others or turn inward with our bitterness, but both of these options only lead to graves of craving.

Or we can turn toward the One who is ready to listen and provide. He is near. He is life. And, as with Moses, he is poised to answer even before we're finished pouring out our hearts to him.

Turn to him. Tell him. And trust him. This is the model we're given in Scripture for lament.

God won't rescue us from the cost of serving him, but he has given us the way through the costs: he sees us and meets us in our lament.

Ten

What No One Else Knows, He Knows

*E*very pastor and pastor's wife carries battle wounds unknown to even the closest around them. The situations they've encountered may be resolved and even be long in the rearview mirror, but scars remain, whether they're from weathering criticism, navigating division in the body, watching someone they've invested in walk away from the faith, or hearing their children describe unrealistic expectations placed upon them. Perhaps a friend broke their trust by sharing their private information, or a congregant's voiced "you should" or "you should not" still hangs heavily in their minds and interactions. Among pastors and pastors' wives, there are even horror stories of vilification, firings, and being treated as an enemy.

What do we make of this? When I was new to ministry, encountering these pains was nothing short of shocking. Now I'm not surprised by much of anything, because I know with greater certainty that "we do not wrestle against flesh and blood, but against the rulers, against the authorities, against the cosmic powers over this present darkness, against the spiritual forces of evil in the heavenly places" (Eph. 6:12). To call the pains of ministry battle wounds is not hyperbolic. We're on the front lines of a spiritual battle, and our enemy wants nothing more than to kill, steal, and destroy the people of God. In my experience, he aims most viciously at two groups: those isolated from God's people and those who lead God's people.

As frontline fighters battling for the souls of men and women, we are what I call "absorbers"—we're generally considered viable options for where congregants can safely bring not only their opinions and preferences but also their hurts, disappointments, frustrations, struggles, and pain. Though their burdens are difficult to carry, this is the great privilege of vocational ministry. However, when people don't know how to *rightly* handle their preferences or their pain and instead release it in the form of anger, slander, suspicion of their leaders, cultivation of disunity, demands, and gossip, we ourselves become the wounded. It helps me to remember that sometimes the sinful overreaction is more about the person's pain than it is about my husband or me, but it hurts nonetheless.

To say that we're absorbers is not saying we don't gently and lovingly reprimand sin and draw biblical boundaries for behavior when appropriate. And I'm also not saying we should avoid difficult conversations or situations. I'm simply naming what it feels like when the sins of others become our own pain and require healing.

We're absorbers because this typically plays out in private. I daresay, as pastors' wives, we are absorbers more than our husband is, because we are more likely to carry pain from others' sin against our husband without having an appropriate avenue to address it. There are a number of relational dynamics to navigate in ministry, and most of our hurts cannot be voiced to others within the community where we're called to live. Some can, but many cannot. So we must continually enter into public spaces, poised to love and serve sometimes the very ones who've hurt us while privately pursuing the Lord's healing.

How do we do this?

With great intention, remembering God knows all.

Resolve to Respond Well

I've made some terrible mistakes in responding to others when I've been hurt. In other words, I've chosen to "absorb" in a way that has turned me sour and, at times, led me to then sin against my brothers and sisters. I've since learned that I must resolve how I will and won't respond *even before hurt comes*. Romans 12:14–21 sets the scaffolding for what we must and must not do in our response to sinful wounds:

> Bless those who persecute you; bless and do not curse. . . . Live in harmony with one another. Do not be proud, but be willing to associate with people of low position. Do not be conceited.
>
> Do not repay anyone evil for evil. Be careful to do what is right in the eyes of everyone. If it is possible, as far as it depends on you, live at peace with everyone. Do not take revenge, my dear friends, but leave room for God's wrath, for it is written: "It is mine to avenge; I will repay," says the Lord. On the contrary:
>
> > "If your enemy is hungry, feed him;
> >   if he is thirsty, give him something to drink.
> > In doing this, you will heap burning coals on his head."
>
> Do not be overcome by evil, but overcome evil with good. (NIV)

What, according to the apostle Paul, must we choose in order to return blessing for reviling we've received?

Resolve Not to Assume You and Your Husband Are Always Right

In verse 16, Paul tells us we aren't to be proud. Pride makes us unwilling to hear constructive feedback, honest questions, and the good ideas of others. Instead, pride and conceit make us unapproachable and defensive.

We must remember we don't always suffer unjustly; some wounds from other believers are "wounds of a friend" (Prov. 27:6). We're not victims or martyrs, and we're not perfect. Sometimes the feedback we receive is right, comes from a loving place, and can be helpful in our growth. We must prayerfully reflect on our hurts and consider that

God may be trying to get our attention through any painful situation we find ourselves in. In other words, sometimes we cause the hurt. Instead of responding with defensiveness to others, then, we must always be prepared to both receive loving correction from others and also acknowledge when we've hurt them.

Resolve Not to Develop an Overly Sensitive Radar for Angry or Disappointed People

Paul also tells us we aren't to be conceited. Conceit is an excessive focus on self, often including an excessively favorable opinion of oneself.

Anytime Kyle and I have walked through difficult church situations, I find myself overly aware and sensitive to what people think of my husband, me, and our church. Every interaction is guarded, every word spoken to me analyzed, and I find myself trying to stay one step ahead of their potential disappointment. This is a form of conceit: I've placed myself and my favorability at the center of things, and I've thought highly of my ability to win over and please all.

But Galatians 1:10 orients me back home: "For am I now seeking the approval of man, or of God? Or am I trying to please man? If I were still trying to please man, I would not be a servant of Christ."

We must resolve to trust the Lord to care for his church and to care for us along with her. Christ is the head of the church and, therefore, we are not responsible to keep everyone happy. We're responsible to trust and serve him as he directs us.

Resolve Not to Avoid People Who've Hurt You

One of the mistakes I've made in responding to hurt is consciously avoiding specific people in church and social situations. I've told myself that it's no big deal, that no one (including the person I'm avoiding) will notice, but it's later been revealed as blatantly obvious and offensive.

Paul exhorts us in Romans 12:17 to resist avoiding and instead honor all equally, no matter how they treat us: "Be careful to do what is right in the eyes of everyone" (NIV). And in verse 18 he adds, "If it is possible, as far as it depends on you, live at peace with everyone" (NIV).

Paul's word choice of *everyone* leaves us without excuse. We're to honor all people in the way we interact and engage, contributing to a church culture of peace, harmony, and love.

Honoring doesn't equate to trust, however. If someone has blatantly hurt you or others and is unwilling to receive loving and careful feedback or correction, they aren't someone to whom you must trust your heart and innermost thoughts.

Resolve Not to Speak Poorly of Others or Attempt to Draw People to Your "Side"

Avoiding slander is one of Scripture's qualifications for an elder's wife. We must never use our words to speak even a hint of someone else's sin to another person, tear down, make fun of a church member, or speak of our distaste for someone. In addition, we aren't to use our words to defend ourselves or our husband through backroom conversations.

If sin is involved, there are proper channels detailed in Scripture for church discipline, but we pastors' wives are rarely called upon to contribute to this discipline.

Paul doesn't just call us to avoid slander or gossip. He says we're to take a proactive stance: "Bless those who persecute you; bless and do not curse them" (v. 14). We're to actively do good and speak good toward and about them. "If your enemy is hungry, feed him; if he is thirsty, give him something to drink. In doing this, you will heap burning coals on his head. Do not be overcome by evil, but overcome evil with good" (vv. 20–21 NIV).

This is a ministry life with no regrets, nothing to hide, and free of reproach.

Resolve Not to Disengage Your Heart

The gist of Romans 12:14–21 is that we must continue engaging the community of faith, rejecting an unhealthy image of God's people.

I heard a pastor's wife say once, "All sheep bite," referring to the way her husband—the shepherd—was being treated by people in their church. The more I thought about her statement, the more saddened

I became for her and her husband. Working from an image of God's people as angry, biting sheep who only hurt their shepherd negatively affects the way we engage the people God has called us to love. Love believes the best of others (1 Cor. 13:7).

Do sheep bite sometimes? Yes, just as shepherds sometimes act cruelly or apathetically toward their sheep.

When sheep bite, we reflexively pull back, just as we do when our hand gets too close to fire. We must be careful, however, that we don't pull back into ourselves and turn our hearts off but rather hide ourselves in the refuge that is God and let him nurse our wounds.

Sometimes when I'm dealing with church hurt, I almost feel like I'm walking around clenched up, fearful and on alert as to where the next dart or arrow will come from. I can go through the motions of church life, but I want desperately to disengage emotionally. I know that's not the way to thrive in community with others, so I must choose to make intentional efforts to "unclench" my heart.

Before I share how I do that, I wonder if you see a theme in the ungodly responses I've mentioned we must reject. The recurring pattern I see is self-protection: *I will not let anyone get close enough to hurt me like that again. I will not let what's been done affect me. I will work hard to make sure people are pleased with me. I will defend myself and my husband. I will live fearful of the sheep, because they bite.*

Self-protection is what causes my heart and even my body to clench up.

Psalm 5:11–12 is my go-to "unclenching" passage:

> But let all who take refuge in you rejoice;
> > let them ever sing for joy,
> and spread your protection over them,
> > that those who love your name may exult in you.
> For you bless the righteous, O Lord;
> > you cover him with favor as with a shield.

The only true protection we have is God. We will hurt and be hurt by people, but we have a safe place in God. He's called our refuge, our protection, our cover, and our shield, so we don't have to constantly protect ourselves. Because we're hidden in him, we're free to engage others without fear.

The God Who Knows Is a Just Judge

How does hiding in God leave us free to continually reengage, even though we will likely encounter pain again? And how is absorbing pain privately for the sake of the whole something God may ask of us?[1]

Because the name of the One we take refuge in is Just Judge.

I take this helpful truth from 1 Peter 2:19–23:

> This is a gracious thing, when, mindful of God, one endures sorrows while suffering unjustly. . . . But if when you do good and suffer for it you endure, this is a gracious thing in the sight of God. For to this you have been called, because Christ also suffered for you, leaving you an example, so that you might follow in his steps. He committed no sin, neither was deceit found in his mouth. When he was reviled, he did not revile in return; when he suffered, he did not threaten, but continued entrusting himself to him who judges justly.

Consider times when we suffer unjustly. For example, our husband, knowing all the details of a situation, makes a biblical and loving decision and someone with only part of the information criticizes that decision publicly. This is an example of "doing good and suffering for it." It's painful because we cannot correct the wrong—the missing information is private and cannot be shared.

Jesus gives us an example to follow. He kept his mouth from reviling, and this passage says *how* he was able to do that: he was "mindful of God" and "entrusted himself to him who judges justly." In other words, he willingly endured by looking at God and seeking to please him. He laid himself bare before God, knowing he sees all and judges perfectly. God deals with all people according to truth, including me and including you.

This is something I learned early on in ministry when my husband and I were deeply hurt. The situation called for our complete silence on the matter. I was deeply wounded but could not talk about it with anyone except my husband and the Lord. In my hurt, I nursed bitterness and anger. I kept going over conversations and situations, convincing myself of how I'd been wronged. I wanted the truth to be known. I wanted to be vindicated.

At some point, the Lord got hold of me. First, he led me to acknowledge that what had happened was truly wrong. My hurt was real, and he saw that hurt. But then he turned the spotlight onto me and showed me what else was in my heart: bitterness and unforgiveness.

God showed me that he judges justly. I realized I'd taken the hurt as an excuse to sin, and this was just as grievous to my Lord as the other person's sin. I needed to repent and do the hard work of forgiving and rooting out bitterness. I no longer could rehash my hurt if I also wanted to obey God.

But he also showed me that, if he judges justly, then it's his job to convict of sin and deal with the person appropriately regarding what they'd done. I needed to entrust myself *and* the person who'd hurt me to him. This began the process of forgiveness, in which I could release the judgment from my own hands into the Lord's.

In ministry, we must have this same mindset as Jesus. He faced sorrow and hurt, far more than we ever will. Acknowledging the difficult parts of ministry can be helpful, but it isn't permission to harbor bitterness or unforgiveness. It isn't permission to avoid our own sanctification.

It means we must entrust ourselves to God, the Just Judge.

eleven

Cultivating the Skill of
Rooting Out Bitterness

A ll callings have their own unique temptations and challenges. For the pastor's wife, I believe the greatest temptation is to allow bitterness to take root and grow, often leading to her own self-isolation and resentment, or even to anger or depression.

Bitterness can take root in a myriad of ways, but I think its easiest avenue into our hearts is when we've been deeply hurt or when we dwell on not being understood. We *do* have a unique stewardship that many, including those closest to us, may not ever fully understand. You may feel that even your own husband doesn't fully grasp how his work affects you. You may feel that your friends don't share your passion for the Lord, for his church, and for disciple-making. And then there are the difficulties we feel inadequate to navigate— the blurred relational lines, the hurts that must remain private, the burden we feel for our husband as he carries the burdens of many, or the expectation of being available to anyone who wants our time.

When we experience these acutely, it glaringly highlights our sense of being different or alone.

Difference from others, if not celebrated as God-given, is the fertile soil for bitterness. Difficulties and challenges, if not taken to the Lord, pour water and fertilizer on the soil ripe for bitterness. No wonder Scripture exhorts us to "see to it . . . that no 'root of bitterness' springs up and causes trouble" (Heb. 12:15).

Comparison

One of the ways bitterness grows in ministry life is through comparison. When Kyle and I were new to ministry, we were young and childless, and many of our best friends were getting married or gathering for social events on the weekends. I hadn't considered that our weekends were forever changed because my husband was now a pastor. We'd always have to be home on Saturday nights so he could be at church on Sundays. Even now, Saturday nights are "at home" nights, my husband's mind already turning toward church and last-minute adjustments to his sermon. I'm used to shortened weekends now, but in the beginning, I compared what I felt was a lack of freedom with the freedom (and the imagined lack of responsibility) I felt our peers had, and resentment developed in my heart toward my husband's calling.

Comparison that leads to bitterness is a destroyer of joy. It keeps us from the work God has given us to do: cultivating our specific plot of land, as we've discussed previously, in order to bring him glory.

When I compare myself with others or am envious of those with a ministry-free life, when I think, *Why has God called me to this but he hasn't called that person?*, I also think of John 21:18–22. In this passage Jesus says to Peter,

> "Truly, truly, I say to you, when you were young, you used to dress yourself and walk wherever you wanted, but when you are old, you will stretch out your hands, and another will dress you and carry you where you do not want to go." (This he said to show by what kind of death he was to glorify God.) And after saying this he said to him, "Follow me."

Peter turned and saw the disciple whom Jesus loved following them, the one who also had leaned back against him during the supper and had said, "Lord, who is it that is going to betray you?" When Peter saw him, he said to Jesus, "Lord, what about this man?" Jesus said to him, "If it is my will that he remain until I come, what is that to you? You follow me!"

In relation to comparison, the last part is what sticks in my mind: "What is that to you? You follow me!" (v. 22). God had a specific plan for Peter, just as he did for John. God has a specific plan for you too, just as he does for your friends and peers. We're called to be faithful in the life God has given us, not in someone else's life. We're not to look around and inspect the plot of land God has given others, even fellow ministry wives. We're to focus on following Christ.

When our eyes are on him, bitterness can't grow.

Facing Bitterness

Many times in ministry I've announced to my husband or to a friend that I'm weary and discouraged and later realized I wasn't weary or discouraged but rather deeply resentful because of unprocessed ministry hurts.

One year, when good friends had left our church, the wife told me on the way out how I'd failed her. I just tried to go on as if nothing happened, attempting to plug the hole of negative emotions with busyness. I couldn't share the details of the situation with others, but I could say I was weary and discouraged, so that's what I said. It was a more acceptable way of saying that I felt deeply bitter and resentful.

Bitterness lurks around the edges of ministry, looking for ways into our hearts. It's deceptive, because it points blame at others when really there is unacknowledged hurt and fear within ourselves. But bitterness is far more than that; it's acid eating away at joy, cynicism that wants to take everyone else down with us, and exhaustion born from carrying compounding unprocessed negative emotions.

After the incident with that couple leaving the church, I told one of my out-of-town friends I was filled to the brim with cynicism, and she said the wisest and simplest thing she could've said: "Take it to the Lord."

I hadn't considered confession. I hadn't thought of telling the Lord that my heart felt so hurt and so hard that no amount of my own thinking, rationalizing, or work could break apart my brittleness. So I did as she suggested and took it to the Lord.

I sat in my favorite chair by the window that overlooks our backyard and immediately sensed the Lord saying, *Tell me how you feel.* I thought of my recent study of Psalms and how the psalmists were so free with their honest feelings, so I took the leap and poured out my heart in the language of lament he'd taught me.

I feel sad, I told him, *a general malaise of believing I've disappointed that person and maybe am currently disappointing everyone. Some have told me so. I feel a sadness of not being able to make things perfect for everyone, a frustration of feeling the pull that I must try. And I hate feeling sad because it feels like a heavy twinge in my chest that, like an unaware houseguest, has overstayed its welcome. I hate it so much that it's hard to even say the word "sad."*

The truths that came next into my mind were so salient and clear that I grabbed a notebook and scribbled them down. This is what I wrote:

> *Do you recognize your unhelpful responses? Take note, because they never serve you well.*
>
> *Your most instinctive response in the face of negative emotion is to work harder—do the things that will un-disappoint or make it different for people. Do what you think others want, just to get the negative emotion gone. But this is you wanting to please people, slavishly trying to win approval.*
>
> *When that doesn't work, you run and hide in self-protection and defensiveness. You're unwilling to consider if there is any truth to what people have said to you. Instead, you think of all the reasons why others should not be disappointed in you. You justify yourself. You want to walk away from all you know God has commanded—to love, to be faithful—because it suddenly appears too difficult.*
>
> *When that doesn't work, you ignore the emotion and wait for it to go away. You just move on. But that never works. It always comes*

back up, and if anyone says or does anything that touches near that sensitive wound, you react explosively, trying to protect what you don't want to acknowledge is still there.

The twinge in your chest has a name. That pain is legitimate. Name the emotion you feel. Tell it to God. Name the emotion out loud to him and hear yourself say it. Tell him why you feel it. Sit with him in the discomfort of that negative emotion.

Read a psalm or two out loud, like a prayer to God for help. Psalms 25–31 are good places to start.

Wait on God to connect the truth of his character and steadfast love that you read about to the twinge in your chest.

While waiting, the unhelpful responses will call to you. Reject them. They only compound pain.

Repeat.

This is what it looks like to root out bitterness, one terrible thorn and thistle at a time.

Confess Bitterness to Others

We partner with a network of churches in El Salvador and come alongside to help them reach their neighborhoods and encourage our brothers and sisters doing the everyday work there. Last year, I went to El Salvador with a team from our church on a short-term mission trip.

It changed my life.

But not in the way you might think.

I loved the people, and I learned so much from the believers boldly sharing the gospel in their communities. I heard them pray with great faith and testify of God's healing and provision for them in dire circumstances.

But what changed my life happened when I was by myself in my hotel room, where I'd gone after breakfast to gather my things for the day ahead. A few minutes prior, our team had gathered in the hotel courtyard to go over the details and logistics of the day. As we prayed together, I felt the unmistakable compulsion of the Holy Spirit, and I knew I would be disobeying him if I didn't follow his leading.

YOU AND GOD

I didn't want to obey, though, because he was asking me to confess something vulnerable in front of the whole team, including nine teenagers, two of whom were my own boys, and all of whom attended our church and knew me as their pastor's wife.

Before I could let myself off the hook, I asked our team leader if I could say something, and I immediately started crying. I even said out loud, "I don't want to do this," and of course every head jolted up to see my face, to listen intently for what was about to come out of my mouth.

I confessed cynicism. I had thrown a thought out in the van ride the night before that was full of disbelief and cynicism about what God had or could actually do, and it had instantly killed the joyful mood among our team. I apologized. Everyone forgave me, and they moved on.

I then went to my room to grab my backpack and was suddenly overcome with a wave of emotion. Inexplicably, I felt as if my insides were being washed clean, as if a heavy burden had been taken from me.

Something happened in that moment that went way beyond confessing careless words on a van ride.

Restoration happened.

The two previous years had been pretty brutal for me. I'm usually quick to discern what the Lord wants to show me or what sin I need to confess, but those years had been characterized by a lack of clarity and emotional pain, and I'd not been able to figure it out nor do anything about it. I'd asked God to speak to me, help me, and show me the core issue, and he'd spoken to me in words that didn't solve but had provided daily salve: *I am with you. I haven't left you* (Heb. 13:5).

Just what I'd needed, but not what I'd wanted.

I eventually came to recognize that the pain and uncertainty had been localized around one thing: church.

Yes, I believed serving alongside my husband in ministry was the specific stewardship God has given me. Yes, I believed that the church is a gift to all believers, including myself. And, yes, at the same time I'd embodied this role, church had become a hard place for me to be. I couldn't have told you exactly why, and still can't. There wasn't a

106

conflict or a specific hurt or person or situation I could point to in order to explain it away or address it. It was simply a culmination of many difficulties.

What I could explain was that somewhere along the way I'd just started wondering if I belonged. I'd started wondering if my presence mattered as a person and not as a performance. I'd started wondering if I was known. I'd started wondering if anyone might notice my need. My deep self-focus drew me further and further inside, and at some point, I'd simply disengaged my heart. My vitality had been drained out by bitterness.

In those years, I looked back at who I used to be and how passionately I'd loved the church—our church, our people—and I wanted so badly to be that person again. But I couldn't make it happen. I couldn't figure it out. And I started to believe that my heart would never come alive again, for it instead felt so hard and apathetic, looking to be served, noticing every slight, envying others.

Of course, you might not have guessed this if you'd seen me in action. I know how to perform when it's required, a little bit too well, if I'm honest.

But if you have not love, it means nothing.

I never asked for help, partly because I didn't know what to ask for or how to put into words what I was dealing with. But I could not practice what I'd preached for so many years—I couldn't take the risk of vulnerability. I felt so fearful that to ask for what I needed from others would just reinforce my pain.

In my Scripture reading, I zeroed in on the Israelites as they traveled through the wilderness. I paid attention to how they responded to God, and I *really* paid attention to God's steadfast provision and love for his people. Like God had never left them, he'd also never left me, even though my heart had gone far away in search of validation and love from other people, in search of some assurance that I was going to be okay.

I had no love left.

Only bitterness. And bitterness will take you right into self-imposed isolation.

So when I say my insides were washed clean there in that hotel room, I mean my insides were washed clean. God answered the prayer I'd been praying for months upon months upon months. It wasn't my prayer for clarity; it was my prayer for heart change. For joy again.

And it came through one small step of obedience called *vulnerable confession*.

To say to people who I often think expect me to play a certain role in their lives (pastor's wife) that I am a person who has done wrong, that I am a person with great cynicism, that I am a person with needs—that required a vulnerability I hadn't been willing to risk for far too long.

And that confession gave me strength to share more. To pull aside several women in my church and say, with immediate tears, "Church has been hard," and ask them to pray for me and hold my hand and help me. To say to a friend, "I need encouragement and for you to speak what's true to me because I'm not sure anymore." To confess my self-idolatry to that same friend. To simply be a person and not a pastor's wife. To be loved rather than to perform for it.

I thought I'd forgotten what joy was like. I thought I'd forgotten how to love. Cynicism and bitterness had started becoming normal.

But God. He restored to me the joy of his salvation in ways I'd longed for.

Dear pastor's wife, maybe I am saying aloud what you feel. Maybe you think you're the only one, and you've been about ready to give up. My advice to you is what I'll remember and repeat to myself: vulnerability and confession are the keys to God restoring joy. Go to a friend, whether another pastor's wife in your community or a long-distance friend, who will listen and pray and help you release your burdens. May God restore your joy and heal whatever wound you've carried for far too long.

He is able.

And he is good.

And when you do so, bitterness will fly away.

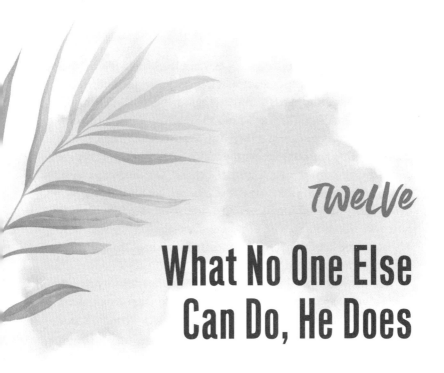

Twelve

What No One Else Can Do, He Does

There are seasons in ministry when it seems the world is closing in and all hope appears lost, times of utter loneliness, times when the well has run dry and we're dreaming of escape. What is going well? What are we doing right? Nothing, as far as our emotions can tell.

"We got no food, no jobs; our pets' heads are falling off." That's the kind of language I use to convey this state of mind to my husband, because he can instantly connect with *Dumb and Dumber* quotes.

I make light of it, but there really is no lightness to times like these. It's all darkness and confusion and heaviness, times when we just need to know that we're on the right track, that we're giving our life to something that matters, that God is somehow using us, that we're appreciated as a vital part of the body of Christ, that we have a friend in the world, that we matter.

This is called *discouragement*.

I always say that ministry is a consistent battle with discouragement. There are always issues to solve, people who are hurting, and something more that needs to get done, and sometimes our empathy muscle gets fatigued. There are truths to be shared so often with others that sometimes our own ability to meditate on and embrace those truths dries up and our relationship with God turns cold. There are people moving away, some leaving the church for another in town, and someone new to town to connect with and get to know; the lack of constancy can easily drain us. And of course there are discouraged husbands who work so hard but sometimes look longingly at those with mindless jobs, wondering what that life would be like, if they're hiring, and how soon he could start.

Whether it's physical weariness, friendlessness, spiritual dryness, opposition, or apparent fruitlessness, our fatigue and frustration can usually be summed up by that dreaded word: *discouragement.* A lack of confidence and courage. Low on hope.

I find that in times of lingering discouragement, I crave words of affirmation from other people. I'm not talking about the healthy, Christ-centered community kind of encouragement. I'm talking about an almost insatiable desire for approval and validation for my contribution to our church family. *If only they would shower me with love and adoration. If only they listened to Christian radio so they could learn October is Pastor Appreciation Month and celebrate accordingly. If only they publicly recognized what I do behind the scenes. If only they came alongside to cheer me on. If only they carried me around on a chariot.*

Do you find, as I do, that when you expect others to sustain your hope through encouragement, God causes them to withhold it the most? And do you also find, as I do, that when others do speak a kind word into the midst of your discouragement, it's not enough—because you've slavishly chased it? Assurance and courage evaporate as soon as the minute passes.

This is God's mercy toward us: no amount of human encouragement will ever meet the deepest needs of the heart. No human encouragement can *reach* the deepest recesses of the heart. And so, he will cause human withholding so that we might turn to the true source of hope and encouragement. God is our hope. His words are the true words of life. His approval is our security and confidence.

When I recognize I'm discouraged, I always think of 1 Samuel 30:6: "But David strengthened himself in the LORD his God." Do you know the story? David and his men came back from battle to find their homes burned and their wives and children taken. His men angrily turned on David, taking up stones to kill him.

He was beyond discouraged, and he was distressed over how his leadership had affected others. "David and the people who were with him raised their voices and wept until they had no more strength to weep" (v. 4).

David, however, sought no person's reassurance about the type of leader he had been. He instead ran immediately to God for wisdom, a sense of his worth, and encouragement. He asked for direction from the Lord, for some discernment in the midst of the grief and confusion. And God gave it to him.

In the end, though his circumstances hadn't changed, David was strengthened and filled with courage for the immense task ahead of him.

David's response has given me a framework for learning to encourage myself in the Lord as he did. Of course, it begins with recognizing that I must allow God to kill any unhealthy desires for words of approval and worth from others, even from my husband. This is always the beginning: confessing sin, confessing when I'm frustrated by unmet expectations, and confessing to God that he alone is my source of hope and courage. When I recognize and acknowledge that my hope is in God and acknowledge what he has done and is doing in my life (and that all hope is not lost), I find he urges me to diagnose the specific source of my discouragement and then ask him for what I need.

Diagnosing Discouragement

We sat in the sun, and its heat beat down in the same way my heart beat up. Like the day, I felt sunny, as if my heart were strolling along and whistling back at the optimistic blue sky. But my friend, who serves faithfully on a campus ministry staff, was a different kind of blue, and she told me why, and her tears sprang easily. I could see so clearly how God was using her and moving in her and gifting her and loving her, but her heart was clouded by that constant and persistent enemy: *discouragement.*

The questions I asked my friend and the words I spoke over her in response to her discouragement came in quite handy, for within the day the clouds had rolled in over my own sun.

Discouragement feels much like an overcast day, doesn't it? Heavy, foggy, and cold. My clouds arrived for various reasons—someone found my work distasteful, a child dodged (again) the wisdom I'd tried to impart, the endless demands kept endlessly demanding my best energy and attention, and several seemingly insurmountable obstacles jumped into my view.

We all face these cloudy days, or what Hebrews 12 calls "drooping hands and . . . weak knees" (v. 12); discouragement wants to trip us and keep us from running the race God has set before us.

No Christian is immune to discouragement. In fact, because the Christian life is a fight against sin and flesh and all their wayward children, we may often find ourselves knocked down, weary, and needing to get back up again while also feeling we lack the strength to do so.

This time, when the clouds rolled in, I thought back to my friend. She'd ask me, "How do you get out of your funks?" And I'd been so certain of my answer on that sunny day. Now, on the cloudy one, I needed to put into practice what I'd offered her. I needed to go back to the questions I ask myself in order to diagnose my discouragement.

What Is Actually Happening?

Emotions easily rise to the surface when the clouds roll in, but they aren't always truth-telling. I may feel discouraged or restless or that my ministry is pointless, but are these feelings correct? My first step in diagnosing discouragement is to prayerfully dig down to the root issue that's causing me consternation. I ask myself these questions:

- What am I actually wishing for or hoping for in this circumstance? Is it a certain outcome or result? And is that outcome or result concerned with self-glory or God-glory?
- What was I doing in the moments before I recognized my discouragement? Was I comparing myself to someone on social media? Was I attempting to control a situation and not getting my way? Was I scrolling through an internal litany of worries or possibilities that make me anxious?
- Am I focused on being faithful or rather on how I (or my husband or my children or our church) appear to other people? Am I doing what I'm doing for the Lord or looking for some form of validation?
- Where is my gaze? Am I staring hard at my discouragement, feeding and fueling it? Or am I making intentional efforts to react with a Godward response?

How Am I or Have I Been Responding?

Noticing and acknowledging discouragement means I must also notice and acknowledge how I've been attempting to assuage it. My natural response is often to attempt to control: to work harder, prove myself, and overcome the obstacles in my life through self-righteousness. This is not a Godward response to discouragement.

In thinking through a response, I then must ask myself these questions:

- God commands me not to be dismayed or fearful or full of worry. He says that I'm instead to cast all my cares upon him because he cares for me (1 Pet. 5:7). Am I casting my cares on him, or am I holding them tightly to myself in worry or despair?
- Am I looking to other people to magically "fix" my situation and, therefore, rescue me from my discouragement?
- Am I acting from a belief that if I work harder next time, I can prevent my own discouragement?

- Am I receiving the gifts of God's care that he's instituted for me? Am I getting enough sleep? Am I getting exercise? Am I spending time with friends? Am I taking time off from work, whether it's paid or volunteer? Am I placing myself within the care of the church through my presence, commitment, and relationships?
- After I've cast my cares upon the Lord, do I need to talk to someone about my discouragement?
- What would it look like for me to trust God in what I'm facing?

What Is True?

After diagnosing *why* I'm discouraged, I need many inputs of truth. And then some more truth.

- What does God require of me? The answer always involves faith and obedience. Am I living from a different answer?
- Have I forgotten that Jesus said, "In this world you will have trouble" (John 16:33 NIV)? How is my discouragement pointing me to him in order to "take heart" by the One who's overcome?
- How is God caring for me? How has he provided for me in the past? How does he promise he will care for me in the future? (It helps for me to write down specifics.) Do I believe him?
- What do I see God doing in and around me? Am I only rehearsing a litany of my worries, or am I purposefully noticing and thinking on the ways I'm seeing and experiencing God's goodness?
- Am I frustrated with a circumstance that is out of my control? How will I trust God in it?
- What specific verses or attributes of God speak to my discouragement?

That last question is the most important one.

Often, when we're discouraged, our view is myopic. More than anything else, we need to zoom out and look at what holds true in every situation and for every person. And that is the character and nature of God.

Fly above the Clouds

Have you ever taken a flight on a gloomy, rainy day? Even as the plane takes off, the eye cannot see far. Fog interrupts the view. Rain trickles down the airplane's window, distorting what can be seen outside. It would seem, based upon what we observe, that the sun has gone into hiding.

And then the plane pushes past the cloud line.

Above the clouds, the sun always shines.

When we're soaking wet in discouragement, God sometimes seems hidden. But when we think about the nature of God and how who he is speaks to our situation, it's as if we've entered the air space above the clouds. We remember his glory and beauty. The big picture comes into view, and we remember he is in control and will never leave us on our own.

Discouragement makes me feel like I'm hanging on an acrobat's bar, high above the ground without a net. What if I can't hang on as long as I need to? What if my patience runs out? What if I fall deep into despair? What if I cannot endure?

Can you relate?

Then come with me now, and together let's remember God. Let's fly above the clouds.

> Jesus is a fountain of living waters. He doesn't run dry. Drink of him in your thirst. (John 7:38)

> Jesus is the bread of life. Consume him and be filled to the full. (John 6:35)

> God the Father is the source of all comfort and compassion. Seek him in your suffering. (2 Cor. 1:3–7)

The Spirit gives us all things we need for godly living. Follow his lead and he'll lead you to demonstrate love. (2 Pet. 1:3)

Doesn't God tell a different story than discouragement does, a truer one?

We're never going to run out of his Spirit, provision, peace, joy, love, grace, strength, patience, help, attention, or care. We can't get to the bottom of him, for he is a well that never runs dry.

Turns out we're not swinging from the rafters without a safety net.

We're safe in the arms of our doting Father.

We are in Security.

PART 3

You
and
Your
Husband

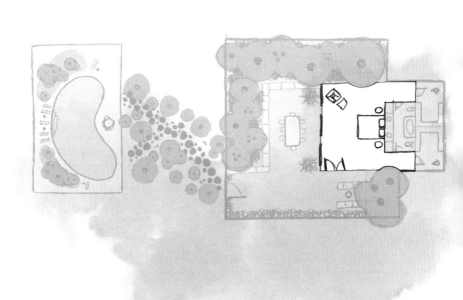

THiRTeeN

Locating Your Marriage

As we enter a new section of this book, we return to the architect's drawing once again, envisioning our life as a pastor's wife and specifically locating our marriage as it relates to other important relationships. In my experience, marriage is an aspect of our life we need great clarity on, because without intentional thought and action, our marriage can too easily become entwined with ministry. If there is any "room" on the Master's plan for our life that most needs protecting but is often most neglected, it's the sacred space of our marriage.

As veteran pastor's wife Jani Ortlund says, "Ministry marriages bear unique strains that often obscure the joys of building a lifelong romance. A woman marries a man, not his ministry, but somehow her husband's calling seeps into every aspect of their one-flesh relationship."[1]

We must learn, then, to draw boundaries around our marriage, not only that we might experience the joy and delight God intends for us in marriage but also that we may protect and maintain it.

Look at the drawing and notice how it visually displays the intimacy and sacredness of the marriage relationship. Now imagine the room without walls, allowing a free flow of children, coworkers, friends, and church congregants into your sacred space. Simply put, if everyone has full access to the pastor (or the pastor's wife) whenever they want, they are *in the marriage relationship with you*. For example, if your cell phone is always in hand (another seemingly innocuous point of access), you are functionally "on call" to anyone and everyone, and the sacred relationship of husband and wife can quickly deteriorate while at the same time elevating the roles of pastor and pastor's wife above the marriage.

We often blame our marital dysfunction on ministry, but we're the ones allowing overly porous boundaries between our marriage relationship and the needs of anyone who comes knocking on our door or texting or emailing.

I write all of this from experience. I know the anguish of feeling like there is a third person—the church—in our marriage. I know the bitterness of feeling like it's my duty to share my husband with everyone. I've resented the almost magnetic pull my husband feels toward his job and meeting the needs of others. I've also enabled our marriage to become less than it should be by driving my husband to perform and enact certain changes or programs in the church.

When Kyle and I sat on the patio beneath the palm trees on vacation, I realized that I didn't just feel apprehension about people waiting at the gate for him with their questions and needs. I felt they'd been invited into our room with us, neither of us had done much to cordon off that space, and it had all become so *normal* to us.

As leaders in ministry, we often feel it is incredibly noble, holy, and right to pour our life out for others. And it is. We know God is pleased as we make his name known and as we consider others more significant than ourselves (Phil. 2:3). But sometimes good things can be twisted and subsequently turn sour.

As married people, the Bible says, we're each half of a living picture: the picture of the intimate devotion between Christ and his church (Eph. 5:32). When we delight in, connect with, and enjoy our spouse—protecting that sacred space together—we display the clearest picture of this beautiful, mysterious, pure love. What could delight the Father more? He is pleased when we devote ourselves to our spouse and creatively express love to each other.

It's been painful for me over the years to realize that sometimes I think of my marriage as a rest stop—a place to sleep or briefly refuel—between moments of ministry. Too often for me, the real work of ministry is "out there," which of course has consequences for a marriage that's "in here." But the Lord has shown me that, as a married person, my marriage isn't a place of "waiting" to then go back out and accomplish his will. When I'm attentive and devoted inside my marriage, I couldn't be any closer to his will and, therefore, his delight.

Your marriage too is sacred and beautiful to God.

Join me now in the bedroom of the architect's plan, and let's discover how we can honor God through our marriage while also serving others in ministry.

FOURTEEN

Wife, Friend, and Lover

*W*hen we planted our church, my husband was given wonderful counsel by many people who had experience with the process. However, he was also given one piece of advice from a fellow pastor that, unfortunately, had a negative impact on our marriage. This particular pastor told him, "You're going to have to sacrifice everything for the first two years, and then you can return to more of a normal life."

That advice sounds good, doesn't it? Ministry certainly requires sacrifice and service, and Kyle and I were both intent on working hard, laying down our life, and giving our all to establish the church God had asked us to plant.

Not knowing what we were getting ourselves into and trusting the wisdom of these knowledgeable others, we did exactly what that pastor advised. For several years, the church took top priority and everything else went on the back burner. Friendship, physical health, protected time together as a couple, rest and renewal, having fun as a family, emotional development, intentionality in discipling our children—who had time for any of that? We had a higher calling, and both of us were meant to sacrifice all for it.

Two years came and went, but there wasn't a significant milestone or marker signaling it was time to come up for air. At two years, it seemed to us, there was more to do and more to sacrifice for than ever before.

Three years in, I found myself increasingly resentful of the church. She'd come between us, and we'd invited her to take that prime spot. Anytime Kyle and I could finally steal away for a dinner together, we spent the entire time talking about her. When she asked for attention, she got it immediately and in large quantities. She devoured our best energy and received our highest devotion. She even dictated our social calendar.

But—this is what we repeatedly told ourselves—we were doing the Lord's work, and we promised one another that at some point in the near future we'd slow down and return to some semblance of normal. So we pressed on, certain this was the sacrifice required.

And then, one day, I realized with horror that I couldn't remember what "normal" was. What did we have to talk about except ministry? What did we have to do except ministry? When was the last time we'd simply had fun together? Who were we apart from ministry? When did we become solely a pastor and a pastor's wife instead of husband and wife, friends, and lovers? We'd given years to cultivating the church and little to cultivating our marriage. We'd coasted in one area because we were consistently moving at the speed of light in another. We'd sacrificed so much that we'd unwittingly even sacrificed our marriage.

And this wasn't a sacrifice we'd ever intended to make.

Your Vow Is Not to the Church

Kyle and I are not alone in this. Sacrificing a marriage on the altar of ministry doesn't happen solely in church planting. Unfortunately, many couples in ministry exist with the ministry itself as the center-piece of their relationship.

I'd like to suggest something better, something more biblical, and something that infuses joy rather than mere obligation into both our ministry and our marriage.

This "something better" stems from the foundational truth that Jesus is the head of the church (Col. 2:19; Eph. 5:23). He is the chief shepherd, and we join him as under-shepherds in caring for his flock (1 Pet. 5:1–4). Christ is the source of the church's growth and holiness (Eph. 4:15–16; 1 Cor. 3:6). Christ is the bridegroom, and the church is his bride (John 3:29; Rev. 19:7).

All of these biblical truths teach us that Christ vows to love, cherish, nurture, lead, and care for the church. While we wholeheartedly serve the bride and bridegroom as groomsmen and bridesmaids, *our covenantal vow is to our spouse, not to the church.*

This is an important distinction because, although we will partner with our husband in fulfilling the work of ministry, the church doesn't take precedence over our marriage. The church is Christ's, and his covenantal vow is to her. We, of course, are members of Christ's bride, a reminder that serves even further to drive home my point: we're not ultimately responsible for the church. Christ willingly takes that role. We're responsible to God and to the spouse he's given us.

Our marriage, then, isn't to be sacrificed on the altar of ministry. Instead, our marriage—the way we love one another, serve one another, delight in one another, and yield to one another—is to reflect the beauty of Christ's love for the church and the church's love for Christ. A good, healthy, happy marriage between a pastor and his wife is a vital foundation from which to raise children and to serve others. And a good, healthy, happy marriage has Christ at the center, not ministry.

Before you are a pastor's wife, then, you're a spouse, friend, and lover to your husband. Your biblical calling to love, respect, edify, and help him is a higher calling than anything you do outside your home. Of course, that calling will overflow into the church and community (as it does through all godly marriages), but it's vitally important that you intentionally cultivate a relationship and partnership apart from ministry, or the foundation and all that's built upon it will crack.

The demands of life, however, constantly pull us away from one another, even more so if we're not purposefully working to stay tethered together. Ministry life perhaps pulls us apart even more, because it multiplies the demands on our time, depletes our emotional and mental storehouses, and networks us with a large quantity of people who have needs, questions, and desires for connection. In other words, ministry constantly fights for the most prominent place in our marriage. The question then for each of us is, *What will I do to purposefully cultivate a thriving marriage?*

For various reasons, many wives wait for their husbands to take the lead in cultivating their marriage. We may feel at times like we have little control over what sacrifices must be made for the sake of others, as if it's his decision more than it's ours. We may feel guilty for wanting more of our husband's time and attention, because perhaps that means we're not gladly sacrificing for the sake of Christ. We may have asked our husband to adjust his work hours or his attachment to his phone, but when he didn't listen or make changes, we simply gave up.

I've written a later chapter directly to your husband, but in this chapter, I'm speaking to you and to what you can do to cultivate a happy and holy marriage. I want you to know that you carry so much influence in your marriage and with your husband. You can't change your husband, and I don't think *demanding* your husband do exactly what you want all the time is right or productive. I do, however, think you can be prayerfully intentional in requesting and expecting him to contribute to the health of your relationship. And you can choose to intentionally cultivate your life, home, and marriage in a way that *invites* wholeness, thriving, and intimacy between you and your husband.

You can choose it, and you must.

Friend and Lover First

When I realized I was both thinking wrong thoughts about who was ultimately responsible for our church and enabling (even encouraging) my husband to sacrifice our marriage for the sake of ministry, I recognized that I primarily thought of myself as a "pastor's wife." In order to place proper boundaries around our relationship, I needed to remember that before I was a pastor's wife, I was simply a wife to my particular husband, and part of being his wife was being his friend and lover. Yes, I was also his helper, but the greatest help I provided him wasn't assisting him in ministry. The greatest help I could give him was doing my part in cultivating a happy home and intimacy in our relationship.

The greatest help, in other words, is doing what a wife alone can do. Let's look together at what it means to be a wife that prioritizes friendship and intimacy.

Be His Friend

The best friendships generally share similar ingredients: quality time spent together, pursuit of activities both people enjoy, mutual vulnerability and sharing, expressions of gratitude and love, giving little gifts that remind you of the other, laughter and tears, talking often about what God is teaching each person, cheering one another on, and providing listening ears that help the other process their life and experiences.

In other words, a friend halves the difficulties of the day and doubles the joys. With a friend, you can escape the responsibility and burdens you're both carrying and simply enjoy one another's company.

This kind of friendship is the goal in our marriage. It must be marked by pursuing focused time, play, and emotional connection. Let's look at all three of those actions.

One: set aside focused time. One of the frustrations many pastors' wives express regards the constant presence of the pastor's phone. That phone represents the constant pulling of the church on the pastor, and a wife can quickly become resentful when she can't seem to get her husband's undivided attention. The problem isn't just the phone (and the problem isn't always just the pastor's) but also the reality that the pastor's work is typically burdensome and weighs heavy on his mind and heart even when he's with his wife.

How can we help our husband set aside work and be mentally present with us?

One way Kyle and I do this is to note and take advantage of pockets of uninterrupted time and spaces that enable us to focus on one another. For example, after the rush of dinner, our children are expected to clear the dishes and clean the kitchen while we sit on our front porch—phoneless—to catch up on one another's day. For whatever reason, sitting outside helps me release the urge to get things done around the house, and it helps Kyle relax and unwind after a busy day.

What helps your husband will, of course, be unique to him. Perhaps he needs thirty minutes of alone time when he gets home to shower and have space to think. Perhaps he wants to tinker in the yard or the garage. Perhaps he wants a hug and your undivided attention right when he comes through the door. Because he is unique in his needs, ask him directly, "What can I do to help you set aside work and be mentally present with me at the end of the day or on your day off?"

Included in this question should be discussion about how much he wants to talk about anything related to work. Your husband may want to download the day with you, or he may not want to talk about it at all. For Kyle, it's usually somewhere in between: he wants to tell me some but doesn't want to talk in so much detail that it puts him right back in the mindset of work. And although I like the details, I instead want to prioritize being a refreshing escape from the burdens of his day by talking about other things, like what we're reading and learning, what the kids are up to, or what we're dreaming about for the future.

And, of course, there has to be a plan regarding your phones. If there is no plan, you're choosing divided attention. Once again, this is a conversation that will be unique to you as a couple.

Two: play together. When was the last time you and your husband had fun together or tried something new as a couple? Play is one of the greatest catalysts for friendship and fun in a marriage, and play is often a low priority for ministry couples. However, without recreation, we begin to think life is all work and everything is heavy and serious, and then we begin to take ourselves far too seriously. Play releases pressure, eases stress, creates connection, and gives us something other than ministry to talk about.

Play could be anything from going to a movie or sporting event, taking a day trip, trying a new restaurant, going for a walk, developing a shared hobby, hiking, fishing, working out, playing a sport, taking a class, or playing board games. In other words, anything you do together for fun can be categorized as playing together. If you have children, get creative on involving them in a way that doesn't take away from your play as a couple. For example, when our boys were younger, Kyle and I would play tennis together and pay our kids five cents for every ball they retrieved for us.

When you're in ministry, sometimes play can seem frivolous. Who has time to recreate when your task is changing the world? After coming close to burnout, however, I now see that play and recreation are vital components of how God renews and refreshes us and keeps us happily connected as a couple. When we're renewed and refreshed, we have so much more to give to our children and to others.

Three: cultivate emotional connection. Friendship grows deeper upon vulnerability, which can be defined simply as sharing at an emotional and spiritual level. Despite being people who deal with emotional and spiritual issues for a living, pastors often have few people and spaces where they can express and process their own emotions. As pastors' wives, you and I have a wonderful opportunity to be a friend to our husband by helping him name and process his emotions.

I've learned that well-timed, gentle questions help draw Kyle out. He doesn't always know how he feels, but when he tells me the situation he's in, I can reflect back to him, "Does that make you feel _____?" I may not hit the exact emotion on the head, but he can then clarify, which leads to further conversation and understanding on both of our parts.

Be His Lover

Generally speaking, developing and deepening friendship (focused time, play, and emotional connection) with your husband typically makes affection and sexual intimacy much easier to cultivate. Sex and affection can be a catalyst for emotional intimacy, but emotional intimacy cultivated between husband and wife is also a catalyst for physical intimacy. In other words: to affect one we cultivate the other, and vice versa.

Sex is a gift from God to every marriage, but specifically for a pastor and his wife because it creates a private cocoon. Though you may share your husband at most other times, when you have sex, you get his undivided attention, and he gets yours. When you offer yourself freely to your husband, you minister to him in a way no one else can. If he's discouraged, defeated, or feeling rejected in his work, you can express love and desire to him physically. And when you share in this physical act, it is an expression of the focused time, play, and emotional connection you've each been building into your marriage.

This small section is certainly not a full treatise on sexual intimacy, but here are a few ways that, as a wife, you can do your part in cultivating a thriving, intimate sex life.

One: be free with verbal affection. Respect and admiration are expressions of love to a man. Tell your husband frequently what you admire about him and why you respect him. Thank him for how he serves your church and family. In other words, think about the good you see in your husband and don't assume he knows these things; speak them out loud as often as you think them.

Two: let your respect for him be a catalyst for desire. The sexiest thing my husband does, aside from power washing the siding, of course, is faithfully preaching the Word of God. I'm not joking. I find him irresistible as I listen to him preach and proudly think to myself, *That's my husband! And he has chosen me! I am the one who gets to be with this good man.*

The same is true for you. The more you think of the ways you respect your husband, the more you will desire him. Try it and see.

Three: communicate frequently about sex. Sex and sexual desire change over the course of a marriage. When your children are little, you may not want to be touched in certain ways. When your children are teenagers, you may have difficulty finding time for sex. And when you're middle-aged, your hormones and his hormones may change the way your bodies respond. What works for the two of you in one season may not work in a different season. I believe God allows these changes so that we continue to communicate and connect with one another. By frequently discussing your sex life, you can work together to implement changes or tackle an issue that's affecting one or both of you.

Four: make time for rest. Under each point in this entire chapter, I could make a case for Sabbath rest and healthy rhythms that create space for a healthy marriage to grow. Certainly, if either of you is constantly exhausted, you will struggle to have energy or desire for sex. What can you encourage your husband to do that would give him rest? And what can your husband take off your plate so that you can physically and mentally prepare to give yourself to him sexually? Rest is a good gift you can give each other in your marriage, especially in your sex life.

When You Need Something from Your Husband

A friend doesn't just bring lightheartedness and a listening ear; a friend also speaks truth we need to hear. We must be that kind of friend to our husband: a wife who is willing to challenge when challenge is needed, yet doing so with a tone and demeanor of honor, love, and respect.

For example, let's say your husband has committed to himself, the church, and to you that he'll take one day a week off work. In reality, his heavy workload has encroached more and more on his day off. At first, he promised you, "It's just one meeting, and then I'll take the rest of the day off." But now his "day off" is not a day off at all and is, in fact, filled to the brim with "just a few things" he needs to take care of. You've continued encouraging him to take his day off each week, but he feels so much pressure at work that he's pushing dangerously through his need for rest. You're starting to grow resentful, not only because he's not heeding your wise counsel but also because when he doesn't take time off, it affects your own workload and ability to rest as well as the amount of time you get with him.

What do you do? Do you bring it up again? Or is that considered nagging?

One thing I've noticed is that ministry can at times create a dynamic for pastors' wives where we can feel that we're just an additional person on the pastor's plate—an additional person with a problem to fix. In the spirit of mutual sacrifice, we tend to feel like we have to say yes to everything and can lose the ability to discern when we need to say no, when we need to share a request or need with our husband, and when we need to draw a line in the sand.

How do we communicate our needs and desires? And what recourse do we have if our husband isn't listening? It's not like we can do what everyone else in the church does and go to the pastor for counsel.

The most important consideration, in my opinion, is not whether or not you express a need or concern to your husband. This is your biblical right and duty. A marriage is meant to be mutual. The primary concern is *how* and *when* you broach the conversation. Are you asking him about taking his day off because you know you're right, or are you asking him out of love and concern for his well-being? Are you hoping he'll figure out you're upset if you are quiet and cold toward him? Are you calling him when he's at work on his supposed day off and demanding he come home right that instant?

I've learned a few things the hard way when it comes to expressing my needs and desires. In the past, I tried bringing up my needs over and over—the "If I say it again in a slightly different way, he'll hear it this time" tactic. But I wasn't just bringing up my needs; I was also blaming him, putting him on the defensive, and doing it all with, shall we say, *great emotion*.

Surprisingly, that didn't work.

I rethought my approach. Here's what I've learned.

Needs and Desires Are Good and Right to Have

We don't have to diminish ourselves in the name of sacrifice. We don't have to allow ministry to be the constant priority and centerpiece of our marriage. We are human beings, designed to need rest, help, and community.

As wives, knowing that God commands marriage to be honored by all, we have a sacred position in our husband's life. If you have a need you're keeping from your husband so as to not burden him further, you're doing yourself and your husband a disservice. You're contributing to an unhealthy dynamic that *will* have future effects on your relationship.

Discern What Needs to Be Voiced

Not all needs and desires are to be voiced every single time we have them. Sometimes we have preferences that are selfish or unrealistic. We have to first learn, then, to discern when we have a legitimate need or right desire. As human beings, we often *feel* things before we think them through or understand why we're feeling that specific way. If we take a moment to consider what we're feeling and thinking, we will be able to get to the root of the issue before we ever say anything to our spouse. Sometimes what we're feeling, needing, or wanting is something only the Lord can meet.

I'd certainly share the experience with my husband—what circumstance bothered me, what I thought about and felt, and how the Lord ministered to me—even though it doesn't require a response or change on his part. But sometimes my need or desire is for my husband to change. How do we know when it's right and necessary to make that request? We ask the Lord to help us sort through our thoughts and emotions. God gives us discernment and wisdom to know not only if we should approach our husband but what the specific issue at hand really is.

It's possible that, when we take our emotions and concerns to the Lord, he'll ask us to address a blind spot of our husband's with him. We must remember that we are an important part of our husband's growth as a person. If we see glaring issues, it's our responsibility to lovingly bring them to his attention.

Approach Him Wisely

We must approach our husband with our thoughts, needs, or requests at the right time and with love, gentleness, and truth—not with an attitude of conflict or confrontation. We should not be overly demanding, expecting that our husband should make life and ministry more palatable for us, but we can and should ask directly for what we need or point out what issues we see. The more specific and concrete we can be, the better.

Let's return to the example of a wife's frustration over her husband's work hours, which is a conversation Kyle and I have had in the past. If I need to bring it up again, what should I do?

After thinking and praying about whether or not I should say something (again) and also praying for my husband to be receptive to the Lord's conviction, I'd wait until after the kids were in bed (as experience had shown me was best) and then say to Kyle, "Do you mind if we talk about something that's been on my mind?" He, of course, would be receptive. I might then say, "I'm concerned for you that you're not taking time to rest and be renewed each week. I recognize that you have so much on your plate and feel pressure to get it all done, but I see that a lack of rest is affecting you. You're getting run down. I'd like for you to begin taking your day off again. Can we talk about what a true day of rest would look like for you, and how I can help ensure it happens for you?"

When you approach your husband, be prepared to state a concrete change that you're requesting ("I'd like for you to take your day off") and ask how you can help him make that change.

Finally, as we consider a wise approach to sometimes difficult conversations, it's important we approach our husband in the same way we'd want him to approach us about our own blind spots. We want to exude an attitude of togetherness and teamwork, not one that communicates being at odds with the church or with our husband.

Pray for Him

Ultimately, heart and lifestyle change for your husband come from the Lord, the Lover of his soul. We influence our husband in the best way when we ask God to influence him. God influences him perfectly and has constant access. I learned this early in marriage when I went to visit a friend whose husband led a large parachurch ministry in our town. Before our meal together, she led us in extended prayer for our husbands, praying for their integrity, character, wisdom, and strength to carry out that day's work. She poured out her desires for the Lord to work in and through our husbands with such passion and earnestness that I took note. I hadn't been praying for my husband like that. In fact, I'd been so wrapped up in the routines of my own days with a baby at home that I'd hardly considered the spiritual support I could provide my husband simply by praying consistently and specifically for his heart and mind the way my friend demonstrated for me.

We each have this incredible opportunity to support our husband through prayer. We can channel our desires for his strong character and ministry faithfulness into prayer to the One who can affect both these things. And through prayer, we can cultivate a love for our husband and a respect for the challenges he faces, both of which enhance our marriage relationship.

FiFTeeN

Pastor to the Pastor

I'm often in awe of what my husband does as the lead pastor of our church. He's a strong leader, cares for people well, preaches truth, and genuinely tries to balance ministry and family life in a God-honoring way.

But from our private conversations and our day-to-day life, I'm fully aware that he also gets weary and needs pastoring himself. He needs encouragement, rest, and reminders of God's presence and character spoken into him. And I know I'm the primary person who can do that—sometimes I'm the *only* person aware of his needs. I'm the one who can counsel him, champion and celebrate his strengths, gently bring blind spots into his view, and point him to Jesus and God's Word.

My words to him carry weight, especially in regard to his decisions. My perspectives on other people affect how he views and relates with them. My attitude toward his job shapes his own attitude toward it.

I influence the influencer.

I pastor the pastor.

I care for the caretaker.

I am like an Aaron to his Moses.

Though it is often unseen and unrecognized by others, you too play a significant role within the kingdom of God, because you influence a man who has considerable influence on the spiritual well-being of others. How you and I wield this influence is important. We can either give our husband wings or weights in ministry. In other words, we can significantly multiply his ministry or significantly divide his attention from what God's called him to do. One of our most important contributions to the church and to the kingdom of God is to encourage God's under-shepherd as he cares for the flock.

I liken my influence on Kyle to being a sounding board for him. In musical terms, a sounding board can be a thin, resonant plate of wood placed in a musical instrument to *enhance* the power and quality of the tone. In other words, it takes sound and makes it better, clearer, and more beautiful. A sounding board can also be a board used in floors or partitions for the purpose of *deadening* sound.

We've appropriated this definition beyond musical terms to describe a person whose reaction serves as a measure of the effectiveness of the methods and ideas put forth by another. This definition speaks of our ability to influence our husband well or influence him poorly. As our husband's sounding board, we can listen and respond in a way that either *enhances* his effectiveness in ministry or *deadens* it.

I know what it means to hinder my husband, because I've done it. I've spoken bitterness into him concerning people in our church who have offended me. I've manipulated him in my discontentedness. I've been emotionally unrestrained. I've too confidently trusted my own wisdom and discernment and pushed my preferences onto him. I've failed to recognize his need for encouragement and support. And I've harshly spoken my resentments at what his job has required of me.

Each of us has this level of influence.

We affect our husband's perspectives on God and on ministry itself, his sermons, other people, and his decisions. This is great power and also great responsibility. We must consider, then, how we can be good sounding boards for our husband—to pastor the pastor well.

Purposeful Counsel

How can we positively enhance our husband's effectiveness in ministry? Part of being a good sounding board is offering him wise counsel. Following are important components that constitute wise counsel.

Purpose to Listen and Ask Good Questions

We must first be alert to when our husband is turning a conversation toward weighty matters. Typically, your husband will not sit you down and say, "I need you to listen and give me feedback." Sometimes he may simply be talking, sharing about his day or about a specific situation, and you'll recognize that he's wrestling with a decision or response.

We must be discerning about when our husband needs feedback and when he simply needs a listening ear. This discernment comes from the Holy Spirit.

Proverbs 18:13 says, "If one gives an answer before he hears, it is his folly and shame." As we sense a conversation turning weightier, we ask the Lord to help us listen carefully, know when to speak, and know what, if anything, we should advise. Good sounding boards don't jump to conclusions, immediately move to our husband's defense, or spout off an answer without knowing everything we can know about the situation.

Our goal must be, then, to gather information that will help him process. The way we do that is to ask questions. First, we should ascertain *factual* details. Then we can move our questions to the emotional level and ask, "What are you feeling about the situation?" He may not know exactly what has frustrated or hurt him, so we can help him pinpoint those emotions. And finally, we can ask questions that help him discern if he needs to take action and, if so, what he should do.

We want to listen well and ask well-placed questions because it gives us an opportunity to listen to the Holy Spirit and think biblically about the situation at hand. Otherwise, we'll counsel him according to our instincts, experiential wisdom, or preferences. We don't want to influence him according to our preferences but rather according to God's preferences.

As you listen and gather information from your husband, ask the Lord to give you his heart for the situation and that his thoughts and ways would trump your preferences or instinctual response.

In relation to Kyle's work, I've found it is a very rare occasion when I am to help him make the decision, but often I can help him *arrive* at the decision. I provide this help through the questions I ask and the ideas we brainstorm together.

Purpose Not to Compound the Problem

Seeing my husband stressed and uncertain can be extremely disconcerting, because I hurt when he's hurting. I want to erase his pain, whether it's giving people who've hurt him a piece of my mind (which typically means complaining to my husband and compounding his difficulties), entirely discounting criticism he's received without helping him search the criticism for nuggets of truth, or diving headlong into situations I believe I can "fix" when God and my husband haven't asked that of me.

However, my husband is much like me when I'm hurting. I don't need a solution—at least at the beginning—but rather a listening ear, comfort, support, prayer, and love. And these are the very things he most needs from me.

Every wife's instinctual response is to defend her husband, but I've learned that when my husband is sharing his frustrations, there is no benefit in venting my own frustrations. Empathy is helpful—"I can understand why you'd feel discouraged"—but piling on is not—"Yes, I'm frustrated at that person as well, and let me tell you all the reasons why." I have tremendous power to cloud my husband's perspective on people in his life. Even with words spoken in private conversation, I can cause division in relationships and cause frustrations to grow.

Therefore, when our husband is expressing frustration or discouragement, we must purpose to do two things: trust the Lord ourselves and respect our husband's ability to handle the situation.

These situations *always* call upon us to entrust them to the Lord. Will we have faith in him and allow the process of sanctification for our husband or for others, or will we fear and worry in a way that increases our husband's stress? Will we trust the Lord to work out the situation, or will we jump into everything and further tangle and confuse it? When we choose to trust the Lord, we're able to speak truth to our husband and draw him back to the foundational realities that God is trustworthy and will sustain him. We convey the peace of Christ that passes all understanding (Phil. 4:7) and offer that same peace to our husband. Our faith often breeds faith in our husband.

Our trust in the Lord will instinctively lead to trusting him to lead our husband. For me, I feel freedom remembering that the pastor role is not my job. It's my husband's, because God has called *him* to do it, and God will enable him to fulfill his ministry.

Purpose to Help Him Respond Well to Criticism

An essential ground rule in being a good sounding board is remembering that criticism is not always a bad thing to be avoided at all costs. My husband reminds me that we want our church to be a place where people can bring their questions and concerns, because we aren't perfect, the church isn't perfect, and we can learn from people in our church.

Proverbs 19:20 says, "Listen to advice and accept instruction, that you may gain wisdom in the future." So when your husband shares criticism he's received, it's important that you help him process whether or not it has any validity and what a biblical response to it might be.

This brings up an oft-repeated question: How much should a pastor share with his wife? Should she know everything that is happening within the ministry and about every conversation he is having with congregants? Or are there limits to her knowledge and involvement?

Aside from adhering to widely accepted confidentiality boundaries for counseling situations, I think the answers to these questions are highly subjective. Each husband and wife need to determine what their personal communication boundaries will be, depending on what support the husband needs and what the wife wants to know or can handle knowing. The answers are also subject to context: if the pastor is the only staff member or the missionary couple is without a team, the husband and wife will likely share much more openly. In church planting too the wife will likely know everything that's happening and be heavily involved in decision-making. But if the wife is working full-time, for example, and is unable to participate in everything pertaining to the ministry, there may be more delineations in what she knows and doesn't know.

Personally, because we're serving in an established church, I work part-time, and my husband shares leadership with a board of elders, I no longer know everything and don't *want* to know everything, especially specific criticism he or others on staff have received. For example, I don't want to know if someone doesn't like a song we sang in church or pushed back about a certain sermon point. These things don't typically bother my husband, and to know them would only agitate me.

I do, however, want to know everything my husband is feeling. If a person is continually antagonizing Kyle and causing him personal pain, I want to know those details so I can emotionally support him. I want to know what's discouraging him. And I also want to know about pain people in the church are walking through, especially if I have opportunity to minister to them in some practical way.

Purpose to Listen for What He's Not Saying

Being a good sounding board means hearing and responding to what is said—but also what is *not* said.

For example, September is often a very busy month for our church. Last fall, my husband made several comments about not seeing certain people, all of whom were men he considered friends. He didn't realize how many times he'd commented about not seeing these friends, but I mentally noted how hard he'd been working, what he'd had on his plate, and how he'd had very little downtime with people whom he didn't have to be "the pastor" with. I told him what I was hearing and seeing, and I encouraged him to get together with his friends. I even suggested dates I would happily stay home with the kids so he could have that time to recharge and have fun. Kyle never said, "I want to hang out with the guys," but that's what I heard when I read between the lines.

Another example common for ministry wives is when every conversation at home revolves around church. Perhaps you're experiencing this now. It seems our husband's whole existence is about work, and he's entirely too wrapped up in it. What do we do?

We don't need to nag or criticize him, but we can help him be a whole and healthy person. If he is talking about work all the time, and neither of you can think of anything else to talk about, that's a sign of him (and you!) not being a whole person. A whole person has family relationships, friendships, recreation, healthy emotions, and varied interests that are life-giving and restful. Influence your one-track-mind husband by encouraging him to pursue activities outside of that one thing and joyfully give him time and space to pursue those things.

Sometimes the situation is reversed, and *I'm* the one talking too much about what is work to Kyle. Perhaps I'm digging too much for information or attempting to provide solutions for a problem during time he'd prefer to relax. When I see Kyle's shoulders slump or he gets quiet, that's often a sign for me that I need to change the subject and revert from being a pastor's wife to simply being a wife.

Purpose to Encourage

Whether or not you give your husband advice, in every conversation you have an opportunity to give him encouragement.

Encouragement comes in various forms. Listening and giving him an opportunity to pour out his soul to you is itself encouragement. Wise, biblical counsel is also a form of encouragement, as are verbal affirmation and physical affection in a moment when he's disheartened—anything that lets your husband know you're on his team, for him, and will always be by his side.

We'll dig deeper into encouragement in the next chapter, but for now know that the best encouragement is specific and concrete. For example, if your husband says you look beautiful, I imagine that means something to you. But if he says he loves when you wear that certain dress because the color makes your eyes pop, that's a compliment that lands differently. How can you be that specific and concrete in encouraging your husband?

> After he preaches, give him specific positive feedback about his sermon without him having to ask for it.
>
> Speak highly of the people he serves with.
>
> Pray for him and tell him you're doing so.
>
> Tell him you're proud to be his wife and why.
>
> Verbally celebrate his strong character and integrity.
>
> Thank him for how hard he works to provide for the family.
>
> Tell him what you see God doing through his ministry.

And most importantly, constantly work at joyfully embracing his calling and what it means for you.

A Question for Any Situation

In whatever situation or difficulty my husband faces in ministry, I not only want to wisely counsel him but also want to help him as I have opportunity. I want to be the person who sees my husband's needs and seeks to meet them. I want to come alongside him and make his job easier. If that is the only thing I do as a pastor's wife, I've done well.

So I've made it a habit to consistently ask him, "How can I help you?"

I'll ask this question after the end of a heavy conversation, at the start of a new workweek, or on a busy Sunday morning. And I ask him this because it also helps me orient my mind and heart. Sometimes, honestly, my heart isn't actually to help my husband, usually because I'm pouting about the sacrifice involved in what we do.

More often, however, when I don't ask Kyle how I can help him it's because I've already assumed I know the answer. I've determined how best I can meet my husband's needs, and I throw myself into it like a dog with a bone—only to discover later I haven't helped at all.

Instead, I've taken on too much and become stressed and frazzled. Or I've gotten involved in one area while my husband would prefer I gave my attention to another.

So it really does help to ask, "How can I help you? What do you need from me?" And when you find yourself in a new role or ministry: "How do you envision me serving? What gifts do you see that God might want me to use in this context?"

If you ask, you must also listen to his answer. He likely knows you better than you know yourself. He sees your place within the ministry more objectively. And he knows what would most help him.

In my mind, I always assume Kyle wants me to lead major ministries and host people all the time. Generally, however, his answer when I ask, "How can I help you?" is something far simpler: "I need a hug. I need you to pray for me. I need to zone out tonight. I need to spend time with you. I need you to remind me why we're doing this."

Sometimes, as I stated previously, his answer is also nonverbal. I can read it on his face when he wants to stop talking about church. I can hear behind his words: *Christine, I need you to serve joyfully. I need you to have faith rather than fear. I need you to create a space of peace and harmony for me. I need you to be for me and not against me.*

If you ask your husband how you can help him, you might be surprised at the simplicity of his answer, yes, but also because it might be something you want too. Recently when I asked Kyle the question, he said, "In the evening, we talk so much about how our days went. I think it would be helpful for me if you ask how I'm doing." This question tends to lead to more heart-level conversation, where he invites me deeper into his thoughts and feelings. And that's exactly what I want as his wife.

Sacred Influence

What if the culture of your marriage or your home is not conducive to these types of conversations? The good news is that you don't have to wait for your husband to take the lead on any of these things. They are all steps you can take to care for your husband and cultivate a healthy marital culture. Your husband may not always respond how you want him to, but if you purpose to approach him in gentle, loving, and biblical ways, he will likely be more apt to listen and respond how you need and want.

You are an extremely influential person.

At least that's what your husband would say, if I asked him who most affects his attitude, spiritual growth, leadership, courage, and decisions both inside and outside the home. You have powerful influence in the life of a man who influences a whole host of people through preaching, leading, counseling, and decision-making.

You influence the influencer. You pastor the pastor. Are you helping him, or are you hindering him?

SIXTEEN

Cultivating the Skill of
Counting Up God's
Goodness Together

No matter the circumstances we face, it's God's will for us to be thankful in our life as a pastor's wife. That's what 1 Thessalonians 5:18 says: "Give thanks in all circumstances; for this is the will of God in Christ Jesus for you."

Thanksgiving is not a natural practice, especially when we're discouraged in ministry.

During an especially discouraging time in our family and our ministry, my husband and I had the opportunity to go away together. We were able to gather our thoughts for the first time in weeks, and I started recounting to my husband all the good things that were happening we'd been blind to in the everyday grind. I quickly saw his demeanor change. I realized in that moment how often we talked about what was going wrong and how little we focused on all that was going right, and I determined that if I did nothing else, I wanted to help my husband pastor by encouraging him. Actively encouraging him, in turn, always encourages me.

As Kyle and I had that conversation, God reminded me of something he'd shown me in my study of the book of Ezra.

Ezra records the time in Jewish history when a remnant returned from exile in Persia to rebuild the temple in Jerusalem. As we'd expect whenever slaves are set free, the people were overjoyed. Some wept because they'd seen the original temple and couldn't believe they were experiencing God's restoration after a long period of exile and discipline. It was a strong start, a good beginning.

As I read, I thought back to when we first planted our church. We'd moved to an unfamiliar place with a huge task in front of us, but we'd also been filled with a sense of excitement and wonder. We'd felt God's pleasure at our obedience and faith. Anticipation had been high.

While starting something is exciting and glorious, we cannot maintain that same level of excitement. Why? The reality is this: gospel work is not romantic. It instead requires day-in and day-out faithfulness that largely goes unseen and sometimes seems unrewarded or unfruitful.

I continued reading in Ezra and discovered that the temple builders' excitement was almost immediately met with resistance. Unsurprisingly, this resistance took the form of discouragement—their enemies actually *hired* professional discouragers to frustrate their efforts. As a result, the restoration work ground to a halt. They were paralyzed by discouragement for fifteen years. Later in Ezra, we discover that they also lost their joy and zeal for the Lord's work.

What happened for the temple builders also happens with us: gospel work is always met with resistance. This resistance leads to discouragement that, if we listen to it, causes us to lose our joy and zeal for the Lord's work. Though we continue working and going through the motions of ministry, our hearts grow hard and "building" stops *on the inside*, where God can see.

The interesting part of the story, however—the part that God reminded me of as I sat talking with my husband—is they eventually resumed building the temple. What made them start again? The prophets Haggai and Zechariah spoke words of encouragement to Zerubbabel, the leader of the rebuilding efforts.

We have their actual words recorded in the Bible, and it's a lesson in itself to see what they spoke over Zerubbabel.

Haggai specifically drew Zerubbabel's attention to the Lord's constant presence:

> "Yet now be strong, Zerubbabel," says the Lord . . . "and work, for I am with you," says the Lord of hosts. "According to the word that I covenanted with you when you came out of Egypt, so My Spirit remains among you; do not fear!" (Hag. 2:4–5 NKJV)

Zechariah specifically addressed the Spirit's power and how daily effort eventually adds up to a great work:

> "Not by might nor by power, but by My Spirit,"
> Says the Lord of hosts.
> "Who are you, O great mountain?
> Before Zerubbabel you shall become a plain! . . .
> The hands of Zerubbabel
> Have laid the foundation of this temple;
> His hands shall also finish it. . . .
> For who has despised the day of small things?
> For these seven rejoice to see
> The plumb line in the hand of Zerubbabel.
> They are the eyes of the Lord,
> Which scan to and fro throughout the whole earth."
>   (Zec. 4:6–10 NKJV)

We may not have prophets standing alongside to encourage us as we serve the Lord, but we can certainly be a Haggai or Zechariah for others and for our spouse. Although ministry tends to be a constant fight with discouragement, if we stop, look, and listen, we can *always* find something to celebrate regarding what God is doing.

We can help ourselves and help our husband pastor by encouraging him the way the prophets did: *one brick at a time. One person at a time. One day at a time. One sermon at a time. One response of faithful obedience at a time.* Eventually it all will add up to the building of a fruitful life lived in honor of the Lord.

Counting the Wins

Kyle and I now call this practice of thanksgiving and praise "counting the wins." We count the wins both individually and together as a married couple. And we count the wins with our kids, giving them eyes to watch for what God is doing and who he is to them, especially in difficult situations.

Wins don't have to be big. In fact, wins are often small, almost to the point of imperceptibility, which is why we have to practice looking for them. A win may be a conversation where a seeker is pricked by the truth of the gospel or a timid congregant starts confidently utilizing their spiritual gifts. A win is an open door with a neighbor or a discipleship relationship forming. A win is a visitor returning to the church for the second week or a day of deep rest and renewal. And of course, wins can be big too: a salvation, a marriage restored, a prodigal child returning home.

Below are some questions to help you begin counting the wins in your own life. Why not ask your husband to join you in order to double the joy?

What has happened today or in the past few days that has revealed God's presence and provision to you? How has he specifically provided for you?

What prayers has God answered that you were praying around this time last year?

What has discouraged you in the past few months? How has God helped and sustained you through that time?

What specific people have been a blessing to you? How have
they been a gift to you?

What are some of the highlights of what God has done in the
lives of those around you this past year?

What is going well in your ministry? What are you thankful for
about your church?

How is your spouse a blessing to you? How do you see God
using them?

Where is God at work in your neighborhood and community?

What opportunities has God given you to form relationships and
have gospel conversations with nonbelievers lately?

What opportunities has God given you to use your skills and gifts?

What has God done to help your children grow in wisdom and
stature? How is he currently at work in their lives?

What do you enjoy about the life God has given you?

Kyle and I decided to make it a consistent practice to count the
wins, because our heavy hearts lifted when we started giving thanks
on that day we went away. We've discovered that thanksgiving is always the result of counting the wins. We see so clearly that we cannot
help but lift our heads and thank God that he has never once stopped
working in the world and on our behalf.

The Biggest Win of All

There is one more question I'd add to our list that must be answered
when counting the wins:

What is God's character? What Scriptures speak to particular aspects of his character? How has he shown his character to you?

The practice of counting the wins is ultimately an act of remembering and worshiping God. Some of the questions I listed above may not have an answer on any given day. Our prayers may still be unanswered. Our relationship with our spouse may be suffering. Our children may present more worries than wins. Our church situation may be a current source of pain.

But whatever life circumstance we find ourselves in, whatever pit of despair we're mired in, there is always one question we *can* answer when reaching for wins: Who is our God? If we can't think of anything to thank God for, we can always praise him for his character.

How little do I stop to consider how God is praiseworthy and speak those praises to him. When I do, it is often to praise him for what he's done for me, not simply to praise him for who he is and how I've experienced his character. It's the difference between my children saying to their dad, "Thanks, Dad, for buying me new cleats," and "Dad, I see in you that you're generous and kind to your children."

When we look to praise God for something he's given us or done for us, sometimes we're facing difficulty and suffering and cannot see his hand at all. But even when we're suffering, his character remains unchanged, and we find him worthy of praise.

For example, we can praise God that he is a refuge for his children and welcomes them with steadfast love. Psalm 33:20–22 says,

> Our soul waits for the LORD;
>   he is our help and our shield.
> For our heart is glad in him,
>   because we trust in his holy name.
> Let your steadfast love, O LORD, be upon us,
>   even as we hope in you.

Though wins may be few and discouragements many, the steadfast love of the Lord will never be taken away. His character and presence, just as Haggai and Zechariah told Zerubbabel, are the greatest encouragement—the biggest win—of all.

SeVeNTeeN

A Word to the Pastor

How to Help Your Wife Thrive in Ministry

*P*astor's wife, I know it's sometimes difficult to explain to your husband how his calling affects you or to communicate what you need from him in order to thrive as his helper, so I've written a chapter just for your husband. My goal in writing is to help him better "see" you and to have specific tools he can use to encourage you in your own ministry. Please invite him to read and discuss it with you.

Pastor, as she serves by your side, your wife watches people pull on you on Sundays and listens as you recount your days. She knows what your calling means for you and how you handle it all. However, there are days when you're exhausted or discouraged, and she notes just how influential she is in this race you two are running together. She helps you, cheers you on when you're low, and smooths the path for you by her emotional and physical support.

Although your wife is your most valuable partner in life and ministry, you are equally valuable to her. Your leadership in your home and marriage and the way you champion her and her own ministry help her run beside you well.

So far in this book I've written to your wife, encouraging her to walk faithfully with the Lord and with you and to embrace the calling God has placed on your life. Now I want to take a moment to write to you, offering you specific ways you can help your wife thrive in a life of ministry with you.

Daily acts of sacrificial service are the biblical responsibility for all husbands (Eph. 5:25–29), but in ministry, because you are in demand relationally, you must be especially purposeful and intentional in expressing your commitment to your wife and caring for her needs. When you do this well, your wife will thrive, much like water and sun fuel the growth of a plant.

Your Opportunity and Responsibility

Before we get to practical ways you can "water" your wife, I want to tell you a story.

Years ago, I stood in front of a roomful of pastors' wives and took questions. Every question broached betrayed some level of desperation, concern, and anguish, and most were about their pastor-husbands. *How do I encourage him? How do I handle my own concerns when I see how much pressure he's under? How can I best help him when I feel so needy myself?*

But there was one woman I will never forget. As soon as her hand shot up, she started crying. "What do I do?" she asked. "I feel like my husband loves the church more than he loves me."

Every woman in the room cried along with her, because all pastors' wives know that feeling. *We all know what it feels like to compete with the church.* We all know what it feels like to realize that, at some level, we've had to sacrifice ourselves and our marriage for the sake of the church.

We are the first to feel the effects, brother, when you cave to the pressure of success.

I tell you this story because I hear this woman's sentiment far too often. Learning about strategy, leadership, and ministry paradigms is vitally important, but please make it a priority to consider how you can treasure the resource at your side and help her flourish as a wife, mom, and minister.

Not a wife in that room cried because we don't understand the pressure pastors like you are under or because we have unrealistic expectations of our husband. Your wife feels the pressure—albeit different pressure—as much as you, and she cares about your success probably more than you do. She loves you, respects you, and sincerely wants to be a help to you. Although she is not merely a resource to be used to further your ministry, she is your best resource in life, family, and ministry. And while she is your helper, she needs your help too. She needs your understanding and listening ear.

Earlier I used the analogy of water and sun fueling the growth of a plant. If your wife is not watered and nourished, she will become brittle and dry and not produce beautiful flowers. In other words, she'll grow bitter, resentful, and spiritually dry. Of course, her spiritual walk and faithfulness to God are her responsibility alone. But your nurture enhances her vibrancy, and Ephesians 5:25–33 calls you to the holy work of tending carefully to your marriage.

One of the struggles many pastors' wives face is that very rarely do their churches intentionally encourage them. People in your church, as you well know, don't see most of what your wife does to serve you and them. So your wife will, above all, look to you for encouragement. This is right and good. Proverbs 31:23 says the godly woman's husband "is known in the gates when he sits among the elders of the land." He is considered an honorable man and leader, likely dealing with conflicts and receiving adulation. Certainly, his wife joins in respecting and lauding her husband. But where does the wife receive her praise? Her good works speak for themselves, earning her respect (v. 31), but her verbal affirmation comes from within the home. "Her children rise up and call her blessed; her husband also, and he praises her: 'Many women have done excellently, but you surpass them all'" (vv. 28–29).

In other words, you have a wonderful opportunity—and responsibility—to bless your wife.

Help Her Find Her Place of Service

When my husband and I first entered ministry, I looked around at the other women serving as pastors' wives in our community and assumed they were certainly not feeling all that I was—fear, uncertainty, and doubt, among other things. I understand now that those emotions are common for young ministry wives and even seasoned pastors' wives who go through a time of transition.

A pastor's wife may have a mental picture of the ideal woman for the role she's in—and in her mind she's not that woman. She may feel confident about her husband's abilities and calling but uncertain about her own. Especially in the early days, ministry seems intimidating and overwhelming, and she doesn't know if she can do it.

Does your wife express insecurity or intimidation regarding her place within your church or ministry?

You would do well to recognize that gospel work can at times be daunting to your wife because her role is unlike yours. Your job description is similar to that of the pastor in the next pulpit down the street, but there is no job description for the pastor's wife. That role is as open-ended (and unclear) as she is unique, and your wife is trying to figure it all out.

One way you can help your wife thrive is to help her discover her sweet spot of service. Study her and help her know herself. What areas of ministry give her energy and life? What areas drain her and cause her to wilt? Challenge her to do those things she's good at, and help her see how God is using her as she does them. Even better, help match her gifts with ministry opportunities in your church and community.

In the early years of our ministry, my primary question was, *What am I supposed to be doing?* Eventually that question evolved into, *What am I gifted for? How would God want to use me where we are?*

The best thing my husband ever did for me in answering this question was to frame it as my freedom. He said, "I just want you to be a faithful Christian. What would a Christian do?" He didn't force me to take on tasks or roles I didn't want. He helped me keep my focus on my main priorities: being a disciple, a wife, and a mom, and then serving according to my gifts.

Expressing freedom to your wife gives her the opportunity to experiment and learn who God has made her and what he has for her within your ministry together. It also allows her to step away from certain activities when needs at home or her work, for example, require more of her attention.

Draw Healthy Boundaries

If we were to draw a Venn diagram of what relational overlap occurs for you and your family because of what you do for a living, the circles of family, friendship, church, and work would greatly overlap. This reality creates blurred lines and blurred relationships, making it difficult to draw boundaries around your family and marriage.

In some ways, this can be good. Your wife has the opportunity to participate in your work, which allows you to serve together. Your children can hear biblical truth preached by their dad and then watch it lived at home. Your home is a place of refuge and hospitality for others, allowing your children to meet fascinating people and watch you interact with them pastorally.

But just as it is difficult for you, sometimes the blurred lines can be challenging and even exhausting to your wife.

She may experience *emotional exhaustion*, knowing too much about the burdens people are carrying and experiencing fear over the kids hearing too much. Like you, she may experience empathy fatigue and grow weary of being the counselor who listens rather than the friend who enjoys mutual connection.

She may experience *physical exhaustion* as she cares for the home and children, supports you, works, and seeks to meet the needs of others. She may feel pressure to engage in more relationships and ministry opportunities than she has capacity for. Sometimes pastors' wives feel that pressure from their own husband.

She may experience *church exhaustion* if every social event is with church people and every conversation is about church.

Finally, she may experience *problem exhaustion* if you go into heavy detail about all the problems you're facing and the frustrations you feel but don't also share the good things God is doing or what you're excited about. If you share the criticism you receive but never the words of thanks or encouragement, you cloud her view of ministry with discouragement.

Your wife can't draw boundaries around your work for you; it's your responsibility to do so. Decide together with her what is important to guard and then put your choices into action.

In regard to time, is it a Sabbath day? Is it certain evenings? Is it dinner with the whole family? Is it an early morning walk?

In regard to information, what is important for you to share with her and get off your chest? What, when you share it with her, is difficult for her to handle knowing about?

The boundaries you set speak loudly.

Through these boundaries, you teach your church members what they can expect from you. If you answer the phone every time it rings, they will call you at all hours with needs and requests. If you make exceptions on your Sabbath day, they will expect to be your exception.

The way you handle boundaries not only speaks to your church but also speaks (loudly) to your wife. When you turn off your phone after work so she and the kids can have your full attention, that speaks value and honor to them.

Pastor, what are you saying to your wife with your schedule?

What are you saying to your wife by how you interact with her publicly?

What are you saying to your wife by what you do around the house?

What are you saying to her by the way you handle your phone?

I promise that when you speak louder in action to her than to your church, your church will hear the echo anyway.

Love Her by Holding a Biblical Definition of Success

In the story I told above about the woman saying she thought her husband loved the church more than he loved her, what might drive a pastor like her husband to become all-consumed with ministry?

Many options exist: a desire to please people, a true passion for the work, or the constant pressure of unplanned crises and a never-ending to-do list. But I think one of the main culprits for pastors who become all-consumed by the work is an unhealthy definition of success.

What is success in ministry? In your specific context, what is success? How will you know you've succeeded?

Maybe you've never consciously defined success for yourself, but we all have ideas of what success looks like. It's important to think about our definition, because we'll work, think, act, and give ourselves toward this end.

My husband and I have defined success differently at various points throughout our years in vocational ministry. For example, we've defined success according to such things as numbers, events, activities, growth, a good reputation for our church, ease (no obstacles, no difficulty), and people responding how we want them to respond.

This is not biblical success, because as you may have noticed, what determines our success according to these measurements is the success of the church, and that success hinges on us. This is a formula for massive disappointment and dysfunction.

Unhealthy pastors focus primarily on the success of their church, proving themselves a good leader, and impressing people (or at least not disappointing them).

This idea of success isn't just detrimental to you; it's also detrimental to your wife, because if your success is tied up in the success of the church according to these terms, you'll certainly begin to love and care for the church more than your wife. This sets your wife up in competition with the church for your affections. Nothing will create resentment in your wife faster than you asking her to help you carry the burdens of ministry but also putting little effort into giving her what she needs as your wife.

Clearly, in order to help your wife thrive as your partner in life and ministry, you must have a proper perspective on success. Without the right definition of success, you're in danger of feeling like a constant disappointment, trying to reach an unattainable standard, and trying to please other people rather than the One who called you into ministry.

So maybe a better question is really this: *Who* defines your success? Who is the loudest voice? Who do you look to for validation or affirmation of your success? Is it your wife? Is it a vocal or influential person in your church? Is it yourself and your own standards? Or is it God? And what does he consider to be success anyway?

Because we are one part of a larger body, and we are placed in it just where God wants us, we know we aren't measured by other pastors or by other churches. We are a part of a beautifully woven tapestry of spiritual gifts, personalities, and God-appointed places, so we can't define biblical success on whether we're an extrovert or introvert, whether we serve with one gift rather than another, or what our particular city and church look like.

Because of what we know about the Holy Spirit's role in salvation and sanctification—that we are unable to change hearts ourselves—we know we aren't measured by the spiritual responses of others. It is God who gives the increase, not we ourselves (1 Cor. 3:6).

So what *are* you responsible for? What is it that pleases God? Hebrews 11:6 says, "without faith it is impossible to please him." We, then, are responsible for our faith and the obedience that comes from that faith. *Faith is our success!*

This definition of success puts everything you and I do into proper perspective. It takes you far beyond imitating a list of behaviors you see other pastors doing and far beyond hoping church members like you. It requires you to unrelentingly go to God and ask, "What is it you want me to do as your under-shepherd?", doing those things with boldness and faith, and then returning again and again to him to ask, "Am I doing what you've asked me to be faithful to do?"

When the unbelieving neighbor continues to avoid spiritual conversations, and you feel like you're failing: "Am I doing what you've asked me to be faithful to do?"

When someone leaves your church to go to one vastly different from yours: "Am I doing what you've asked me to be faithful to do?"

When you feel like a disappointment because you aren't like the dynamic pastor down the street: "Am I doing what you've asked me to be faithful to do?"

That question has reoriented me so many times in so many different situations—away from self-focus and feelings of failure and toward what God has asked of me (and what he's ultimately taken responsibility for). It's reminded me over and over that faith and obedience are my success and that I am not called to carry the weight of the world on my shoulders.

Do you carry a heavy weight as a pastor? Are you a steward of the church? Most definitely. But the head, the responsible party, is Jesus Christ. He said he would care for his church. His vow is to her.

Your covenant vow is to your wife, not to a church. The church is Christ's bride, and he promises to sustain her. I know this is a difficult distinction, because pastoring truly does require a large bulk of your time and energy, but I also know this is an *important* distinction. Do you recognize and acknowledge by how you live and lead that this is Christ's church and, therefore, Christ's responsibility? Because if not, you will become a slave to unbiblical success, and your wife and children will reap what you sow.

One question you and your wife can use to evaluate if your marriage is in its proper place in regard to the church is this: Does your wife have to engage in some sort of ministry with you in order to connect with you or spend time with you? Or do you enjoy a connection and relationship that can stand alone, apart from the church? If you or your wife think she's primarily your ministry partner rather than your marriage partner, I would encourage you to consider what needs to be done immediately to return her to her proper and rightful place in your life as the wife for whom you're called to lay down your life. Remember, the church is Christ's bride. He laid down his life for her, and he'll continue to sustain and grow her until he returns.

Walk Closely with the Lord (and Point Her to Him)

The most impactful way you can love your wife is to pursue the Lord daily.

One of the things I respect most about my husband is that he fuels himself with the Word every day. He doesn't look to secondary sources for his sustenance, sources that won't enable him to endure with faith and joy. As his wife and ministry partner, I not only feel secure in that because I know he is following God but I also reap the benefits. He's ingesting heart sustenance that enables him to pour out both onto others and into our family. In addition, by making himself available to the Holy Spirit, he keeps a soft and sensitive spirit toward me.

There are times in ministry I grow weary and discouraged, and out of the overflow of his walk with the Lord, he's able to comfort me and draw my eyes toward Christ.

Your wife also needs this ministry from you, not as a pastor but as her husband. When you see that she needs care from you, and you listen to those needs with a heart to help, you keep her heart. Remind her of God's faithfulness, invite her to celebrate with you even the smallest of spiritual victories, give her specific feedback about how God is using her, and consistently bring her back to the truth of God's grace and love toward her.

Ministry is sanctification on steroids for both the pastor and his wife. You shouldn't attempt to protect your wife from that sanctification by trying to rescue her from any and all difficulty. Instead, pray for her and, while loving and caring for her, encourage her to look to the Lord for everything she needs. That is ultimately the best thing you can do for her—and for yourself.

Pastor, if you care well for your wife, you will never lose her heart, and she'll be your most valuable partner in life, love, and ministry.

Author's note: I believe it's vitally important that pastors and their wives have ongoing open dialogue about ministry and how it affects each spouse. On my website, HowtoThriveasaPastorsWife.com, I've provided discussion questions to get you started.

PART 4

You
and
Your
Children

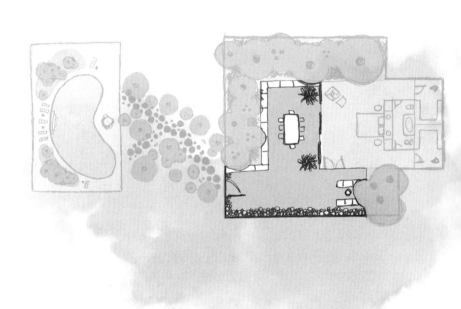

eiGHTeeN

Locating Your Family

Our children do not share our calling in ministry. They are born to a mom and dad who serve in vocational ministry, but they aren't vocational ministers themselves. However, just as we feel pressure to conform to a certain mold as a pastor's wife, our kids face similar pressures. We must make and protect space for them where they can be merely kids, not pastor's kids.

This happens within the family unit, gated off from the rest of the world. As we once again return to our architect's plan, we locate our family in just such a place: the courtyard surrounded by a fence. Within this protective patio, our kids can be the unique, imperfect people they are and find from us love and belonging, as well as training in the ways of God.

And fun! Don't forget the fun! There's nothing worse than a dour, dutiful Christian, not to mention being a kid whose mom and dad find the work God's given them to be miserable drudgery and who allow that miserable drudgery to color every facet of family life.

Notice how, just as the marriage is cordoned off and sacred, the family is as well. Work remains outside the gate. Inside the gate, Mom and Dad can relax with the family, enjoy the hammock, and engage with their children in intimate, deep relationships. They keep the stress of ministry life away as much as possible, while allowing in the joys and privileges of engaging in ministry to others. They're not owned by their cell phones or to-do lists, so they're not disengaged mentally. Rather, they're intentional about caring for their children's needs and bringing them up "in the discipline and instruction of the Lord" (Eph. 6:4).

Shepherding our children is not just a good thing to do; it's a foundational qualification for pastoring "outside the gates."

> [An elder] must manage his own family well and see that his children obey him, and he must do so in a manner worthy of full respect. (If anyone does not know how to manage his own family, how can he take care of God's church?) (1 Tim. 3:4–5 NIV)

As pastors' wives, we're not elders, but we're equal and pivotal partners in providing for the spiritual, emotional, and physical nurture of the family.

How do you envision the space on the architect's plan as it represents your family?

Perhaps extended family and friends who are like family are invited into this space—that's your choice. Perhaps as your children get older, they're invited into more details of your vocational ministry life. Again, that's your choice. Certainly, they will step outside the gate with you and accompany you to worship and into your service within the community. However you envision it, ensure they have their own sacred space, safe within the confines of your grace-filled family.

NiNeTeeN

Seasons of Ministry with Younger Children

Our boys were ages five, two, and six months when we planted our current church in our living room. Every Sunday, before our guests arrived, I'd clean, move furniture around to make it feasible for worship, bake goodies for our guests, greet folks as they came through the door, and run interference so my crawler didn't drool all over the worship leader's guitar. Once the teaching began, I'd take the boys to an upstairs room to play. I did this for the first three months—and every Sunday for three months, I cried after everyone left. I felt so disconnected from what was going on and from the relationships that seemed to be forming without me. I had no idea how to be a mom and a church planting wife simultaneously, especially when I was the childcare. Sundays were exhausting and difficult days.

Prior to church planting, we'd served at a large church with overflowing options for childcare, but I'd still found Sundays to be the hardest day of the week in regard to parenting. When our first son was born, it felt like decoding an encrypted war message to determine how I'd shower, nurse, squeeze in his nap, prepare a bottle for the nursery, and get us both to church on time without spit-up all over my dress and a diaper blowout.

When we had our second child, the number of bags I needed to pack and carry in to church doubled, as did the number of blowouts to avoid on the way and the chances of a meltdown from either a child or a frazzled mother. And that was just getting in the door of the church building!

Once inside—as many pastors' wives know well—we may have to manage a child throwing a tantrum in the middle of the church service or the knowing look when we're the last one to pick up our kids in the nursery again. We've all had to navigate the situation where one more person stops us to talk just as we're trying to get out the door with a visibly exhausted child, or when our child needs immediate discipline and everyone seems to be watching our every move. And we can't count the number of times we haven't been able to find our school-aged kids in the building when it's time to lock up and go home.

Sundays really are the hardest days of the week for pastors' wives. How can we make them as smooth as possible?

This question is especially pertinent when our children are young, so we'll focus first on the combination of ministry and parenting young children in this chapter. In the following chapter, we'll discover the unique challenges and joys of parenting teenagers while also serving in ministry.

Keep Your Parenting Goal in Mind

At church, those of us who are parents wear three hats: wife (relating to, being aware of, and helping our husband as needed), mom (relating to and parenting our children), and pastor's wife (relating to and loving people in the church). Actually, we wear more: Christian (relating to and encountering God), friend (relating to those we know personally), and servant (ministering in whatever capacity we may be serving that particular morning).

When my children were young, the most difficult balance or "hat combination" for me was being available to others while parenting solo on Sunday mornings. My loneliest and most exhausting Sundays were those when I corralled kids while helping tear down after the service while having a conversation with a hurting congregant while holding in my own tears of weariness or hurt. I'd thank God every week for Sunday afternoon naptime and for the kids' naptimes too.

However, I've since learned that raising kids in the ministry isn't just about managing Sunday mornings; it's about so much more.

It's about the very hearts of our children.

This seems obvious to say in regard to parenting, but when we live from a primary identity of "pastor's wife," we're more prone to consider our children as tools for ministry, props in the picture-perfect pastor's family image we're trying to portray, what we "do" when we're not doing "true" ministry, or as PKs (pastor's kids) rather than the unique human (read: fallen) beings they are. We may expect them to behave so as to reflect well on us, to keep quiet and out of the way so we can go about our noble work, or to be longsuffering about the endless attention needed by others.

Children must receive their rightful place in our families. They aren't the center of the universe, but they *are* our primary ministry and disciples, and they're given to us by God as blessings to enjoy and gifts to steward. Rather than props or even obstacles to ministry, they are children to love and rear in the fear and admonition of the Lord. This monumental task requires time, attention, energy, thoughtful care, and relational capital.

That's why we must keep our parenting goal ever-present. The goal in rearing our children isn't our sanity, our comfort, perfectly behaved children, or smooth Sundays. It is to give our children a lifelong love of God, his Word, and his church.

With this goal in mind, the stage of parenting young children is very much a foundation-building time. Your children may not be old enough to remember what you do now or understand everything you're saying to them, but you and your husband are setting the culture of your family now that will help you reach your goal later. Here are five aspects of your family culture to consider implementing in the midst of ministry life.

Security

Security for young children is established within a peaceful, loving, routine-based family culture. Where does this warm and disciplined culture originate from? From a mom and a dad who follow Jesus and find their identity and purpose in him. In other words, the security of the home is based upon your security in the Lord.

Do you trust the Lord to lead and shepherd you? Do you trust the Lord to speak to and empower your husband with wisdom and discernment? Do you trust the Lord will shepherd and nurture your church? And do you trust the Lord with your children? Do you believe ministry life is an opportunity not only for your growth and flourishing but for their growth and flourishing as well?

At various times, I've worried what ministry life might mean for my kids. Were we harming them by moving far from grandparents and other extended family in order to fulfill God's call? Would the demands of church planting and being a lead pastor's family eventually be detrimental to them? Anytime I met an adult pastor's kid, my attention would perk up and I'd pepper them with questions about what their parents did that paved the way for their salvation and love of the church.

I've learned that the best thing I can do for my kids is give them the security of my bedrock trust in the Lord—that his ways are perfect and right. Just as this calling on my husband's life is for my good and growth, it's also for our kids' good and growth. God is using this particular slice of life we live to form and mold them into the people he wants them to be.

Setting a secure culture in the home helps our kids know their needs come before the needs of others outside the home and that they are deeply loved for who they are, not what they do or don't do. In time, this security develops in them an appreciation and affection for the church and her people, rather than a resentment that the church and her people have usurped their proper and rightful place in Mom's and Dad's hearts.

One practical way you can foster security in your home is to keep watch over your mouth. How do you speak about the church? About going to worship? About people who are sinners and in need of grace? About other pastors, churches, and leaders? About your husband's job, busyness, and demands for his attention? About God and what he's called you to do? Rather than focusing solely on keeping negativity to yourself, focus instead on genuinely "[giving] thanks in all circumstances" (1 Thess. 5:18) within listening range of or in conversation with your children.

For example, sometimes at the dinner table, my husband talks with our children about the extreme generosity of the people of our church and what their financial giving enables us to do for the hurting and hungry in our community. Not only is it a teaching moment for them but it also makes my heart sing.

Separation

When our children are small, they don't have lives of their own, so they go where we go and fit into our calendar and agenda. We must make a conscious effort, then, to build in a gated boundary between church life and family life. There will be times when church and family life overlap and *should* overlap, of course, but willingly closing the gate to the "patio" enhances the security of the children's identity apart from being PKs and gives them a sense that they're a priority when so many are pulling at Mom and Dad. It also sets the stage for when they're teenagers and have interests and schedules of their own apart from our ministry—they have space and opportunity to become individuals according to who God has made them and parents who champion their uniqueness.

What does *separation* look like? Anything that affords our children undivided attention. Family fun. Play. Relaxation. Doing things or talking about what our children take interest in. Helping our kids pursue interests and friendships. Connection.

The important component of separation is that we leave ministry outside the gate, focusing solely on those inside. Though we may close the gate and be physically present with our children, what often hinders separation and invites distraction and unnecessary overlap between family and ministry life is technology. Phones are out and calls are taken. Without an intentional choice regarding how we'll manage phone use, we parents are figuratively letting any and all through the gates into the sacred space where our children are being shaped and molded.

Another hindrance to separation between church and family life is conversation between Mom and Dad. If we're not careful, every conversation during every car ride, dinner table discussion, or family walk turns back toward church, church people, church decisions, and the church calendar. Sometimes, if we're honest, we wonder what else we have to talk about.

Perhaps separation isn't just for our children.

When we choose separation, our children see us living a well-rounded life, not just focusing on a job. They see we have friends, read our Bibles separate from sermons and church events, take vacations and time off, and are real people who aren't constantly stressed.

By building separation into our family life, we're teaching our children how to be healthy people: to have interests and passions, be physically active, have friendships, enjoy creation with people we love, to rest and have fun, to attach to the right things and resist being attached to the wrong—and that it's good and necessary to say no sometimes. And of course we're also reminding *ourselves* that we're human beings who must persistently choose what makes for a healthy marriage and family. We're demonstrating and protecting our children and ourselves from letting church become a tyrant, an owner. In other words, we're giving them a vision and love for the local church as it is meant to be. And we're giving them a vision and love for marriage and family as they are meant to be.

Salvation

Every Christian parent's greatest desire is for their children to know and walk with the Lord, and pastors' wives are no exception. When our children are young, we long for them to come to faith. And like all other parents, we wonder if we're doing enough to pave the way for the Lord to call them to himself.

The temptation in the pastor's home is to think that our kids pick up the gospel through osmosis, simply by being at church and hearing their dad preach, and perhaps by seeing all the ways their mom serves others. These are both wonderful perks of being a pastor's kid, but they don't involve one-on-one, consistent relationship.

I always tell new moms in our church that the day-in, day-out work they put into discipline and building a warm relationship with their young children pays off in dividends later, especially in their spiritual growth.

In terms of discipline, we can use their disobedience as an opportunity to share about the gospel: "When you disobeyed Mama, you dishonored God, because the Bible tells us that we are to obey our moms and dads. He calls this disobedience sin. You can pray to God and tell him what you did and ask for forgiveness, and he will forgive you. You can then tell Mama you're sorry, and I too will forgive you. The way you show you are sorry is by doing it different next time. But even now that you know you've done wrong and want to obey, can you obey Mama perfectly? No. Mama also can't obey God perfectly, and God knows that. None of us can obey perfectly. That's why God sent Jesus to us. Jesus obeyed God perfectly and then died on the cross to take the punishment for our disobedience . . ."

In other words, these are opportunities to talk about Christ's death and resurrection, how we come to him by faith, and how he gives us his Spirit to convict us of sin and lead us to obey God. The necessary ingredient is not the exact right words; it's relationship. We *live out* the gospel in front of them by exhibiting gentle yet firm correction, offering quick forgiveness, and demonstrating a restored relationship when sin has marred the connection.

In an interview with Barnabas Piper, a pastor's son, I asked him, "How can moms of PKs help their children develop a personal faith and a genuine love for the Lord and for the church?" He said:

> The best thing parents can do is present Jesus to kids *personally*. This means exemplifying grace and speaking of your own relationship with

Jesus. PKs don't need lessons. They need living proof that Jesus is great and close.

Give them room to ask questions, and even encourage it. Indoctrination will do more harm than good in the end, whereas honest conviction will do great good in helping your kids come into their own faith.

The biggest piece of this is overwhelming grace. PKs need it because too often they don't receive it from those in the church. They need it because they will screw up. They need it because it points them to Jesus.

Don't preach at them. Don't Bible lesson them. They need counselors, confidants, and conversations. PKs need to connect with their parents, not just hear from them.

Build relationships with your kids that surpass the sharing of morals and information.

The biggest thing, then, is having a personal faith and living it so your kids see it. They need to see your patience, grace, and peace. And of course you will fail because you are human and being a mom is hard. So then they need to see you repent and ask forgiveness. This might be even bigger than getting it right the first time. It sets a precedent of forgiveness both from God and within the family. That helps make God accessible and personal.[1]

Service

Kids are never too young to learn that serving others is better than serving themselves (Acts 20:35). Teach them that cleaning up after themselves, helping to carry in the groceries, and putting away their clean clothes isn't for their own reward but for the good of all within the family. Teach them to honor those who serve them by saying thank you to the one who prepared their meal and looking the restaurant server in the eye while speaking politely. In other words, teach them that the greatest among us is a servant.

Invite your children into the joy of serving with you in your ministry. The way we communicate that joy is by continually helping them understand why we do what we do. When taking a meal to someone suffering, explain the importance of the body of Christ coming around those who mourn. When preparing for a church service, explain that you are committed to a local church not because it's your husband's job but because the church is a gift God gives every Christian. Take any occasion you can to tell your children, "These are things we do because we're Christians. We'd do them whether Daddy is a pastor or not."

With your husband, determine one or two ways you will incorporate your children in service at church. Young children can set up chairs. They can put bulletins on seats. They can write cards to people special to them. They can help make cookies for your small group gathering.

When my boys were small, we had many guests in our home for meals. Each time, I tasked them with setting the table and choosing table decorations. Most of the time, this meant they wrote name cards and selected a LEGO minifigure to pose at each place setting, personalized for the person coming. Sometimes it meant LEGO creations spread out in the middle of the dining room table. Although certainly not beautiful by Martha Stewart standards, the boys loved it and were eager to see our guests' reactions.

They didn't realize they were also learning to serve.

Sundays (and Other Church Events)

The best tip I can give you for navigating Sundays as a solo parent is to prepare your kids in every way possible for the day ahead before you enter the building.

Over breakfast or on the drive to church, go through the schedule of the morning from start to finish. Will they be sitting with you in the service or attending their own classes? If they're sitting with you, do you have materials you brought for them to engage with the sermon? Will you be observing communion and, if so, how will this affect them? Will you and the kids or your husband alone be attending scheduled lunches or meetings after church? Do they need to stay with you at all times, or are there instructions you can give them about managing themselves as they play with friends? Going through the schedule enables you to explain certain elements of worship (communion or baptism) and also cheerfully lay out expectations for the morning.

Another way to prepare your kids is to help them know what they can expect and what is expected on any given Sunday. Explain to them how you'd like them to get your attention if you're talking with someone and how you'll communicate if you need them to patiently wait for a stopping point in the conversation. Teach them to look others in the eye and answer basic questions politely and to sit attentively and quietly. And let them know by word and practice that, when needed, you'll discipline them privately at church or later at home; they won't get away with poor behavior at church simply because Mom and Dad may be engaged with other people.

As you navigate Sundays, the most important tip to keep in mind is that you don't have to go it alone. *Help others know what you need.*

Our church was built on a foundation of college students and young, newly graduated singles, which is a beautiful base. But for over a year, I was the only mom in our church, and we were the only family. After our Sunday evening gathering, everyone else would flit away to a movie or restaurant, and I'd stay home to put kids to bed while longing to be with them. I started feeling resentful about this, but my husband gently reminded me it wasn't that they didn't want me around or didn't want to help me with cleaning up the house after our gathering. It also wasn't that they didn't want to help with my kids—it was that they didn't know what my needs were. If I actually voiced what I needed, people would probably be eager to help me.

I've learned he's right.

If you need help with your kids, ask someone. Most people would be happy to serve you in that way. Perhaps you could ask a teen to meet you at your car on Sunday mornings and help you get your young children where they need to be. Perhaps you could ask a friend to get your children from their classrooms after the service is over so you can connect with people. When are the times you most need help with your children? Who could you ask to help you with those times? Ask them today.

Of course, one person you can always ask for help is your husband. Let him know what is most important to you and ask him to help.

After I had months of those Sunday evening tears, the best thing my husband did for me was to ask an established church in town to provide childcare for our kids during our church times so I could participate. That church sent two college girls to our house each Sunday evening, which totally saved my sanity!

My husband helped me when I most needed it.

While acknowledging there are some instances when he cannot help, when are times your husband *can* help? Does he know you need that help? You must voice your needs to him.

As part of the discussion with your husband, consider these questions: What are the most important times and events for you to have his help? During what occasions at church do you most want to be together as a couple or family? What are the times and events during which your husband feels he needs to give his undivided attention to others? As you discuss these questions together, you may find that you're able to meet in the middle and work together as a team, both in ministry and in parenting.

For example, when our kids were small, my husband often couldn't help me with our children on Sunday mornings, but he could help me at social gatherings or small groups when he wasn't teaching or needed for a specific task. He helped get our children their plates of food and dealt with behavior issues. Not only did we parent together but our church also saw a model of a pastor who cared for his wife and was engaged with his kids.

Remember, when your children are young, you are setting the culture of your family. Your goal in all you do is to give your children a lifelong love of God, his Word, and his church. With a grace-filled, joy-filled, security-filled foundation set in the younger years, you will reap the blessing through *relationship* in their teenage years and beyond.

TWENTY

Seasons of Ministry with Older Children

A round ninth grade, my oldest son started to struggle with church. He didn't complain to us about anything in particular, but every Sunday, as soon as the service ended, he'd ask for my keys and retreat to our car. Knowing his personality, I let him, but I also broached the subject (and my concern) on many of our rides home. With a recent influx of teenage boys coming to our church after a long drought of boys his age to befriend, I'd anticipated wonderful new friendships for him. I wondered aloud—Had he considered finding that new boy he really enjoyed and talking to him before he left for the car? I also gave him a few suggestions on how he could initiate conversation with his peers, but still, each Sunday, he retreated. It felt like we were losing him to apathy and disengagement at the very time we most wanted to connect his heart to the Lord and the Lord's church.

We'd stepped into a new season of parenting while in the ministry. Instead of schlepping our kids everywhere we went, whether to a church activity or to someone's home for dinner, we now needed to help our boys develop as individuals and give more concentrated time to their discipleship.

As we stepped into this new challenge, I felt inept and scared. The stakes felt high.

When my children were much younger, on any occasion where the subject of parenting teenagers came up in conversation, I paid close attention. I also felt my heart seized by panic at the thought that one day my dear little boys would grow into tall, hairy-legged teenagers who, I assumed, would declare their independence from me at every turn. I myself was a terrible teenager, moody and turned inward, unwilling to hear my parents' counsel, and so I braced myself for the day when I'd parent some form of me.

However, in those conversations with more seasoned parents, my assumptions were consistently challenged. Not only did these parents speak about the joy of relating with their teenagers but I saw their relationships with my own eyes and recognized the possibilities and opportunities ahead of me. These parents (and their teens) taught me through word and deed that I didn't need to fear parenting teenagers, yet they also taught me that I should be prepared to parent differently than I had when my boys were young.

That's what I thought of as I drove my sons home from church, worrying over my eldest's retreat. No longer was I "preparing." I had come to the starting line of parenting teenagers, with the added pressure of the church spotlight shining on all of us.

And the starting gun had already sounded.

The Parenting Goal

The goal in raising our children never changes—we're cultivating in our children a lifelong love of God, his Word, and his church—but the methods we use to meet this goal *do* change as our children grow in wisdom and stature. This is our goal, because these loves act as a solid foundation as they navigate any situation, location, vocation, or relationship in life.

The difference in seasons of parenting young children and parenting teens is our teenagers' growing independence and individualism—both very good things.

When our children were young, parenting was physically exhausting. But they went to bed at 7:30 p.m., took naps, and didn't have their own social lives. I had uninterrupted hours with my husband in the evenings, our kids went with us everywhere we went whether they liked it or not, and the family calendar was dictated by our relationships and ministry choices.

Life with teenagers is still physically exhausting—they stay up so late!—but it's also emotionally exhausting. We now layer our children's social schedules, extracurricular activities, and needs with our own. We make decisions about what we can and can't do differently than we did when they were young, because we don't want to drag our kids to everything we're invited to and because we also want to protect time when we can all be home together. Life feels full and often overwhelmingly exhausting.

But there are also great joys that come with their growing independence and individualism. The greatest joy is my deepening relationships with my children. We have conversations of the sort friends would engage in about everything from movies to the deepest issues of life. Their witty comments make me laugh, and they needle their father and me in fun. They are growing into themselves—into who God made them—and I delight in pointing it out to them because they don't yet have eyes to see it fully.

In other words, it's vital to help our teenagers hone their independence and individualism in a way that honors the Lord and serves others. And as pastor's kids, our children have unique opportunities and avenues in which to learn these lessons in their teenage years.

As we did in the last chapter, we'll highlight a few aspects of family culture to consider implementing in the midst of ministry life and parenting teenagers.

Security

As it is for any teenager, a properly defined identity is paramount to our children's well-being. Every teenager receives messages from social media, pop culture, teachers, youth leaders, and friends about who they should be and how they should conduct themselves. Kids growing up in a pastor's home face additional pressures and complexities that often confuse and burden them. Rather than just worldly pressures, our children also face pressure that comes from people they love—church folks, teachers, peers who often remind them they're a pastor's kid, and sometimes even Mom and Dad—making it difficult for them to separate "PK" from their identity.

They are simply kids, just like their peers, and they need to be taught their true identity: a young man or woman created in the image of God and loved by God. Because we ourselves often struggle to keep our identity separate from "pastor's wife," we must be cognizant of common statements or actions that may have a tone of "get in line" and work against their true, biblical identity.

Barnabas Piper says one of the most detrimental things we can do as parents is the

> heaping on of expectations PKs already feel. I suspect the pressures on pastors' wives are similar to those of PKs, so if you take what you feel and think about that placed on a twelve-year-old, you have a decent sense of things. They feel the need to be better behaved, be more attentive, and have all the answers. They know they are being watched, so to say things like "Now we're going into church; make sure you're on your best behavior, people are watching us" is just piling on. Make sure they know that the standard for behavior is honoring Jesus and loving others—period. Being a PK neither adds nor subtracts from that.[1]

In other words, our children should not feel like they have a part-time job as "the pastor's kid." Our kids aren't a public commodity. We must resist presenting ourselves as perfect mothers and our children as perfect too, because our children won't feel secure as long as they also feel a simultaneous pressure to behave according to a false identity.

So what can we do in order to cultivate security in our children?

One: understand their world as best you can. Talk with your children about the expectations, burdens, and pressures they feel in regard to having a dad who is a public person. Ask them questions to understand what life is like for them: Do strangers talk to them at church? How do they feel when that happens? Does anyone remind them they're a pastor's kid when they either do something right or something wrong? What are the perks of Dad being a pastor? What are the hard parts for them? Do they like being a sermon illustration or is that embarrassing to them? Do they feel like they have to have all the answers?

Two: listen. Don't try to convince them of the positive side of every situation they face. Don't be afraid if they're wrestling with or frustrated by certain experiences. Perhaps you can empathize with them by sharing some of the funny or weird things people say to you or by sharing what joys and challenges you face as the pastor's wife.

Barnabas Piper again helps us here:

> A big thing moms can do to ease these burdens for their kids is to talk through them. Help them see that you know their frustrations and are *with* them. Give them a safe place to vent and sort through stuff. And give them the stability of love so they know you are always in their corner. Sometimes this means pep talks, sometimes an encouraging or challenging conversation, and sometimes it means just listening. Moms are usually really good at knowing which is needed.[2]

Three: set boundaries. In addition, we must consider how we can stand as a guard and shield between the church and our children. Boundaries with both time and conversation are important to give our children healthy space to grow as individuals.

In our home, when it comes to conversations, we rarely talk about church with our kids, aside from when we have a good story to tell or news about someone they know and love from the congregation. We don't involve them in conversations about conflict, criticism, or personal hurts. However, we also don't shield them from suffering. We may share with them about a church member's miscarriage or a difficult health diagnosis so we can pray for that person as a family.

Regarding time and commitments, we rarely involve our teenagers in commitments that they'd have to do solely because they are a pastor's kid. For example, sometimes our family gets invited to someone's home for dinner solely because Dad is the pastor. If our children know this family or if they have similarly aged kids, we say a happy yes. But if our kids don't know them, we generally shield them from dutiful commitments that are really more about Mom and Dad, perhaps by suggesting an alternative get-together with just adults.

Sanctification

In the teenage years, emotions run high and low—and I'm not speaking of the actual teenagers. I'm speaking of *myself*, the parent of teenagers. The stakes feel so high, and they are. As our children are exposed to more choices, more independence, and more of the world and its nature, there are land mines everywhere. As a parent, I know my children don't have the full extent of wisdom they yet need, but I also know I can't hover over and control every aspect of their lives. Parenting a teenager is ultimately an ongoing lesson and test in whether or not I trust the Lord.

As moms to pastor's kids, we must know that our children will inevitably need grace. They will make mistakes, intentional or otherwise, and how we view those mistakes is vitally important. Are their poor choices solely reflections on the pastor and the pastor's wife? Are they signs of bad parenting? No; rather they are opportunities for our children (and us!) to grow and learn about confession, repentance, mercy, grace, forgiveness, and sanctification within the safe environment of a grace-filled family.

This past year, one of my sons found himself in a situation I would not have preferred. He'd done nothing wrong; he was very open with us about it, but I was nonetheless surprised at my own reaction. I was at various times angry, fearful, distrusting, panicky, and grasping for control. I also knew he was in over his head and didn't know exactly how far. Looking back on that time now, I see how good it was not only for him but for me to walk through that situation. We were able to have many good conversations as he navigated a difficulty, and he saw our predictions and warnings actually play out in real time.

Letting our children fail or fall is one of the hardest things to do as a parent. However, mistakes and difficulties can be good for teenagers (and for their parents), especially if the relationship between parent and child is strong and characterized by open communication. Mistakes and difficulties grow their faith, and they grow ours as well, although the emotional stakes are nonetheless high.

While we must not protect our kids from difficult things, there are specific ways we as moms can protect and nurture our PKs as they navigate these things in full view of others.

First, we can help them maintain their privacy. When our kids are facing consequences from their mistakes or are struggling, we should not share that information with anyone else without their expressed permission, and even then we must be careful how we speak about our children. We should never shame our kids in front of others.

Second, our children aren't a public commodity. We can demonstrate this by refraining from using them as teaching and sermon illustrations unless they've given their expressed permission to do so. One pastor I know pays his teenagers $20 each time he uses them as a sermon illustration, because he knows that, even though he's received their permission, the illustration will cost them in some way, as person after person will talk to them about it.

Finally, one of the most important things we can do for our teenagers is to vocalize our own struggles and uncertainties and how God is speaking to us through his Word. Share with your kids when God is calling you to repent and change, how he's challenging you, and how the gospel is applicable to you personally. In other words, demonstrate how to apply the gospel and teach them to turn to the Lord in any and every situation.

Sundays (and Beyond)

When our oldest continually retreated after church services, it was an alert to me that something needed to change—because my boy had changed. He was no longer a duckling following wherever I led but rather was becoming an independent person who needed to integrate into the community of the church on his own. Kyle and I had a choice: we could force him to do what we wanted because we knew it was good for him, or we could help him cultivate a faith and connection to God's church that was his own apart from his parents. We chose the latter, although some of this cultivation did involve firm expectations—not all decisions were left to him.

Soon after, our men's ministry announced an upcoming retreat, and my husband invited our oldest son to go with him. Our son expressed reluctance, but Kyle sold him on all the fun activities he'd get to enjoy. When the weekend arrived, they headed off together, and upon their return Kyle reported some fantastic moments where the men in our church interacted with our son as a man, encouraged him to see his influence as a leader in his school, and expressed interest in him as a person and in his spiritual growth. In other words, they invited him into the community of the church as one of them. He came home a different person and, as soon as he walked in the door, asked me, "When's the *next* men's retreat? I can't wait!"

I praise God for the men of our church who demonstrated the joy of Christian fellowship to our son and, in one weekend, completely altered his engagement with God's church.

You too can and must look for ways to connect your teenager to the life and community of the church. Invite people who show an interest in them to their sporting events or band concerts. Have people in your home who love your teenager well. Encourage your child to engage in a discipleship relationship or join a Bible study at church apart from you. Invite them to join with you as you interact with the sick and suffering. If you're far from family, cultivate a relationship with adoptive grandparents who can celebrate your teenager's special days and accomplishments and spoil them a little.

Helping your teenager engage the church will certainly come with challenges. One challenge, of course, is threading the needle between firm family expectations (i.e., attending church is nonnegotiable) and freedom to choose as an individual (Will they be expected to attend every opportunity provided for youth at the church?). We must keep in mind, again, that our goal is not molding them into an example of the perfect pastor's kid. Our goal is helping them develop a deepening love for God, his Word, and his church. With this in mind, we can have ongoing conversations with our kids about what feeds their faith, what the Bible commands God's people to make a priority in our life, why these priorities are for our thriving, and what activities are negotiable.

Another challenge we face in these years is the creep of required time commitments for community and extracurricular activities that may, without intentionality on our parts, interfere with our family life, our teen's devotional life, and their integration into church life. Each pastor's family may handle these situations differently, but if our goal is ever-present and if we've cultivated open communication with our teenagers, these difficulties make for excellent opportunities for our teens to learn how to make wise and biblical decisions, how to say no, and how to handle disappointing people, experiencing disapproval, and setting priorities.

As parents, we may experience tension when our decisions set our children apart as "different." In the teen years, other teenagers (and their parents) come into play. When should a teenager get a cell phone? When should a teenager be allowed to go on a date? These are questions we've discussed and decided on together as Mom and Dad, but the influence of other families' choices cannot be overstated in the life of a teenager. I'm not saying we allow other parents to make decisions for us; I'm saying we have to work hard to know our children's friends, we must be willing to ask uncomfortable questions of our children's friends' parents if needed, and *we have to be okay with our children being different from everyone around them.* I think this last one is perhaps the hardest and most important of all. I have often had to ask hard questions of myself about why I wouldn't want my children to be considered "different" by their peers even though I know the "different" decision we've made is absolutely best for my children. As we parent teenagers, we must be intentional in decision-making and willing to stand our ground according to our convictions.

Service

In addition to helping them integrate into the community life of the church, one of the greatest joys in parenting teenagers is teaching them to serve others, helping them find a place of service within the church that best fits their interests and gifts, and then watching them overcome setbacks in order to flourish.

When it comes to helping PKs learn to serve, the key phrase is "helping them find a place of service within the church that best fits their interests and gifts." As your children blossom into unique individuals, study them. Is he a people person? Is she good with details? Is he naturally gifted with leadership skills? Is she someone who prefers serving behind the scenes? Is he good with kids?

Teenagers often cannot see in themselves what their God-given talents or gifts are, so we as parents have the joy-filled opportunity of helping them discover how God made them and then encouraging them to step out in faith and use those gifts. We can help them match their gifts to specific opportunities within the church or among the ways the church is serving the wider community.

Serving together is a great blessing for the pastor's family, and we've found that one of the best ways to serve together is through mission work, both locally and globally. For the past few years, either Kyle or I have annually taken a child with us on an international mission trip through our church. On these trips, we're careful to interact with them as team members while at the same time letting our kids know we're available to them as their parents whenever they need something. Watching them engage international partners—pastors and leaders in a different culture from our own—and seeing them come alive to God's work across the world has been a true gift. Not only that but they've learned to serve in reliance on the Holy Spirit rather than their own energy and strength.

One often overlooked area of service we have countless opportunities to train our teenagers in is hospitality—and this is not limited to having people over for a meal. In a world where many are glued to their screens, we can teach our teenagers the value of relationships.

By example and by having continual conversations about it, we can teach them to truly "see" people, initiate engagement with them, and honor and show interest in others by asking good, intentional questions. For example, when preparing to host a family in our home, we've asked each of our boys to think of one question they can ask our guests during dinner. Or similarly, we've given them language to help them in conversations at church, whether answering questions or asking them of others. And when their friends come over, we talk in advance about offering their friends snacks and drinks and what they can do together that doesn't involve screens.

Have you noticed a theme in these lessons? I'm learning in this season of parenting and ministry how necessary *relationship* is with my children, and how necessary it is to know my *specific* children.

Moms of teenagers, your children need you now more than ever. They need your presence, awareness, structure, questions, discipline, and engagement in their lives. As PKs carrying additional pressure, they need to know that you're there, you love them no matter what, and you will always sacrificially help them. Above all, they need to be close enough to you to see and hear your trust in the Lord for them.

PART 5

You
AND
Your
Friends

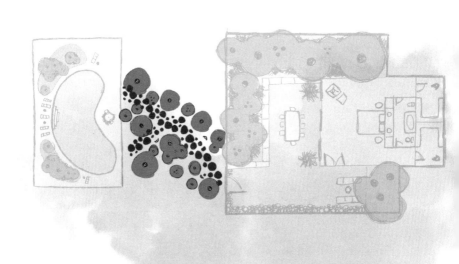

TWENTY-one

Locating Your Friendships

*N*otably, we've spent the entire book up until this point focused on what's inside the gate: your relationship with God, your husband, and your children. These relationships are your priorities and must get the bulk of your energy, time, and intention.

But of course there are many other people we have the privilege of interacting with and being in relationship with. As we return to the architect's plan, it's time, then, to step outside the gate and discover how we can thrive in other arenas of life.

Previously I described the conversation I had with my husband and how I felt the church staff, elders, and congregants were lined up just outside the gate, ready to engulf him with their questions, needs, and concerns. What would you say waits outside your gate, perhaps even bangs on the door, begging entrance? Is it your own work? Your husband's work? A certain relationship? The church's expectations for you, as their pastor's wife?

In other words, what feels most pressing and demanding in your life?

For most of us, it's something involving church life—an event to plan, a shower to host, a community group to lead, a woman to counsel, a Bible study to prepare for, or a long list of activities on the calendar to attend.

When I created an outline for this book, I originally planned to focus on community and friendship *after* focusing on our relationship to the church. Friendship can feel like a luxury—something we may or may not have time for, something we may or may not enjoy at the moment—and for many pastors' wives, the subject of friendship can be a source of pain and consternation. We often think of our work within the church as more important than any effort or time we put into cultivating friendships.

But as you can see, I switched the order to focus on friendship before church. Why? Because friendship is personal. We can't hide behind a façade in friendship, and if we're going to grow instead of becoming spiritually malformed, we must be in deep relationships with other women. If we hope to thrive in ministry, we need friends.

Let's locate friendship on the architect's plan.

As we leave the gate, following the garden path toward work, community life, and church, there are benches where we can stop, sit, and refresh with a friend. Without these benches, our life outside the gate is all work and no play. The lush tropical plant life surrounding the benches reminds us that sanctifying friendship is a vital component to our flourishing as Christians—and to our flourishing as pastors' wives.

Join me now on the garden path.

TWENTY-TWO
What Friends?
Identifying and Cultivating Friendships

few years ago, I took questions from an audience of women. One woman, knowing I was a pastor's wife, raised her hand with a question about her own pastor's wife. She asked, "I really want to care for her. What do you suggest?"

I smiled, affirmed her desire, and began listing various options for how she could specifically show love to her pastor's wife: pray for her, let her know she's being prayed for, say thank you for the many unseen sacrifices she makes, and perhaps, if applicable, help her with her small children on Sunday mornings.

The woman then interrupted me to rephrase her question. "But how do I become *friends* with the pastor's wife?" She appeared frustrated that her pastor's wife seemed hard to get to know.

Afterward, her question sat heavy with me for days. When she'd asked it, for a reason I couldn't quite pinpoint, I'd bristled inside, feeling defensive. In the weeks following, I realized why: the questioner presumed friendship with her pastor's wife was inevitable—a right—and she seemed personally offended that her pastor's wife hadn't welcomed her into her confidence.

I bristled because I've sensed those very expectations many times before, and in general I tend to feel like I'm never quite navigating well the many blurred lines between friendships, social relationships, and church life. At times, I feel like I engage church and church people with a little too much caution. Other times, I realize my actions have over-promised relational closeness that I cannot fulfill. And then there are the times when I want so badly to tell a friend something that's weighing on me, but I can't without dishonoring confidences. Is true, vulnerable friendship even possible for me, the pastor's wife?

The topic of friendship feels vulnerable and sensitive, not only because I've gotten it wrong far too many times but because I've also nursed silent wounds that I worry may lace my words with bitterness. In addition, it seems that everyone has an opinion about how the pastor's wife relates to others, and I wonder if people who ask me about how I experience friendship will listen—*really listen*—to my flustered, fumbling answers.

I also wonder about the pastor's wife my questioner referred to. I don't know her name or anything about her, but it's highly probable that, like me, she's somewhere out there struggling to navigate all of her relationships within the church. Are they friendships? Or simply warm church relationships? What can she share, and with whom? Can people see her as a real person? Who can she bring into her confidence, and will there ever be a person like that for her in her own church?

A pastor's wife, as one recently told me, often feels as if she's relationally a mile wide and an inch deep. She may even believe the oft-repeated charge that she is not to have personal friends within the congregation, or she may feel church-related demands have stretched her so thin that friendship isn't logistically possible for her.

I've felt and believed all of these things at various points and even tried to live as if I were responsible to maintain friendships with everyone within our church. For many years, I resigned myself to the idea that I didn't have a choice in who my friends were—*I should be friends with everyone!*—and, in trying to be friends with everyone, I was deep friends with no one.

Pastor's wife, I have good news for you. You *do* have a choice in the matter, and friendship is a very real possibility for you. In fact, it's a *necessity* for your emotional well-being and spiritual flourishing. Without friendship, we're susceptible to blind spots, sin, and an "all work and no play" mentality. And we're forever the counselor with no one to whom we can go to seek counsel.

Friendship requires your intentional vulnerability, however, and this is the first obstacle you'll have to hurtle yourself through, because vulnerability is something we pastors' wives tend to tightly lock away. We often point ourselves to the caveat—"But make sure you are vulnerable only with safe people"—as permission to remain holed up and self-protective. Self-protection doesn't win friends, dear reader.

So let's talk about what does.

It starts with learning to identify categories of relationships.

Know the Difference between Relationships and Friendships

My husband recently told me we'd been invited, as the pastor's family, to dinner at someone's home, and we discussed whether or not we could commit to the date they'd offered. I felt immediately overwhelmed, because I thought about the emails with similar requests waiting for a reply in my inbox. I'm grateful for these invitations, and I also want to remain openhearted to everyone in our neighborhood, community group, staff and elder team (and their spouses), parents of the kids on our children's sports teams, and everyone in our church at large, but the deepest truth is that what I really want is *friendship*. I'm surrounded by lovely people and countless relationships, but relationships don't always equate to friendship, and I tend to forget that.

As pastors' wives, we must have a hearty understanding of what friendship actually is, because after years of being accessible to many people, we tend to lose the ability to discern between a *relationship* and a *friendship*. We may even feel as if we've lost ourselves or our ability to make friends underneath the weight and busyness of ministry. So let me remind us: relationships only require an association or a commonality. We go to the same church. Our kids attend the same school. We live in the same neighborhood.

Friendship, however, involves *mutuality*: a back-and-forth, a give-and-take. If there is not mutuality at some point, we cannot label that relationship a true friendship.

Many times, being openhearted to others as the pastor's wife means being a listener and an initiator, reaching out to those we encounter at church and in the community. It may help to mentally label these types of relationships as "ministry relationships," and we should absolutely seek to bless, encourage, and minister to anyone God brings into our sphere. In fact, this is a template for ministry that fulfills the Christian's mandate: "Love one another deeply as brothers and sisters. Take the lead in honoring one another" (Rom. 12:10 CSB).

In *every* relationship, honor others. When you go to church services or gatherings, honor people with your words, demeanor, affection, attentive listening, and help.

However, as we've already determined, not every ministry relationship is friendship, *nor does it have to be*. You don't have to be everyone's friend; in fact, it's not possible to be everyone's friend. Friendship's distinctive, again, is mutuality: mutual vulnerability, mutual pursuit, mutual responsibility, and mutual care and concern. When we consider friendship in that vein, it's clear that not only are we unable to be friends with everyone but also that it would be unwise to try. It also makes clear that what some women want or pursue with us is not actually friendship but merely to be known or helped by the pastor's wife without also knowing the pastor's wife.

Pastor's wife, honor all, be friends with a few, and engage in ministry relationships how God leads you. Friendship, in which you share your innermost thoughts and feelings, is reserved for the one or two who've proven trustworthy, godly, and persistent in reciprocation. Friendly with all, deeper in friendship with a few—that's my own motto that I'm passing along to you.

Many pastors' wives worry they'll be criticized for showing favoritism or being exclusive if they pursue deep friendships within the church. One way we can avoid unintentionally causing hurt feelings is to keep our social calendar to ourselves. For example, I refrain from posting pictures online of informal gatherings, birthday dinners, or anything non–church related where I'm socializing with women from church. I also never drop lines into conversation like, "Last week, I was having coffee with so-and-so. . . ." I am fairly tight-lipped, even among my friends, about what I'm doing and with whom. Of course, I can't control what others share online or in conversation, and I can't control (nor am I responsible for) any feelings of jealousy others may feel. But I can certainly do my part to honor the women in my church by refusing to flaunt my friendships in full view of others.

Where Are These Friendships to Be Found?

You may be thinking, *Where do I find these friendships? I'm semi-friends with everyone, and I'm not sure there is anyone in the church I can share myself with.*

We must first learn to identify potential friends or those who fit in the "friendship" category.

As we attempt to do this, the blurred lines and overlapping spheres of life can make it confusing and complex. (And this is often where we give up, assuming it's too difficult.)

I think back to the invitations in my inbox. Does the woman inviting me to coffee need counsel, or does she want to get to know me as a person? Does the dinner invitation come from a place of desired friendship or from a place of pastoral need? I often don't know until I'm sitting across the table from others or until time has revealed the true nature of the relationship. If there are sparks of mutuality, in which I'm asked questions or there is some sort of reciprocal interest and care shown toward me, I may have a potential friend. A relationship, in time, *may* evolve into a friendship.

Again, the key word is *mutuality*.

Sometimes a relationship stalls out from becoming a friendship because of the other person's inability to reciprocate. Perhaps she can only seem to approach us as "the pastor's wife," holding us up on a pedestal. Perhaps she sees us only as a wise counselor, the person with the inside scoop, or a messenger to the pastor. Because this is how they relate to us, these women place themselves squarely in our ministry relationships category, and we'll gladly honor and serve them. But we don't have to reveal ourselves vulnerably to them.

I daresay, however, that mutuality is primarily our own problem. We pastors' wives are notoriously guarded, and there are good and right reasons for that. But if we want friendship, we must be willing to return vulnerability with vulnerability.

So, first, identify: Who are trustworthy, godly women you can share yourself with? Look for those who approach you not as a role or according to who you're married to but rather as a person with strengths, faults, passions, emotions, convictions, and weaknesses.

Look for those who don't keep or allow you to keep the church as the main point of connection or conversation.

Look outside the church, in the community and in your neighborhood. Befriend nonbelievers, who often hold no special reverence for clergy, and let their perspectives and needs both challenge and grow your ability to express your faith.

Look for friends among your fellow pastors' wives in town. They can be sources of empathy and encouragement to you.

Look up and down the age spectrum, perhaps inviting a younger woman into a discipleship relationship or asking an older woman to have lunch so you can glean from her wisdom. These relationships can easily turn into friendship.

Learning to identify is the necessary first step toward friendship. We must allow ourselves the freedom to distinguish friends among the many relationships we have. We cannot steward or pursue friendships we can't name.

Who are the trustworthy, godly people in your orbit?

Identify, initiate, and invite them into your life. And if they're already there by your side, invest time in cultivating those friendships.

Get Out of Your Own Way

When it comes to friendship, I think we as pastors' wives are often our worst enemies. We get in our own way relationally when we try to avoid criticism, getting hurt, or disappointing people, and when we're attempting to appear as if we have it all together. Or, when the blurred lines feel a little too complex to navigate, we retreat and resign ourselves to the fate of never having good friends. We stay busy in ministry relationships to mask the occasional bouts of loneliness and isolation.

Here are five ways you can get out of your own way and keep friendship as an important priority in your life.

One: root out bitterness and self-pity. Other women sniff out bitterness or self-pity and don't know what to do with it, especially if it's emanating from the pastor's wife. More importantly, however, bitterness is sin against God. God sees how you've been legitimately hurt in the past or when you've felt isolated and alone. His Word calls us not to ignore how we've been hurt but instead to acknowledge it both to ourselves and to the Lord, and sometimes—with the Lord's leading—even to the person who hurt us. If we don't deal with our hurts, friendship will be difficult for us. So know that God saw what that person did to you, and he'll deal with their sin, but don't become the sinner yourself in your inability to entrust yourself to the Lord's care and comfort. The Lord is your defense (Ps. 5:11–12) and gives such secure love that you can put yourself back out there and keep trying relationally.

Two: think of yourself rightly. You are introduced everywhere you go as "the pastor's wife." You may feel unspoken expectations regarding the role. You may find yourself trying incredibly hard to be what you think everyone wants you to be. *But you are ultimately not a role; you are a person.* As I've stated in previous chapters, the more you think of yourself as a role, the more you'll find yourself performing and overanalyzing relationships and the less you'll be able to engage other women as the real person you are. Don't think of yourself first as the pastor's wife. Think of yourself as a Christian who needs the gift and sanctification of community and friendship.

Three: don't take the attitude of a martyr. If you want deep friendships, you absolutely must reveal your physical, emotional, and spiritual needs to others. Think about how you would feel if you tried cultivating a relationship with another woman who never expressed an uncertainty, a discouragement, or a physical need. You wouldn't want to be friends with her! Start with small things, but start somewhere.

In addition, know that friendship struggles aren't unique to pastors' wives. Don't use your role as an excuse. Friendship rarely falls into the lap of any woman. Those who have friends have intentionally cultivated them and taken the risk of vulnerability.

Four: make friendship a scheduled priority. We all feel the tyranny of the urgent. Ministry can, at times, feel very reactive. We don't have time to stop and think about who we'd like to have coffee with or get to know better, because we're just reacting to the latest need. What can we do? In order to move away from mile wide, inch deep relationships, we have to plan ahead. Who do you want to get to know better? Who are you growing friendships with? Which people fill you to the brim with life and fun and joy? Schedule time with those women on your calendar before church-related activities fill it up. Make time in your schedule for friendship.

Five: take the initiative (yes, again). One of the risks we must take in order to gain friendship is taking the initiative to go first with invitations, hospitality, vulnerability, planning, and conversation. In other words, many of the actions you and I take all the time in social and church situations.

In the past, I've felt extremely frustrated that I consistently found myself in the initiator position in relationships, but at some point, I said to myself, *Do you want to have friends? Then keep putting yourself out there!*

It seems that primarily being the initiator (rather than on the receiving end of care and questions) is something that comes with being a pastor's wife. We can either embrace initiation as an opportunity for influence or we can nurse bitterness, and as we've already discussed, nursing bitterness does nothing to help us make friends or maintain connection with the friends we already have.

With closer friends, consider sharing with them how much joy and relief you feel when they initiate or take the lead in hosting or planning get-togethers or when they pursue you. And thank them for asking questions and ministering to you in intentional ways.

Pastor's wife, friendship is possible. And not only is it possible but it's also *necessary*. You may navigate social situations that others don't, but every believer has a need for life-giving community, and you are no exception.

Take the risk and initiate today.

TWENTY-THREE

Navigating Difficulties in Friendship

*O*ver coffee a few years ago, I tried (because it's difficult to put into words) explaining to one of my closest friends (who is not a pastor's wife) why I sometimes get so tangled up in knots about relating with other women within our church (which she attends). I don't remember exactly what I said, but I do remember what she said in return: "Christine, I experience many of those same things."

She referred to, at various times, feeling left out, uninvited, lonely, hurt, isolated, misunderstood, and unknown. And she gently cautioned me against believing I was the only one experiencing complexity and difficulty in friendship within our church.

Friendship, she said, is difficult for everyone.

She's right.

Every woman has obstacles to overcome or difficulties their circumstances present that they must navigate when it comes to friendship. The single woman may feel out of place in a sea of married women. The depressed and anxious woman may struggle with the energy and motivation friendship requires. The working woman may have limited time available to give toward cultivating relationships. The woman new to the community may feel like an outsider and desperately lonely.

While it's helpful to remember that we're not alone in navigating difficulties in friendship, the unique difficulties we pastors' wives face typically involve some level of risk. In order to have deep friendships, we must be willing to take those risks.

I hear from so many pastors' wives who are desperate for friendship that involves mutual care, conversation, enjoyment, and initiation. Too often, however, they've been told they can't have good friends in the church, they've carefully crafted excuses that have only served to keep them isolated, and they've been hurt—painfully, devastatingly hurt—in ways they usually must keep silent about. Perhaps some have even heard from others that they aren't allowed to have friends at all. They also want to be wise about what they share and with whom they share it, but often they take it to the far extreme of keeping themselves completely unknown. The messages we've received about what it means to be a pastor's wife and the experiences we've had have made us fearful of taking the necessary risks friendship requires.

What if the friend ends up leaving the church? What if she shares a confidence with someone else? What if she doesn't reciprocate vulnerability because she fears the pastor will find out what she said? What if the friend won't understand what ministry demands of our time? What if she disagrees with our husband's decisions and then distances herself? What if the friend is also a staff member's wife and, therefore, our husband is her husband's boss? What if something weighty happens in our marriage—can we tell her? What if she's just sidling up to us in order to get information or to pass along her preferences to the pastor?

But taking risks is worth it, *even if* some of our fears come true. As I wrote in the last chapter, we need friends to help us grow, to carry our burdens as we carry theirs, and to help us be whole, healthy people who are not stuck in ministry mode all the time.

In considering risk, we must remember that no relationship we ever have will be ideal and without risk.[1] As a pastor's wife who struggled with long years of loneliness and isolation and finally decided it wasn't working for me, I can tell you that the benefits of finding and enjoying friends far outweigh the risks (and realities) of getting hurt or stumbling our way through.

Let's look at some of the specific risks we encounter in ministry and how we can mitigate them.

"But I Can't Share Everything"

The biggest risk of all, of course, is vulnerability. We know vulnerability is a necessary ingredient for friendship, but we are also downright scared to let down our carefully crafted walls and invite people in.

You might say, "But I can't share everything with my friends." No, you can't, but that shouldn't stop you from sharing as much as you can. Discuss with your husband what subjects he's comfortable or not comfortable with you sharing, and then, based upon that conversation, hone the skill of knowing how and what to share that allows growth in a friendship.

It may help for us to define our terms.

Vulnerability is not spewing every thought and emotion out on every woman, hoping it lands on someone who will resonate and be our friend. Vulnerability is intentionally sharing what is presently on our minds and hearts with the people in our life who have the *ability* and *authority* to respond. Over the years, I've sometimes found myself, in the spirit of empathy, sharing snippets of what's weighing on me with people I have little to no relationship with and, when they then haven't sought to care for me, I've felt hurt. In retrospect, however, I realize I've shared information about myself with someone who, because we have no ongoing relationship, likely felt they had inadequate avenues for responding to me. They had neither the ability nor the authority to come to my aid.

I've learned that when I need counsel or comfort, I must instead share with those closest to me—those who have access to me, know me well, and can actually help or challenge me. But telling my closest people often feels the most vulnerable of all.

Many pastors' wives resist vulnerability in general because they know some parts of their experiences within church life cannot be voiced. However, if being vulnerable means sharing on an emotional and spiritual level with trustworthy, godly women, there remain many areas in our life we can talk about, things like confessing sin, sharing deep joys, asking for help or prayer regarding heart-level issues we're facing (or physical needs that require assistance from others), and sharing deep encouragement with one another of how we see God at work in one another's lives.

I think we can even talk about our behind-the-scenes church life with our close friends from church. Of course, there are often *details* we can't share, but we can share generally about ourselves—such as what we're feeling or what we're wrestling through spiritually—without crossing any lines.

For example, if there is a difficult situation going on at church, I can say to my closest friends, "Kyle has been dealing with a difficult situation and it's spilling over onto me (or our marriage). I'm feeling nervous and fearful. Can you pray for me that I will trust God to care for his church through this and lead Kyle in what he should do?" I can share my feelings, worries, hopes, or requests for prayer without going into details about other people involved in the situation. Good, godly friends will respect our boundaries and hold our confidences while also caring, praying, and coming alongside us.

But what if the difficult situation or trouble is in our own marriage? Can we share authentically with friends who attend our church and call our husband their pastor? Aside from our relationship with the Lord, a healthy marriage is far and away the most important relationship in our life.

In other words, it's always good to consider how we can grow as a wife, receive wise counsel from seasoned wives, and pursue deeper intimacy with our husband. There are multiple avenues we can take: receiving counseling, attending marriage conferences, reading and discussing books together as spouses, and, yes, talking with friends. With trustworthy, proven women with whom we have long-term friendship, not only *can* we share about difficulties in our marriage but we also *need* the insights and accountability of others. Take two goals with you into any conversation involving your marriage: to honor and respect your husband and to focus on how you can grow and change. With these two goals in mind, we will never turn a conversation into a complaint session.

I know what I'm saying comes with situational caveats and may even cause you fear and apprehension. You don't have to approach vulnerability just as I do, but I want you to consider if you're overly protective of yourself and your husband. Where do you need to take more risks relationally that may release you from the confines of your loneliness and isolation?

Instead of sharing, we're more prone to hiding behind the pastor's wife shield when what we're really doing is hiding our uncertainties and insecurities from the sight of others. We're more intent on impressing people than connecting with people. *Impressing* is about image, perfection, performing, and evaluating. *Connecting* is about relationship and vulnerability.

There *is* inherent risk in friendship. The truth is that we will get hurt. And we will hurt others. But the reward of friendship *only comes through the risk*, because biblical friendship—the "one anothers" of Scripture—is grounded in vulnerability. Galatians 6:2 says, "Bear one another's burdens and so fulfill the law of Christ." How can we help carry a load unless we know the load is there? How can someone help us carry a load unless they know what we're trying to carry?

"But No One Tries to Know Me for Me"

We often fall into church mode in relationships because of the way others relate with us. We might not want to talk about church all the time, but they sure do. There is an expectation that we're an answer person—an encyclopedia of church knowledge, a systematic theology textbook during women's Bible study, a walking church directory, and the keeper of the church calendar. We're also seen as the wise counselor, the shoulder to cry on, the extroverted greeter, the conversation carrier, and the direct path to the pastor's ear. We listen, answer questions as best we can about church-related things, point people in the right direction with their concerns, welcome new visitors, and ask polite questions to keep the conversation moving.

Of course, we love serving people and being available to them, but every so often the thought creeps in, *What about me? No one asks me anything about myself. No one seems to want to get to know me.* And then the pity party commences.

Instead of attending that pity party, try a different tack. Here are a few that have helped me.

One: give space in conversation for returned questions. Or just start sharing. I feel great pressure to carry the conversation with other women from church, and I have a treasure trove of questions stockpiled from which to draw. I tend to fire them one after another without taking a pause, and then I wonder why people don't ask me more questions. Well, I don't allow space for them!

I admit, sometimes this is intentional. I can hide behind rapid-fire questions and keep the attention on the other person. I can also circumvent the pain of sitting in silence and not being asked anything. Either way, in the end I'm still not known.

I've learned, instead, to allow space for uncomfortable silence. If the person sitting across from me is socially astute, that silence is often a signal for them that they should fill it, and I find they often do so by asking me a question. When they do ask about me, I may feel slight discomfort with the attention on me, but the discomfort is more about my fear of vulnerability than anything else.

My husband often reminds me that people may not ask questions because they don't know what to ask. They may be intimidated, interacting with me as a role or spiritual authority rather than as a person. They genuinely may not realize that the pastor's wife has feelings, needs, or struggles. Think of someone you consider a spiritual mentor. Can you imagine that they have uncertainties, struggles, needs, or negative emotions? Perhaps the women in your church struggle in similar ways to see you as a person. So give them reasons to see you as a person—just start sharing. Don't wait to be asked a question.

I often use what they're sharing with me as a jumping-off point. I certainly don't immediately turn the conversation onto myself, but after careful listening and purposeful questions, I can typically empathize with them in some way by sharing something from my own life. And by all means, if someone asks me a question, I encourage more by answering as deeply and in as much detail as I can.

Two: talk about something other than church. If all you talk about is church, you'll only feed the idea that you are a role instead of a person. So first consider: Do you talk about things other than the church? You should! Just as in marriage, you can't build a relationship around the church. Christ? Yes! But church politics, conflict, decisions, and activities? In the eyes of other women, these topics put you squarely in the pastor's wife role, not the friend role. Take the church out of the middle of your friendships. Talk about books you're reading, what God is teaching you, your kids, your work, your passions, current events, what you're studying in the Word, sports, or whatever else you enjoy. Yes, church is a big part of your life, but it shouldn't be the *only* part of your life that a friendship has to be built around.

Three: know that only One can truly understand. We easily convince ourselves there's no point in risking vulnerability, because we can't tell everything, and even if we did, no one could fully understand how we experience being a pastor's wife. There've been many times I haven't shared with proven, trustworthy friends because I know they can't walk in my shoes and can't carry some of the load I'm carrying.

In reality, no one can actually walk in my shoes. And although you and I are both pastors' wives and have much in common, I don't know what it's like to be you, just as you don't know what it's like to be me. If we could be fully known, understood, and helped by others, we wouldn't depend upon the Lord. He is the only One who can truly know any one person, pastor's wife or not.

Remembering this truth takes the pressure off and is a steady balm in the face of risk.

"But I Already Feel Spread So Thin Relationally"

Despite how desperately I wanted our little church to grow at the time and how much I feared it wouldn't, I sometimes look back at those beginning days of our church plant with longing. We had no idea what we were doing, but we could invite our entire church over for dinner, and we were a happy little band of brothers and sisters.

Then the church began to grow. As we passed certain milestones, I began feeling pulled in many different relational directions. We could no longer have everyone over for dinner at one time, or even everyone a handful at a time. People were coming to us faster than we could know them all, but still we *tried* to know them all, even as we tried to maintain relationships with those we'd known and loved since the church's inception. As a result, I lived in perpetual motion. At the same time, I couldn't figure out how to navigate all of the relationships, I constantly felt guilty that I couldn't be all things to all people, and my new normal became various levels of bone-tired.

The truth is I didn't want to admit to myself that I couldn't do it all. I didn't want to disappoint people, so I searched for some magic formula that would enable me to do all the things and have all the relationships. More than anything, I didn't want to have to say no. As a result, I became spread so thin relationally that I lost track of God's voice beneath the persistent human voices, and I felt devoid of purpose and joy.

I think many folks in ministry feel this way at one time or another, especially if they're leading or serving in a growing church. In a church plant, there is a low-grade pressure to be and do things how you've done things from the beginning, even when the church has evolved entirely.

When I looked at my life during those years, all I saw around me were good things. A happy family and marriage. A growing church full of absolutely wonderful people. Opportunities to serve the larger church through writing and speaking. Personal relationships with women I adore to this day. In other words, all I saw was *abundance*. So why was I struggling?

One day my husband used the phrase "choking on the abundance," and it stunned me with its accuracy. We'd been given an abundance of relationships, and we needed to consider how to navigate them all in a way that honored others but also didn't move us away from what God had originally called us to do.

Perhaps you too feel spread thin relationally, whether you're in a church plant, a small rural church, or an urban megachurch. Maybe you feel like you're juggling many roles and responsibilities. Know that God intends you to steward that abundance he's given, not choke on it. *Stewarding* means making purposeful and intentional choices—saying yes and also saying no.

I needed to learn to discern God's leading again so that I could separate "best" from "better" and "good," relationally and otherwise. I had to go through the excruciating pain of learning to say no when I'd just been saying yes, yes, and yes. Here are a few things I've learned along the way about stewarding a relational abundance.

One: praise God for abundance. If your ministry or your life has vitality, praise God. If you have relationships and friendships, praise God. If you have more coming at you than you know what to do with, praise God. Thank God for the influence and opportunities he's given you. Don't allow your heart to become embittered because of the pulling and pressure that come with the abundance. Don't allow yourself to swell with pride, thinking you've done something to earn this abundance. God and God alone has given you what you have.

Two: check your heart. Are you spreading yourself too thin relationally because of self-idolatry? This has been the case for me far too often. When I set myself up as a god to myself or others, I believe things about myself that are an affront to God and act in ways that are detrimental and harmful. I will actually try to be all things to all people. I will try to fix everyone's issues. I will also seek glory for myself in the form of respect, admiration, and appreciation. When I recognize my position before God, I'm humbled and able to embrace my limits. I'm encouraged to trust God for my own needs as well as the needs of others. I'm also reminded that my life is not my own but is to be poured out for God by serving others.

Three: make connections. Be a connector. Use your opportunities and influence to connect people with each other, with small groups, and with ministry opportunities. Not only does intentionally looking for ways to connect others keep us from becoming the hub of the relationship wheel but it also sets us up to experience the unique joy of having connected women to one another.

Four: clarify your people priorities. Ask God to give you laser focus on those people in your life he wants you to cultivate relationships with. After your spouse and kids, who are the people he most wants you to invest your life in? Who do you need to dive deep with? I've heard it said, "Do for one what you wish you could do for everyone."

Give your friends your best time. Say yes to your friends as much as possible. Give margin and space in your life for friendship. Even if you know it's a sacrifice, get up earlier or stay up later. Go out even when you don't feel like it. Make space for your husband to pursue friendships as well.

As we put away our excuses and take risks of vulnerability, we find that friendship is not only possible but also ripe for the taking. We too can enjoy friendship within our church and community.

PART 6

You
and
Your
Church

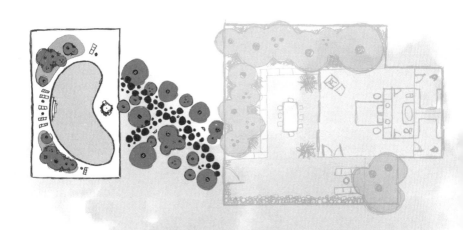

TWENTY-FOUR

Locating Your Church

When Kyle and I together developed the visual plan, the most helpful part of my life to "locate" on the map was our church.

Throughout the decades I've been a pastor's wife, my "closeness" to the church has varied wildly. When we were newly married and didn't yet have children, I enjoyed being intimately involved in everything my husband did. After we had children, although my heart was very much still in ministry, logistically I couldn't be as involved. When we planted our church, I *needed* to be involved as much as possible in order to help get the church up and running. And as our church became established and our leadership team expanded, I could once again choose what I'd do according to God's leading, my life season, and my own interests.

Having served in all these ways, I'll tell you that the early church planting days were both the easiest and hardest for me in all our years of ministry. They were the hardest because, as any church planting wife will tell you, the work was endless, exhausting, and uncertain. But they were also the easiest because I didn't have to wrestle with my relationship to the church—my life and the church felt one and the same. With such little separation, I didn't have much choice, and that lack of choice blurred the lines so drastically and became so normal that years later I'm *still* learning how to have a healthy relationship to our church.

The visual map has helped tremendously, because it reminds me that there is distance between the church and me, and that this distance is right and good. I am not the church and the church is not me; my identity, in other words, is not defined by the church and my role within it. My emotions don't have to rise and fall according to what is happening within the church body. I don't need to know everything that's happening within the church, nor am I to be a part of solving every issue or meeting every need. The church is not my job.

But the church is certainly a gift to me, and I have a place in it.

I am one member of the body that makes up my specific church. I join with the other members to corporately worship God, exhibit love to the world, experience sanctification, and use my gifts to edify my fellow saints.

My husband shepherds this group of saints—it is his job, his calling, and his life's work. As I look at the architect's plan, I envision him stepping outside the gate and walking the winding garden path every day to go do this work for the glory of the One who called him to do it.

How do I both support my husband, knowing what is going on behind the scenes of the church, and also engage the church as a Christian? How do I love and care for God's people while also maintaining a healthy distance from what is not mine to carry?

Sometimes I've struggled with feeling that any distance is wrong—as if it's disengagement or not loving my brothers and sisters as I'm called to love them. The overlapping circles on the Venn diagram of marriage/ family life/friendships/work/church can create confusion, so much so that I tend to feel guilty for trying to make any distinctions at all.

But if we are to thrive, distinctions are needed.

Here is the distinction we can make regarding church, specifically on Sunday mornings: imagine stepping outside the gate, following the path through the garden—past the benches where you sit with friends—and stopping at the V at the path's end. You can turn left or turn right—both lead to the public space where people gather, which represents the church. It matters which direction you take. If you take the path on the left, you follow in your husband's steps to church as work, and you prepare to encounter people. However, if you take the path on the right, you go to church as church—a gathering of the saints to worship the Lord—and you prepare to encounter *God*. Will going to the house of the Lord mean you also encounter people? Of course, but it's a slight mental distinction that makes all the difference in how we engage church.

We must choose the path on the right, going to church not out of duty or as an extension of our husband's work but rather as a child of God preparing to worship.

Practically, what this means is that as I drive to church and walk in, I prepare my heart to encounter God. My husband and I have taken up the habit of briefly meeting at the car when I arrive with our boys, reading a Psalm of Ascent aloud as a family, and walking in together before he separates from us to continue preparing for the service and engaging people.

We do this in imitation of the Old Testament Jews who, as they walked to the temple, sang the Psalms of Ascent aloud, preparing their hearts to encounter God. My favorite is Psalm 121:

> I lift up my eyes to the hills.
>> From where does my help come?
> My help comes from the LORD,
>> who made heaven and earth.
> He will not let your foot be moved;
>> he who keeps you will not slumber.
> Behold, he who keeps Israel
>> will neither slumber nor sleep.
> The LORD is your keeper;
>> the LORD is your shade on your right hand.
> The sun shall not strike you by day,
>> nor the moon by night.
> The LORD will keep you from all evil;
>> he will keep your life.

The Lord will keep
>> your going out and your coming in
>> from this time forth and forevermore.

These words remind me that, as I enter the house of the Lord, my mind is to be set on him, anticipating what work he'd like to do in my heart that day. They remind me that I do not go in alone. He will lead and help me to love others well. He will move among us as a church.

He alone is God, worthy of worship.

TWENTY-FIVE

Sunday Mornings (and Beyond)

or the pastor and his wife, Sunday is the most challenging (and rewarding) day of the week. Sundays stand to remind us: there's a weight to bearing responsibility and influence within the people of God. And that weight often feels more like going into battle than anything else.

When the Word of God is preached and the Spirit is moving in the hearts of people, it *is* a battle: "For our struggle is not against flesh and blood, but against the rulers, against the authorities, against the powers of this dark world and against the spiritual forces of evil in the heavenly realms" (Eph. 6:12 NIV).

Perhaps that's why my kids always get sick at 2:00 a.m. on Sunday mornings. Or why Kyle never seems to sleep well the night before he preaches. Or why my mind inexplicably is stirred toward irritation the moment I awaken on Sundays. The enemy would like nothing more than to paralyze, numb, or distract us from focused, Spirit-empowered love and service to the flock of God.

Being involved in spiritual work means spiritual warfare; therefore the pastor's wife must be prepared for battle on Sunday mornings.

Prepare before Sunday

For the pastor, as you well know, Sunday begins on Saturday.

I got used to staying in on Saturday nights a long time ago, although when we were newlyweds, as I mentioned before, I resented that our weekend plans were limited by Kyle's work schedule. Now I know that by late Saturday afternoon, Kyle's mind and heart have clicked over into preparation mode for Sunday. After dinner and family time, he'll settle into his favorite spot for the remainder of the night, memorizing the sermon he's been preparing all week.

On Sunday morning, he gets up long before me, sits in that same spot, and makes last-minute adjustments to the sermon, ensuring he knows it by heart. Later that morning, among other things, he'll spread the feast for the saints before the eyes of God. What a blessing it is to be married to someone who faithfully shepherds the flock, not from compulsion but eagerly and with great love (1 Pet. 5:1–5).

How can we prepare in similar fashion? If we serve on Sundays in a particular way, we can plan fastidiously, but certainly the greatest preparation—and a boon to our husband as well—is through prayer.

With Sunday coming, pray for your husband. Pray he'd know the Father's love and, therefore, know he has no one to impress and nothing to prove. Pray for the Spirit to encourage and empower him to serve by the strength God provides. Pray he'll walk in integrity and humility.

Pray for the church that will gather. Pray for the Spirit to humble the prideful and encourage the disheartened. Pray for an increase in love and unity, a sensitivity to the Spirit, and salvation for those who don't yet know Christ.

Pray for individuals God brings to your mind and regarding needs you are aware of, repeating Paul's own petition for those he loved, asking God that they may be filled with the knowledge of his will in all spiritual wisdom and understanding, so as to walk in a manner worthy of the Lord, fully pleasing to him: bearing fruit in every good work and increasing in the knowledge of God; being strengthened with all power, according to his glorious might, for all endurance and patience with joy. (Col. 1:9–11)

If you're praying, you're preparing, alive to God's heart toward his people.

Prepare on Sunday Morning

The most challenging time on Sundays for me is the period before church starts. I feel like a boxer in my corner of the ring, warming up for a fight. As I get my kids moving, blow-dry my hair, put on makeup, and choose what to wear, I'm also preparing mentally by fighting off the fiery darts of the enemy.

What am I fighting? Myself, of course. I'm fighting thoughts that are eager to render me spiritually useless for the day ahead: *What do I have to offer anyone today? Another Sunday of going to church with the kids by myself. I'm just going to turn my heart off, put my head down, and get through this day.*

Every Sunday, I must beat these thoughts into submission. Every Sunday, I must square off against small deceptions, digging through to the truth of who God is and fighting for an others-focused perspective.

My internal boxing match doesn't happen because I don't love God, the church, or the people in my life. Not at all. It's that my flesh loves itself most of all. The fight is a spiritual one. If I surrender to doubt, resentment, insecurities, and apathy, I stay inside my head the rest of the day, focused on myself, paralyzed, and unaware of others. When I surrender in defeat to my flesh, I'm rendered useless in ministry.

At least now I recognize the war I am in. In the early days of ministry, I'd go to church alone and walk around in a bubble of self-doubt and self-consciousness. *Who will talk to me? What do they think of me? Am I good enough? Am I doing the right things?* I cringe to think of the opportunities I missed to hear from God and encourage others.

YOU AND YOUR CHURCH

Now, I fight hard. I recognize that the battle is not evidence of my incompetency and inability but rather evidence of a spiritual reality every believer faces.

Now, I fight back with truth, working it out while I also work out the tangles in my hair:

No, I have nothing to offer anyone, but the Spirit works powerfully through me in my weakness (2 Cor. 12:9).

Yes, I'm tired and needy, but God will provide the strength I need (Col. 1:28–29).

No, I'm not sufficient for the task ahead, but if I cling to God, he will produce fruit in and through me (2 Cor. 3:4–6).

Yes, it's a possibility and a risk that I'll be overlooked, but there are others I'll interact with today who feel the same. Might I be God's answer for them through my attentive listening or my words? I will seek to serve and not be served. I will seek opportunities to be a blessing rather than seeking a blessing (Phil. 2:3–4).

By the time I have brushed my teeth, put on some earrings, and slipped on my shoes, the skirmish is done. There will be others, certainly. But I know I am ready for church—not because of the primping I've done in front of the mirror but because the eyes of my heart have turned upward to God and outward in anticipation of those I will encounter.

Prepare for People

I've spoken with many pastors' wives who struggle to know what to do with themselves on Sunday mornings. I've been there myself: wandering around and talking to people while also feeling aimless and wondering if I should be doing something else. Our husband's place within the church is clear, but ours is often nebulous and shifts from season to season.

Here's my advice regarding Sunday mornings: consider if you're more of a "task person" or a "people person." A task person thrives on completing an assignment, whereas a people person thrives on relating with people. Neither is right or wrong, nor is one better than the other, but knowing how God made you will help you tackle Sunday mornings.

A people person will have no problem moving from conversation to conversation, greeting and interacting with people. The pastor's wife who is a task person, however, is usually one who struggles to know what to do with herself on Sunday mornings.

I myself am a task person. I like to have a specific list of things I can accomplish that benefit the greater good: passing out bulletins, greeting visitors at the door, teaching a lesson, praying for people at the end of the service, or volunteering in the children's ministry. Having a task or two on Sunday mornings helps me focus my worship of God and love for people into specific, concrete things. I inevitably feel lost when I don't have an assignment for the day, and one day I realized that whether or not I had official areas of service on Sundays, *I needed to assign myself tasks.*

And, as all tasks should be, those I assign myself are related to people. Before I get to church, I ask God to direct me to at least two people with whom I can have deep conversation, that I may love, bless, pray for, or serve them in some way. My task, then, is to be aware of people around me—Who is a new guest? Who is attending alone? Who have I not seen in a while?—and initiate conversations with them as the Lord leads me. It may be semantics, but simply thinking of this as the Lord's assignment helps me be intentional and purposeful on Sundays.

Another way I prepare to encounter others is to be conscious about people the Lord has brought to mind throughout the week or as I'm getting ready for church on Sundays. I take this as the Lord's direction for who I should seek out at church. These "assignments" I often leave for after the church service, and as the service closes I pray for these encounters to be encouraging and fruitful.

Contributing to a Healthy Church Culture

Many years ago, when Kyle led a large church-based college ministry, we partnered with a missions sending agency to help our students connect with missions opportunities throughout the world. The agency took responsibility for training and sending students from many different churches based around college campuses in the United States, and at the beginning of each summer, all the students heading out on mission would gather together for an incredible and notoriously intense training time.

One fall, the leader of the missions agency, John, came to our church to meet with and recruit students for the following summer. He told us how, having spent so many years of interacting with students during their training weeks, as soon as he met a new student, he could guess where they went to college and what church they'd been sent from.

Curious, Kyle asked, "How?"

John said, "They pick up on and imitate the mannerisms, phrases, and passions of their college ministry leader. Because I know you well, Kyle, I see parts of you in them."

He then proceeded to tell us specific things he'd seen in our students, even down to word choices Kyle repeatedly used that he had unwittingly passed on.

That was the first time I considered the significant influence Kyle and I have in whatever ministry we're leading. I assumed that our intentional teaching, whether in leaders' meetings or Sunday school, could potentially influence the students. But what I hadn't considered were the *intangible* things they were picking up on: passions, loves, demeanor, character, and even humor.

When John relayed this story to us, it was incredibly sobering to me.

There is a reason leaders are called to be above reproach (Titus 1:7). We have positional influence and, in everything we do, we're in some sense imprinting our spiritual DNA into the personality and culture of the church.

I discovered this to be especially true when we planted our church. A few years into the life of our church, I realized that the church reflected the personality and passions of Kyle and me. Our passion for discipleship and hospitality had become central in our congregants' lives as well, but our weaknesses also seemed to be reflected in the church. We realized the importance of having a strong team of lay leaders with various skills, gifts, and perspectives around us.

The same is true for you. No matter what context you serve in, you have positional influence in your church. You can try to run from this influence because you don't like the fishbowl effect, or you can embrace and use it to bring glory to God. How you engage with the life of the church is modeling for others how they should do so as well. If you love people, your church will love people. If you are vulnerable and quick to confess your sin, your church will see the value of humility. This influence shouldn't "puff up" or make us feel entitled. It should humble and sober us and cause us to take our engagement with the church seriously.

To conclude, let's look at two ways we can use our influence to contribute to a healthy church culture.

Model Grace

Grace is universal to all who come by faith to God through Jesus Christ. If our churches exhibit this grace, it will be because we have decided, like Paul, to "know nothing among [our people] except Jesus Christ and him crucified" (1 Cor. 2:2). If we're laser-focused on Jesus Christ and him crucified, how will this be demonstrated in our relationships with people in the church?

One: we'll be mindful of and patient with the weaker brother or sister. Paul tells the Corinthian church that those who are "stronger," or more knowledgeable about and sure of the grace given them through Christ, should bear with those who are "weaker" and perhaps new to the faith or observing strict guidelines they think others should adhere to related to secondary issues. Secondary issues are those in which Christians have freedom to act according to their conscience, such as food, drink, dress, and education. Paul says,

> Food will not commend us to God. We are no worse off if we do not eat, and no better off if we do. But take care that this right of yours does not somehow become a stumbling block to the weak. For if anyone sees you who have knowledge eating in an idol's temple, will he not

be encouraged, if his conscience is weak, to eat food offered to idols? And so, by your knowledge this weak person is destroyed, the brother for whom Christ died. Thus, sinning against your brothers and wounding their conscience when it is weak, you sin against Christ. (8:8–12)

Do we have freedom to drink alcohol, for example? The Bible prohibits drunkenness and being addicted to much wine but doesn't explicitly condemn its use in moderation. Our freedom, however, must always be considered in light of our brothers and sisters and what is best and most helpful for them. A leader models grace well by doing so.

In addition, perhaps a "weaker" brother or sister is one who has not yet developed spiritual maturity and is stumbling as they seek to understand and apply the Bible to their former patterns of living. Instead of judging and condemning, we model grace when we're patient and come alongside them as a loving, older sibling.

Two: we'll keep our convictions on secondary issues in the background and the gospel in the foreground. We all have personal convictions on secondary issues: political views; medical decisions; parenting choices regarding technology; social media use; what we think is beneficial or unbeneficial to watch, read, or listen to; and so on. Many of these are convictions we've developed in our relationship with the Lord or in response to personal struggles we've had in the past that we want to avoid in the present. In other words, they aren't wrong.

But they also aren't the gospel.

If we use our positional influence within the church to "preach" the primacy of secondary issues, and specifically *our* view as the *right* one, we easily create for others a false understanding of the gospel. Whether or not we intend it, people in our churches who look to us as the "stronger" sibling often equate our personal views with the commands of Scripture. We must, then, be especially careful to not only know what primary issues are (salvation, sin, repentance, mercy, grace, love) but also make sure the bulk of our conversations are concerned with those issues.

If someone asks my opinion on certain issues, I will give it, but I'll also note that it's a secondary issue and that many wise and godly people fall along different thought lines than I do. I also note how I reached the conviction I have and encourage them to seek the Lord's conviction personally on the matter.

One way we can ascertain whether or not an issue is primary or secondary is to consider if it's globally applicable in all generations and cultures. Some may say, for instance, that the Bible instructs all mothers to stay at home to raise their children rather than working outside the home. Does this instruction fit single moms whose husband has left or died?

We must be careful not to add burdens and yokes to others unnecessarily.

Consider the flip side: Is God's love available to all generations and cultures? Is salvation and forgiveness of sins available to all who come in repentance and faith, no matter who they are, what they've done, or what their life circumstances are? Yes.

The gospel is freedom for the people in our churches and communities, so let us keep it at the forefront of our conversations.

Three: we'll extend grace when others sin. Grace isn't a free pass that allows us to throw off all restraint. Grace—the unmerited favor of God poured out on us by our faith in Christ—is a compelling change agent that, when received, teaches us how to live. Tim Keller says, "The gospel devours the very motivation you have for sin. It completely saps your very need and reason to live any way you want. Anyone who insists the gospel encourages us to sin has simply not understood it yet, nor begun to feel its power."[1]

How is grace different from a free pass? A free pass says, "I see your sin, friend, and will not call it what it is but will simply ignore it." We often call this love when, really, it's a love only of self. A free pass is easier than the temporary, self-inflicted pain of bringing up a difficult subject with a friend.

God communicates, in his grace toward us, that he sees our sin. He names our sin specifically to us through the conviction of the Holy Spirit, because he has made a way for our specific sin to be dealt with at the cross of Christ. We don't have to cover or ignore it or try to deal with it on our own. We have an avenue to be free of our sin: confess and repent to be forgiven and cleansed. Not only that but he will help us change to reflect his holiness.

In other words, grace looks directly at sin and specifically names it because of love. God loves us enough to pull us out of the pit of sin, discipline us, prune us, and give us joy instead of bondage and despair. The love he has for us is what makes grace so powerful: the favor of the Almighty is given to us so richly that it compels us to present ourselves to him as instruments of righteousness (Rom. 6:13). Grace changes us.

So what does it mean to extend grace to others? It primarily means we see one another as new creations in Christ (2 Cor. 5:17), and we recognize the grace we received at salvation is continuing its work as a change agent in our life (Phil. 1:6). In other words, we're all in process. However, that's not another way of giving free passes. It's a call for us as individuals and as the church to engage the process God himself has given us: looking at sin rather than ignoring it (like God), calling it what it is with gentleness and truth (like God), reminding others of the path of confession and repentance available to them (like God), cheerleading alongside as our friends change (unlike God, because he actually leads the changing), and doing it all out of deep love for one another (like God).

Galatians 6:1–2 paints a picture of a Spirit-led grace-giver:

> Brethren, if a man is overtaken in any trespass, you who are spiritual restore such a one in a spirit of gentleness, considering yourself lest you also be tempted. Bear one another's burdens, and so fulfill the law of Christ. (NKJV)

This kind of grace-giver doesn't delight in calling out sin and isn't prideful about being a truth-teller. Rather, this is a person deeply committed to the spiritual vitality of others and deeply attuned to their own spiritual poverty without Christ. There is humility, a willingness to go the extra mile for others, and a committed devotion to the family of God. And, perhaps most importantly, a grace-giver is positioned to receive from friends the very same truth and grace they're committed to giving.

Love Always

A healthy church culture is also built upon love: the love between God and humanity and the love we share with one another as brothers and sisters. As the apostle Paul says, we may have prophetic gifts and great faith, but if we don't have love for others, we have nothing (1 Cor. 13:1–2).

As pastors' wives, if we do nothing else but focus on loving people, we've done well. The hardest part, though, of loving people isn't cheerfully greeting them at church but loving genuinely, from the heart.

What does genuine love look like? It involves thinking of others as more significant than ourselves and setting aside our preferences for the sake of blessing others. If we were to apply Paul's famous passage on love in 1 Corinthians 13 to our life as a pastor's wife, it might look something like this:

Love is patient and kind. When requests are made of the pastor's wife or someone needs a listening ear, she gives that person her undivided attention and genuine care. When she is overlooked or someone says an unkind word about her or her husband or children, she bears the provocation or pain calmly, without anger, retaliation, or figuratively shunning another.

Love does not envy or boast. The pastor's wife doesn't envy church members who seem to thrive in their leisure and lack of weighty responsibility or who bring in a more comfortable income. She doesn't envy her husband's honor in the spotlight. She doesn't draw attention to herself or to the "successes" of the church. The name on her tongue is not the church's name, her husband's name, or her own but rather the name of Jesus.

Love is not arrogant or rude. The pastor's wife doesn't embrace the perks of ministry—positional honor and influence—at the expense of servanthood. She honors all people equally, not showing partiality to those she likes or who like her. She doesn't use the demands of ministry as an excuse to ignore people or treat them callously. She expresses appreciation for the ways others serve her.

Love does not insist on its own way. Knowing she has great influence on the pastor, the pastor's wife doesn't insist church decisions go her way. In areas of service, knowing people will generally yield to her ideas, she is careful not to overrun or overrule others just because she can. She graciously submits to the elders of the church as Scripture commands. She uses her power to see and serve the vulnerable rather than seek her own elevation.

Love is not irritable or resentful. Sometimes the pastor's wife is hurt by others, intentionally or unintentionally. When she's hurt, instead of retreating and allowing resentment to build and fester, she's diligent to keep a soft heart before the Lord and to do whatever it takes to maintain a genuine affection for God's people.

Love does not rejoice at wrongdoing, but rejoices with the truth. The pastor's wife never engages in gossip, backbiting, slander, or dropping hints of confidential knowledge regarding others. She thinks the best of others and speaks of others positively, both to them and about them to others.

Love bears all things, believes all things, hopes all things, endures all things. Love never ends. The pastor's wife can engage in the difficult work of ministry because God's love for her never ends. She can serve even the hardest to love because she knows she's been welcomed into the very heart of God.

TWENTY-SIX

Dealing with Church Hurt

*I*n a previous chapter, I shared with you the importance of lamenting before the face of God—taking our griefs and cares to him and allowing him to match his truth to the flood of emotion we experience when we're hurt. This lament is inward facing, just between you and the Lord.

However, you and I both know well that there is an outward facing component to how we navigate church difficulties. We must continue to engage in relationships with those who may have said an unkind word to us, spoken ill of our husband, or are causing ongoing conflict within the church.

In the evangelical world, we increasingly use the term "church hurt" to describe pain inflicted upon people within the church by other church members or by church leaders—a pain that affects fellowship with God and causes a loss of community or friendship.

While many associate church hurt as being inflicted by a church's leaders, congregants may be surprised to learn that pastors and their wives also experience it. The difference is that when a pastor's wife experiences church hurt, unless she and her husband move to a different church, she must learn how to process the hurt while remaining in the environment that has caused her pain. She can't withdraw for an extended period of time in order to work through her grief and, in fact, must in many ways continue to be a comfort and resource for others in their pain. Sometimes her own husband—the pastor of the church—is the source of her hurt when he places the church as his first priority over her, for example, or when he's made a foolish decision, causing backlash to come his way and, by association, to her as well. Sometimes she is aware of conflict within the church but cannot address it directly herself, although it greatly affects her husband and therefore her very heart.

Church hurt is real for the pastor's wife and, by nature of the role, can be extremely difficult to handle.

So how do we navigate it well?

Navigating Church Conflict

Church conflict is inevitable. In fact, many of Paul's letters to the churches recorded in the New Testament are about church conflict: navigating internal squabbles, dealing with unrepentant sinners, forgiving and restoring repentant sinners to relationship, and addressing disagreements over theological issues and church practices.

Sound familiar?

We shouldn't be surprised by conflict but rather be prepared to address it directly with a tone and actions of love, compassion, and gentleness—as Paul exemplifies in his responses to various churches.

However, as pastors' wives, we're not typically in a position to directly address conflict. We can encourage our husband to respond similarly to Paul, but our own opportunity is primarily to *model* a biblical response to conflict.

That response falls under the umbrella of 1 Timothy 3:2: "An overseer must be above reproach." Being above reproach means acting in such a way that no one could assign blame or fault to us that causes them to discredit the name of Christ. In other words, we don't want—because of our own pride, defensiveness, or unbiblical acts—to cause others to walk away from the church or Christ himself.

How, then, can we offer a biblical response to conflict?

One: we model repentance and restoration. If God convicts you that you've hurt or offended someone, be quick to confess, ask for forgiveness, repent, and seek to restore the relationship.

For example, I once told an unflattering story about a congregant to our elders and their wives at a social dinner. I immediately knew I'd crossed a line and, as the lead pastor's wife, I not only needed to ask for forgiveness from those who heard the story but also acknowledge and model for them what is acceptable and unacceptable in our conversations with one another. So I did, even though it was painfully embarrassing that I'd told the story.

One of the primary ways we model restoration is by taking the lead to push through any awkwardness that's been caused by conflict or sin in relationships. Once, in misunderstanding a situation, I expressed my hurt to a woman in our church, but the way I did it hurt her in turn. After several conversations and expressions of love and forgiveness, I knew that because of my role within the church, after all was resolved I also needed to intentionally show expressions of restoration and friendship so all awkwardness could be removed from between us, and she could feel safe at church.

The same could be said for anyone we struggle to love because they are divisive or difficult: our natural bent will be to avoid them. Instead, we should intentionally go toward them, looking for ways to express honor and love. We don't ever want to be the reason for ongoing awkwardness.

Two: we are willing to calmly receive and respond to feedback. In other words, we resolve to resist defensiveness.

I tend to get the most defensive when it comes to others critiquing my husband to me. Instead of leaping to defend him, however, I've learned to briefly listen. Then before the conversation goes too far I encourage the speaker to go directly to him—specifically to set up a meeting with him to discuss their concerns—rather than asking for clarification or explanation beyond what they've given. Additionally, by my calm and receptive demeanor, I model what I remind them they'll find from my husband: a pastor who wants to know their concerns and will gladly receive them as a beloved member of the church. He'll listen and take their concerns into consideration. (Note: we should never handle conflict or potential misunderstandings through text or email.)

Three: we don't take ownership of extrabiblical expectations. This too is teaching and modeling regarding conflict, because it keeps the focus on the gospel and the black-and-white commands of Scripture rather than opening the door for division over secondary issues.

For example, a mom in our church asked me why I was not homeschooling my children and expressed that she thought my choice was wrong. After quickly asking the Lord in that moment for help to not get defensive and angry, I calmly explained to her not only why we were educating our children the way we'd chosen—namely, that we'd prayed fervently about it and the Lord had led us in a certain way according to what our unique children need—but also that, as Christians, we have freedom to choose. I told her that I admire and support all of the moms in our church as they pursue the Lord's will for their children, including her.

Four: as much as it depends on us, we don't exacerbate conflict. One big way a conflict can catch fire and consume more and more people? A wagging, slanderous tongue. Resolve to never speak critically of others in the church. Resolve to avoid gossip. If a conflict is unfolding, do not share the details with others. This is a critical choice we must make in order to protect the culture of the church, not only for others but also for ourselves. If gossip is an accepted practice within your church, it will eventually set its sights on you.

These guidelines follow biblical commands, but they are difficult to put into practice when we've been hurt, we're afraid the church is going to fall apart, or we fear our husband being slandered in the community because of one person fomenting dissent.

But forgiveness, loving all people, and repentance are the ways of Jesus and, though we may not always feel these practices are easy, his ways are certainly perfect. His ways, though they often feel counter-intuitive, are the way we obey him and the path to peace.

When They Leave the Church

One of the ways pastors' wives experience church hurt is when people choose to leave the church.

We've all had it happen: a church member to whom we've ministered, have loved dearly, and have considered family leaves the church. Sometimes they are faithfully forthcoming as to why, sometimes they leave a wake of hurt and tears behind them as they go, and sometimes they simply disappear, never to be seen or heard from again.

For pastors' wives, a church member leaving can be especially excruciating. The church is personal to us, as it should be, because serving the church is the unique and specific way God has called us to lay down our life in honor of him, and the practical implications of that mean we're laying down our life for people. We not only love the people we're serving and have high hopes for how God will use our church in our community but also long to experience the unity and community on a personal level as a part of that larger body. It's painful, then, when those we love and have labored with leave, even if they leave in the best possible way.

That's why we must carry with us a foundational understanding that there are few, if any, who will relate to our church as passionately or as personally as we do—the pastor and the pastor's wife. This isn't a value statement on the passion or heart of others, it is simply reflective of what comes with the ministry territory. It's good to care. It's good to have vision and passion, but this truth also gives us a warning: hold people and the church loosely. *Neither belongs to us; all belongs to God.*

I try to think about that when someone leaves, because it assuages the hurt of their having left. Perhaps God is truly shepherding them toward a different flock. Perhaps our church is truly not a good fit for what he wants to do in and through them. And even if I believe it's not a wise decision for them, perhaps God plans to use it for their eventual sanctification. I release them into God's hands, recognizing that they belong to him and trusting that he is working for their good. In my experience, it's also been helpful to voice these thoughts to the people leaving well, because it keeps the relationship open and unhindered and offers them a blessing as they go. All of this is a process of wading through emotions to get down to that foundational truth, but it helps to have it ever handy: people and the church don't belong to me.

But what if people leave for other reasons, such as disagreement over practice, frustration with decisions or direction, or conflict in relationships? What if I feel they've misunderstood or mischaracterized my husband or our church? What if they leave with slander on their tongue? What if they simply stopped coming and are unwilling to return texts or calls? What if I'm angry and hurt regarding their departure but am unable to voice my feelings because of my husband's role? What if people ask why so-and-so left and I can't tell them the reasons?

This is where the pain of people leaving is compounded, because sometimes it involves the sin of others or tempts us to sin by means of anger, slander, gossip, bitterness, or lack of forgiveness. Thankfully, the foundational truth above applies here as well. The people of your church are being shepherded by God, *but you too are being shepherded by God.* You too belong to God. You too are being cared for by God. Your church is being nourished and knit together with Christ as your head. Unless you are in a position and relationship to have gentle and truthful conversations (both as a speaker *and* as a listener) with the leavers, you must quietly trust the situation to the Lord.

This means your husband or your church may be mischaracterized in your community and you are to do nothing. This means your heart will hurt but you aren't to bring others who remain in the church to your "side" to validate your feelings. This means you are to prayerfully look for the truth or lesson in it all and be willing to acknowledge that you are not perfect, and neither is your husband or your church. This means you must actively work for likely a long period of time to root out bitterness and self-pity in your heart. This means you trust the

Lord sees all and judges perfectly, he convicts and deals with all perfectly (including you), and *in due time* his will shall be done. If you feel you've been sinned against or your husband has been sinned against, it's important that you not respond in a way that makes you the sinner.

You can only do this in light of Christ, who "when he was reviled, he did not revile in return; when he suffered, he did not threaten, but continued entrusting himself to him who judges justly" (1 Pet. 2:23).

I'm not saying this is easy but I am saying it's necessary, and that it's a process of faith, time, and allowing God's sanctification. When someone leaves, it is always an opportunity to return to the question that steadies my soul: *Am I running the race God has set before me?* In other words, am I being faithful with what he's given me to do? That's all I can do. I can't make everyone happy or cause everyone to love everything about my husband or our church, but I *can* be faithful to run the race ahead of me and invite others to love Christ, who is the true focus of all our work.

When You Feel Lost in Your Own Church

Aside from feeling lost relationally, there are times we may experience disorientation or feel uncertain about our place within the church. This feeling can act as a barrier for our enjoyment of and engagement with the people in our church.

And sometimes this disorientation can make the church a painful place to be.

I experienced this acutely in church planting. I was heavily involved in the process, from the preplanting to planting stages. I had my hands in everything, but then the church grew and, by God's grace, became an established church with a larger leadership team around my husband.

When I began stepping back my involvement, I also began experiencing a great sense of loss. I wasn't quite sure what to do anymore. Where did I fit in the church? What was my role in the church? I never thought I'd want to go back to the beginning years of church planting, but I found myself longing for those early days when I could partner with my husband in almost everything. I had led out in so many ways and, suddenly, it felt like those glory days were over.

A wise friend said to me, "Christine, it sounds like, by the church plant getting off the ground and doing well, it feels to you as if you've lost something and your husband has gained something."

And that's exactly how I felt. I loved the excitement and partnership Kyle and I'd experienced together, and now I wasn't as necessary to the life of the church. Although I'd gained freedom of choice in how I wanted to serve, in my mind my husband gained so much more—he'd gained a role at an established church and a wonderful team to work alongside him. But I'd lost my sense of place, and I needed to give myself room to grieve that loss and also learn to navigate a new season in our ministry life.

These changing seasons of ministry often affect women much more than men. Kyle's job has been fairly steady and consistent all along the way, while my role has changed drastically. When we first started in ministry, I was able to be a part of everything Kyle did. When we had kids, I had to adjust what I could and couldn't do. As our kids grew, I was able to get more involved and be a partner in what he was doing again. And now with teenagers, it's almost like having preschoolers again, as I've had to pull back once more to be available to them as they prepare to launch from our home.

Changes in seasons of ministry can produce grief, because we may have really loved a season we were in and, by God's providence, he's moving us into a new season with different opportunities.

But we may feel a little lost for a time as we figure it out. And that's okay.

If you're lamenting a change, don't think only about what you're losing but also about what you're gaining. Where is God directing you? What new opportunities do you have? For me, as I moved out of the church planting phase, my new season offered me freedom to choose, though that freedom was a bit overwhelming and frightening at first. However, throughout the years I'd had my hands in everything, I'd discovered gifts I didn't know I had, and I was able to look for ways I could use those gifts as I moved into a new phase of life.

TWENTY-SEVEN

Cultivating the Skill of
Responding to Criticism

*M*any years ago, when Kyle and I were involved in ministering to college students in Texas, we decided to plan a barn dance for a fun fall social event. We reserved an outdoor arena, hired square dance callers, collected hay bales for photo ops, dusted off our cowboy boots, and began advertising the event to the students through the church bulletin.

Within a few days, a church member who saw the ad called Kyle to express her deep concern. She demanded to know if we planned to serve alcohol at the event. Didn't we know, she asked, that dancing could easily lead to drinking alcohol, and drinking alcohol to you-know-what?

Clearly, she didn't understand our intentions, the character of our students, or the nature of the event. So Kyle and I had a good laugh and moved on.

Most criticism, however, doesn't elicit a laugh and isn't easily forgotten. Criticism can be harsh, discouraging, and off-base, and a person's negative words can even become a lens through which we see ourselves. Criticism can be shared directly, indirectly, or anonymously. It can also be grouped with the dreaded "everyone is saying" or "my friends agree with me," leaving us to untangle a web of thoughts and ideas in order to get to whatever the true root issues are—if there are any at all.

We tend to think of criticism in negative terms, but criticism is not always negative, nor is it to be avoided at all costs. In fact, I believe the church is far more secure and healthy for all involved when there are pathways for people to bring concerns, questions, and preferences to their leaders and for leaders to consider how they can grow, adjust decisions when appropriate, and affect the greater health of the body. These pathways also allow leaders to address problems or misunderstandings outright and to apologize when necessary. Having open pathways for constructive criticism involves trust on the part of layperson and leader, of course, and trust is built when we're willing to have hard conversations with one another without defensiveness or anger.

I've noticed that when a church is marked by gossip and backbiting, these actions have often been allowed to continue unchecked and have even been practiced by the leadership. But another important distinction is that these churches often do not have viable and clear pathways for church members to share concerns, frustrations, and feedback with their leaders. Congregants resort to talking about their concerns with others, and an ample opportunity is then opened for gossip, spreading of misinformation, and conversation that demeans or questions church leaders.

There is security and safety for a church when all involved practice healthy, constructive criticism.

The Public Side of Criticism

Having a clear pathway for handling criticism sounds ideal, doesn't it? However, critique is usually aimed up the food chain, so to speak, and requires leaders who know how to process difficult conversations. In reality, we're often completely shocked and sent reeling by criticism. We want to react by telling people off, explaining just how hard our husband is working (when he is the one criticized), defending ourselves (when we're the one criticized), running and hiding from darts and arrows, or throwing our hands up and walking away from ministry entirely.

When the apostle Paul wrote his letters to the churches, people he served were constantly questioning his credentials, his calling, and even his preaching ability. I think this is important to note because it speaks to us, as leaders, that we shouldn't be surprised when these very things happen in our churches. Working with people means navigating criticism.

Because criticism is inevitable from a leadership standpoint, healthy ways of expressing it must be both taught and modeled. Although we may have opportunity to counsel another woman, for example, to share a concern with the elders (our husband included) and give her language for how to do so, our husband does far more of the teaching and also experiences far more of the *receiving* of criticism than we do.

In terms of teaching, our church leads prospective members through a two-day membership class, which includes steps on how we expect leaders and members to handle differences of opinion or conflict. Difficult conversations are to be handled face-to-face, not by text or email. The conversations are to be carefully thought out in advance and approached humbly, with a heart for unity and, if necessary, reconciliation.

Just because our husband, as the face of the ministry, receives the lion's share of criticism, it certainly does not mean we're unaffected by it. At times, I take criticism of Kyle harder than he does. And of course, I am not immune to criticism myself.

This is where modeling comes in. We must practice what we preach and receive each critique in a biblical way, not only because it's honoring to God and loving toward the church member but also because it models for them how to be in healthy community with others.

Let's dissect two examples of criticism we typically encounter and consider how we might respond in those moments.

One: criticism of our husband spoken directly to us. Perhaps a decision he made is second-guessed or a question implies frustration. Perhaps a "suggestion" is given that we're expected to pass along to the pastor. Or perhaps a comment is dropped into conversation that is critical of the church in general (and, in our minds, the church and its pastor are often interchangeable). How do we respond?

In the past, I considered it my responsibility to explain and defend, with a smile on my face and as happy a tone as I could muster. When I left those conversations, I felt icky and second-guessed everything I'd said, feeling almost as if I'd engaged in an immature tug-of-war. I found too that it confused the lines of communication. I'd tell my husband the details of the conversation, but he would not be free to address whatever issue was presented, because the person hadn't approached him directly.

I've since learned that I hold zero responsibility to defend and explain. My response to anything related to the church or my husband is now some form of, "I'm sorry you're feeling this way. I think it would be helpful to you and to Kyle if you went to talk to him about this. I know he'd want to know about this and, knowing him, I can tell you that he'll be receptive to what you have to say."

Two: criticism that centers around relational disappointment. This type of criticism stems from a belief that we can be available to and friends with everyone equally or in the quantity of time each person would prefer. Sometimes this type of criticism can be veiled: "I don't feel like I know you," or "I've been at the church for several years, and this is the first time we've been out for coffee."

One way I preventively respond to this type of criticism is to severely limit how much I tell people about what I'm doing or who I'm meeting with. As I wrote in a previous chapter, I rarely post pictures of myself with women from our church on social media unless it's a picture from a church event. I don't think of this choice as being private or secretive but rather an act of love for the women around me. If I can prevent someone in my church from feeling left out or uninvited, I want to do that.

The second response is to consider how I can positively honor the person expressing relational disappointment. After all, their heart, as my husband often reminds me, is in a good place. If they say, "I don't feel like I know you," I can say, "What would you like to know? I'll tell you!" If they say, "I've been at the church for several years, and this is the first time we've been out for coffee," I can say, "Well, I'm so glad we're here!" If they ask to get together, I can try to make it work, even if I have to offer something that seems pretentiously far off on the calendar. I don't have to kowtow to every relational demand and expectation, but I can certainly honor and love as the Lord gives me opportunity.

The Private Side of Personal Criticism

All that I've written so far is about the public side of criticism, or how we respond in the moment. The most difficult consequence of criticism, however, is what happens afterward: the personal experience of harsh or frustrating words as they sit in our mind and heart for hours, days, weeks, and sometimes for far longer.

How must we navigate the "afterward" of criticism?

We must process what was said with the Lord.

First, we tell God how the criticism stings, because even constructive criticism stings. Second, we ask him to help us lay down our defenses and objectively consider the critique, mining it for truth. We open ourselves in prayer to the conviction of God. Does he have something he wants to teach us through the criticism, however imperfectly it was verbalized?

Mining criticism for truth means we must consider several questions.

One: Who is it from? Is this a close friend or an acquaintance? The closer the person is relationally, the more intently and humbly I should consider what's being said. They know both my patterns and my heart with much greater clarity than an acquaintance does.

For example, when I felt unsettled about what I'd shared at our staff and elder social gathering, I broached the topic with one of the other elders' wives the next time I saw her. She gently and lovingly said, "Yes, you were wrong. That type of sharing is not befitting of us as leaders and doesn't have a place among us." Ouch. Her directness hurt my pride, even though I'd brought up my unsettledness to her. But because I know her relational commitment to me, I also knew the truth of her words. I asked for forgiveness, which she gladly gave, and although it was a short conversation and a small act, I felt secure knowing that my sister would urge me toward holiness.

Two: How well do they know the situation? Do they have the partial story or the whole story? Are they speaking from firsthand experience or repeating secondhand information? Are they creating an outsized scenario ("everyone is saying") or directly addressing how a concrete situation affected them? These questions help me, because if they're close to the situation and are addressing it directly, they may have an accurate read and a perspective I've missed.

Many years ago, a young woman I'd previously discipled asked to meet with me. I agreed, and when we met, she expressed that I'd hurt her. She'd felt "dropped" after our formal discipleship relationship was completed. Outwardly I apologized, but inwardly I was annoyed. Didn't she see all the demands on my time? Didn't she understand I was trying the best I could? And I had given her the best of myself. For a time.

Then, a few years later, another young woman I'd previously served closely with asked to meet with me. Can you see where this is going? She told me I'd hurt her, because after we completed our service together, she'd felt "dropped." She literally used the same word, and I saw for the first time that both of them were right. I'd exhibited a pattern of moving on in relationships that was hurtful to others.

Both of these women approached me well: they had firsthand experience and shared concrete examples, and I couldn't escape that they were accurately reflecting back to me a blind spot I didn't want to see.

That leads to the third and fourth questions to consider.

Three: Is there anything we can learn from what they said?

If we take a learner's perspective rather than a defensive perspective, God will make it clear to us if there is truth he wants us to glean from criticism. Perhaps it has nothing to do with the actual criticism, but we can learn lessons in how to relate to people or respond in the moment of criticism.

Four: What response, if any, is needed? Do we need to apologize? Change how we conduct ourselves? Forgive what was spoken in anger?

Sometimes, when I prayerfully consider a criticism, God helps me see that the person who criticized my husband or me perhaps speaks from a place of hurt and woundedness. Or they may have distinctly drawn preferences because they are a newer believer, much like the "weaker brother" described in 1 Corinthians 8. When I see this, God gives me compassion in place of anger and frustration, and I'm able to pray for the one who has hurt me (Matt. 5:44) and interact with them from a place of mercy and patience.

No matter the response needed, we must always seek confirmation from the Lord that we're being faithful to do what he's called us to do. If we're obeying him, whether criticism comes or not, then we can truly say all is well and press on in what he's asked us to do.

TWeNTY-eiGHT

Relating to Other Pastors' Wives at Your Church

*I*n our first ministry position, I learned a hard lesson about relating to the wives of the pastors on staff at our church. That hard lesson was that I was a greater sinner than I'd imagined myself to be prior to entering ministry. Ministry itself revealed the depths of pride, competitiveness, and lack of love I had in my heart, and the behaviors stemming from those sins most deeply affected my relationships with other pastors' wives at our church and my attitudes toward other churches in our city.

When I look back at that time in my life, the lack of grace in my heart toward others was astounding, but I also see that I didn't fully understand Christ's grace toward me. Without an understanding of the gospel, I was tangled up in what I call the goodness gospel: do all the right things and God will bless you. My spiritual health and fruit fully depended upon me rather than God.

This belief, of course, had a stunning effect on my ability to love others.

The thing I didn't yet understand about God is that we don't move toward him but rather he comes to us. He is a pursuer, a wooer, and an initiator. He waited until I had only fumes of self-effort left, and then he came. As I can see so clearly now, he knew I needed to understand my need. Only when I was aware of the depths of my sin could I understand the extent of his grace toward me.

During this time of my life, sitting across from two college girls one afternoon, I attempted to explain how God works by starting with "if": *If I obey him, then he will approve and act.* That one statement summed up everything I'd believed and everything that formed the foundation of my Christian life.

One of the girls respectfully responded, "Christine, I don't think that's right." And God came to me. In my heart, I knew instantly things were changing, that God wanted to show me some things about his true character, about grace.

I drove home, praying all the while, "God, I know nothing of grace. And I desperately need to know. *Show me.*"

He sent me to the book of Galatians, where I discovered that, because I am in Christ, I'm holy and righteous before God, and nothing I do or don't do can change my status before him. I also discovered that he's given me a Helper—the Holy Spirit—to help, guide, and convict me. I don't have to lead and convict myself but can depend fully on God to do so. My external behaviors are not what make me loved and approved by God; once I receive the love of God given through Jesus, his love will compel me to love him in return through obedience and devotion (2 Cor. 5:14–15).

As I received this amazing grace, I finally understood why Jesus said his yoke is easy and his burden is light (Matt. 11:30). He carries the burden of my sin, my ministry, *my life.* I am loved, so I am freed to love. The posture of the Christian is not performing in order to receive, which bears bitter fruits of pride and condemnation. The posture of the Christian is primarily receiving, because we're given something that wells up in us and compels us to joyfully respond.

Rivals Rather Than Teammates

You may be wondering, *What does this have to do with my relationships with other staff wives?*

Well, during that grace-less time of my life there was one staff wife in particular whom I struggled to love. Instead of loving her and seeing her as an invaluable gift in my life, I was envious of others' admiration of her. I felt I was in competition with her, longing to be seen as better or more spiritual than her. To my shame, I both subtly undercut her and attempted to outshine her.

Serving outside of an understanding of Christ's grace, in other words, has a compounding corporate effect. And despite what we tell ourselves, having poor relationships with other staff wives (and people in the church in general) is a significant issue, because it defies God's commands in Scripture and hinders the health of the entire body.

One example of how discord or disunity among leaders affects the church is found in Galatians 2:11–14:

> But when Cephas [Peter] came to Antioch, I [Paul] opposed him to his face, because he stood condemned. For before certain men came from James, he was eating with the Gentiles; but when they came he drew back and separated himself, fearing the circumcision party. And the rest of the Jews acted hypocritically along with him, so that even Barnabas was led astray by their hypocrisy. But when I saw that their conduct was not in step with the truth of the gospel, I said to Cephas before them all, "If you, though a Jew, live like a Gentile and not like a Jew, how can you force the Gentiles to live like Jews?"

Peter's brief turn away from the grace and truth he'd come to know in Christ and his return to an adherence to religious tradition caused him to seek approval and validation from certain people based upon what he did and didn't do. This led to sharp division between him and Paul and even further between Jews and Gentiles in the church.

When I read Galatians, I saw myself in Peter, and I saw the significance of my sin against my fellow pastor's wife. I was looking for validation from people rather than God based upon my abilities and performance, so when someone so different from me received validation for who she was and what she did, I couldn't stand it. I was looking for approval and appreciation from people rather than from God, so when I didn't get it and she did, I worked even harder, striving for self-glory.

My actions set us up as rivals rather than what we really were: sisters, fellow grace-recipients, and colaborers for the gospel.

This same undercurrent of competition can (and often does) affect our relationships with other churches in our community. If we're seeking self-glory instead of relating to other pastors, pastors' wives, and churches as colaborers and brothers and sisters, we keep them at arm's length out of wariness, competition, envy, and rivalry. Rather than multiplying our reach together and encouraging one another, we're instead territorial and remain siloed.

It doesn't have to be this way.

And for those who not only claim the name of Christ but proclaim the name of Christ, it *shouldn't* be this way.

Good relationships with other leaders must start with our fierce clinging to the gospel of grace. We simply cannot endure in ministry or engage our teammates well without knowing the love of God and his approval. We can't freely love and serve when we're looking to grow our own reputation. Our relational pride affects the church, the work of God in our community, and even our husband's relationships with the pastors and elders he serves alongside.

Rivalry instead of relationship, I believe, is a key strategy that the enemy uses among ministry wives. Why? Because the greatest resource for our thriving—aside from God and our husband—is one another.

So why are we reluctant to tap into this resource?

I believe there are two primary reasons.

Insecurity

What is your greatest insecurity? What is the one belief you have about yourself that you guard, protecting from the eyes of others? Perhaps it's a belief that you're lazy, unwanted, not good enough, weak, or too much. Whatever it is, it's likely general in nature rather than specific and is difficult to pinpoint because it's something that seems almost a part of who you are and how you approach life. Whatever it is, it speaks with a tone of shame—and it's not from the Lord.

Here are a few questions to help you pinpoint your greatest insecurity:

What do others do that makes you irrationally emotional or angry?

What are you afraid someone will recognize and point out in you?

What response toward you are you afraid would paralyze and cripple you emotionally?

Those are the self-protective fears that stand guard around your insecurities.

About a year ago, I was really struggling with a specific relationship I had with a woman in our church. She often directly voiced her thoughts to me about me, my husband, and the church. Eventually, I started taking over for her mentally and emotionally, seeing everything through her eyes and imagining her (negative) thoughts in every scenario.

God nudged me to consider why my response to her was quick irritation, and I discovered it was because of my greatest insecurity. What frightens me most, the lie that my self-protective fears most closely guard, the lie I most quickly believe is this: *I am a disappointment.*

Though she wasn't directly saying so, I received her words as a confirmation that I was disappointing not only her but everyone else in our church.

I saw how I consistently acted from this specific place of insecurity: I went down at the slightest whiff of critique. I retreated from anyone who disagreed with me. I closed off from others whenever I felt I'd disappointed them or *might possibly* have disappointed them.

Acknowledging our insecurities is important because, as ministry wives, we tend to lead and serve from a place of protection around that insecurity. If I fear I'm a disappointment to people, I'll go overboard in serving them so that I'll be approved of, or at least will keep the criticism at bay. I'll compare myself to other women, trying to surpass them.

That's why I asked you to think about your greatest insecurity—because in guarding ourselves from that insecurity being realized or confirmed, we often sin.

But what else does insecurity do? It causes us to hold ourselves back from others. It makes us protect and work and earn validation. We run around begging for affirmation and praise. Everything we do is for this, and we get angry, frustrated, and depressed when we don't get it.

Let's apply this to our relationships with other pastors' wives. For most of us, the picture we hold in our heads of a perfect pastor's wife is the greatest insecurity-maker there is! We think we're the only one who hasn't yet achieved perfect pastor's wife status, so when we look to the side at the experienced pastor's wife or the dynamic pastor's wife or the sweet pastor's wife or the beautiful pastor's wife or the gifted-in-a-certain-way pastor's wife, we then look at ourselves and believe we're no match for her. This woman who is meant to be a sister and colaborer instead becomes someone from whom we hide our questions, weaknesses, or struggles. We'd never reveal our imperfections and ask for her companionship in ministry.

See how quickly division, isolation, and assumptions rear their ugly heads on the back of insecurity? And that just feeds our insecurities even more.

The answer to this problem, of course, is daily rooting ourselves in the gospel. When we live from the security of being a beloved daughter of God, we remember we have a Father who loves and cares for us. We have his ear, his delight, and his approval.

The gospel takes away the need for us to earn validation from others or to cover over our weaknesses. Rather than leading from our insecurities, we can lead from our belovedness. We remember we're not intended to please people but are bondservants of Christ (Gal. 1:10). We don't have to hide our weaknesses for fear that we'll disappoint people, because God says he shows his power in our weaknesses (2 Cor. 12:9). The gospel affords us connection and love, for we then love others as he has loved us (1 John 4:19).

Henri Nouwen says it so well:

> That's where ministry starts, because your freedom is anchored in claiming your belovedness. That allows you to go into this world and touch people, heal them, speak with them, and make them aware that they are beloved, chosen, and blessed. When you discover your belovedness by God, you see the belovedness of other people and call that forth. It's an incredible mystery of God's love that the more you know how deeply you are loved, the more you will see how deeply your sisters and your brothers in the human family are loved.[1]

Expectations

We don't just hold insecurities that affect our relationships with other pastors' wives. We also hold unspoken expectations of them.

Whereas the demand of our insecurities is, "I need something from you, and if you don't give it, I won't feel loved," the demand of our expectations is, "I want something from you, and if you don't give it, I won't love you." With insecurities, we don't believe we're given grace. With expectations, we don't give grace to our sisters.

And, as evidenced by my struggle with my fellow pastor's wife, our insecurities and expectations work in tandem. They are two different sides of the same coin, both displaying a lack of understanding of Christ's gospel of grace.

What expectations do you hold for your fellow pastors' wives, whether in your own church or at other churches in your area?

Some pastors' wives expect they should be best friends with or be mentored by older pastors' wives. Some expect that other pastors' wives should engage in ministry in similar ways to them and have similar personalities, giftings, or time commitments.

Here's where I confess, once again, that I write from personal knowledge and experience. When we first started in ministry, I had unrealistic expectations of the senior pastor and his wife. Although she worked full-time and was raising teenagers, I felt sure she would take me under her wing and help me. In later years, I had expectations of other staff wives—that they should be like me and care about the things I care about. Now that my husband is the lead pastor, because my greatest insecurity is that I'm a disappointment, sometimes I worry that I don't meet the expectations of other elder and staff wives.

These expectations have only served to hinder my relationships with other pastors' wives, not help me connect with them.

Paul speaks a strong word to us as we consider how we can love one another and serve together in ministry. Although he refers to differences in religious observance, we could easily insert our differences in gifts and service.

> Who are you to pass judgment on the servant of another? It is before his own master that he stands or falls. And he will be upheld, for the Lord is able to make him stand.
>
> One person esteems one day as better than another, while another esteems all days alike. Each one should be fully convinced in his own mind. The one who observes the day, observes it in honor of the Lord. The one who eats, eats in honor of the Lord, since he gives thanks to God, while the one who abstains, abstains in honor of the Lord and gives thanks to God. For none of us lives to himself, and none of us dies to himself. For if we live, we live to the Lord, and if we die, we die to the Lord. So then, whether we live or whether we die, we are the Lord's. For to this end Christ died and lived again, that he might be Lord both of the dead and of the living.
>
> Why do you pass judgment on your brother? Or you, why do you despise your brother? For we will all stand before the judgment seat of God; for it is written,

"As I live, says the Lord, every knee shall bow to me,
    and every tongue shall confess to God."

So then each of us will give an account of himself to God.

Therefore let us not pass judgment on one another any longer, but rather decide never to put a stumbling block or hindrance in the way of a brother. (Rom. 14:4–13)

According to Paul, we have no grounds for expectations according to our *personal preferences*.

The gospel of grace allows for differences in the ways we serve God in ministry. In fact, he created us to be different from one another, and we're called to work together with our unique gifts, not separate from one another because we're not alike. Unity rather than uniformity is the goal for the church, and we lead the way in how we relate to our fellow leaders.

With your fellow pastors' wives, acknowledge and recognize how God is calling and using them. Consider: Are you placing an expectation on them that God hasn't? How would you feel if they had those same expectations of you? Remember Paul's exhortation that each person lives by faith as unto the Lord. They will give account only to God for how they live. Don't judge others who minister differently but rather trust God to lead your sister.

In the same way, trust that God will lead and use you.

So do not let what you regard as good be spoken of as evil. For the kingdom of God is not a matter of eating and drinking but of righteousness and peace and joy in the Holy Spirit. Whoever thus serves Christ is acceptable to God and approved by men. (vv. 16–18)

Don't believe the lie that what makes you different from your fellow pastor's wife says something negative about you. God has called you to something unique and good as well. Focus on what God wants for you, because you will one day stand accountable to him.

Paul has told us what *not* to do, but he also tells us what *to do*: "So then let us pursue what makes for peace and for mutual upbuilding" (v. 19).

In other words, we don't just leave one another to our own gifts and callings and passions, as if to say, "You be faithful there, and I'll be faithful here." Rather, we upbuild. We point out to others how God is using them. We celebrate how God is using them. We seek to bless, encourage, and empower.

And I would say this is especially important when we're serving on a team. My husband and I decided long ago that we would always speak about those with whom we serve with great respect. We would point out their gifts and strengths to others. We would express thanks to them personally but also in front of others. We would always support, always build up. We would receive their feedback and correction, and we'd keep short accounts with one another.

In other words, we'd work as if we're connected to a whole body and not just act as an individual part.

What happens when we release others of our expectations? We find that others and their perspectives are gifts to us. Henri Nouwen continues:

> To forgive other people for being able to give you only a little love—that's a hard discipline. To keep asking others for forgiveness because you can give only a little love—that's a hard discipline, too. It hurts to say to your children, to your wife or your husband, to your friends, that you cannot give them all that you would like to give. Still, that is where community starts to be created, when we come together in a forgiving and undemanding way.
>
> This is where celebration, the second discipline of community, comes in. If you can forgive that another person cannot give you what only God can give, then you can celebrate that person's gift. Then you can see the love that person is giving you as a reflection of God's great unconditional love. "Love one another because I have loved you first." When we have known that first love, we can see the love that comes to us from people as the reflection of that. We can celebrate that and say, "Wow, that's beautiful!"[2]

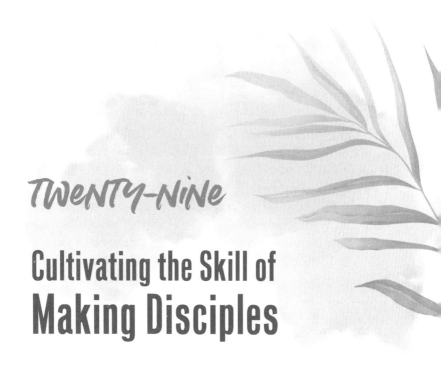

TWENTY-NINE

Cultivating the Skill of
Making Disciples

What is the most impactful ministry you can give your time and energy to within the church?

Teaching a Bible study?

Hosting groups or events in your home?

Leading a ministry team?

Being involved in local or global missions?

This isn't a question just for the pastor's wife. Everyone who desires to impact lives with the gospel should consider what's important in terms of ministry.

Kyle and I began asking this question early in ministry when we were overwhelmed with opportunities, people, and other people's opinions about what we should do with our best time, energy, and resources. As many do, we naturally gravitated toward big events with dynamic speakers and powerful worship that drove big attendance numbers. However, after a few years of this, we wondered if life change was actually happening among the students we were ministering to, and we began reconsidering our approach.

We discovered that the most impactful ministry is not a heavily guarded secret. In fact, Scripture clearly points to one strategy in and above all others: "Go therefore and make disciples of all nations, baptizing them in the name of the Father and of the Son and of the Holy Spirit, teaching them to observe all that I have commanded you" (Matt. 28:19–20).

We reoriented the entire structure of our ministry and eventually planted our current church around one thing: making disciples. Whatever program we created or community event we were involved in, whether teaching a Bible study, hosting groups in our home, or being involved in missions—all we did, we decided, would be an avenue for sharing the gospel and going deeper with a few at a time, helping them grow in their faith and experiencing growth in our own faith at the same time.

And decades later, I'm happy to report: discipleship is a plan that God blesses.

Because it's the plan he wrote for us.

The Biblical Model for Discipleship

As Timothy began his pastoral ministry, Paul told him where his focus should rest: "And the things you have heard from me among many witnesses, commit these to faithful men who will be able to teach others also" (2 Tim. 2:2 NKJV).

Paul essentially told Timothy that in order to fulfill his calling in ministry, he needed to think and act like a teacher. Notice the baton of faith passing from person to person in Paul's instructions and how many generations of teachers and learners there were: Paul taught Timothy, Timothy taught other people, and then those folks taught others. Paul's command involved four generations of gospel transmission and life change. We could say, then, that Timothy was not just to think like a teacher but as a teacher of teachers or trainer of teachers.

What Paul described is discipleship: reproducing reproducers, being a multiplier of the faith.

This model is exactly how Jesus himself structured his ministry while on earth. Consider: Jesus's task was to save all people from their sins, and not just to do the work of saving but also to tell people how they could be saved. "How then will they call on him in whom they have not believed? And how are they to believe in him of whom they have never heard? And how are they to hear without someone preaching?" (Rom. 10:14).

In other words, Jesus's very life was a message that needed spreading throughout the world, across language and generational barriers—a monumental task.

How did Jesus do it?

If it were up to you, how would you do it?

If I wanted to spread a life-altering message throughout the world and make it available to future generations, I'd likely choose for Jesus to walk the earth during this current day. He'd have access to social media, air travel, and the internet. He could rent out stadiums and draw the masses with incredible speakers and celebrity endorsements.

But that's not what God did. He sent his Son before even the printing press was invented, and he planned for his birth to happen in a small, overlooked town in the Middle East. Jesus didn't make any sort of splash; in fact,

> he had no form or majesty that we should look at him,
>   and no beauty that we should desire him.
> He was despised and rejected by men,
>   a man of sorrows and acquainted with grief;
> and as one from whom men hide their faces
>   he was despised, and we esteemed him not. (Isa. 53:2–3)

Not only was Jesus the antithesis of a celebrity spokesperson but he also waited until he was thirty years old to begin his public ministry, leaving him three years to complete in full the work for which he came.

Again, we must consider how Jesus structured his ministry so that his renown—and thus his invitation to salvation—would rocket around the world for centuries to come. Here's what he did: he chose twelve men to accompany him as he traveled and preached in a small region of the world, and out of those twelve, he chose to spend the bulk of his time with three: James, Peter, and John. They lived, traveled, ate meals, and ministered together. The disciples observed Jesus in action and were eventually invited to join him in his healing and teaching ministry.

Why was that his strategy?

Jesus knew close proximity and time with his disciples would lead to their internalization of who he was as a person and what he cared about. They came to know his mission and message in such depth that it became their own. Jesus multiplied himself through the twelve disciples, leaving them to continue the work after his resurrection and ascension.

This is exactly what Paul was trying to communicate to Timothy: that in his ministry Timothy should think in terms of multiplication rather than addition. With addition as a ministry focus, you must gather crowds, trying to get as many people as you can to hear the message. However, just because a crowd of people hears a message doesn't mean they internalize or respond to it.

A multiplier, on the other hand, spends concentrated time with one or two people for a season, teaching them the ways of Jesus and helping them apply his truth and ways to their lives. The impact is deep and wide—life-changing. They can then, as they continue to grow, take what they know and deeply impact one or two others, and so on.

Combined with the verse before—"You then, my child, be strengthened by the grace that is in Christ Jesus" (2 Tim. 2:1)—Paul provided Timothy his job description and what he was to give himself to, whether he was preparing a sermon or counseling a congregant or cleaning up the bagels and coffee. He was to remember how he received the faith and be strengthened in that remembrance of grace (v. 1), and he was to transmit the faith to others (v. 2).

This is our job description as well, no matter where we are in life: working outside the home, raising children, or facing old age. It's our job description when we're the pastor's wife and, if ever our husband

leaves the ministry, a congregant in the church. It's our job description no matter the personality, skills, or spiritual gifts God has given
us. We're to make disciples of all nations, sharing the gospel with
unbelievers and helping believers grow in their faith.

The Bible commands and describes discipleship in this way:

- We, like the Israelites, are blessed by God to be a blessing to
  others (Gen. 12:1–2).
- We're to convert and then help others grow in understanding
  of who Jesus is and in Christlikeness (Matt. 28:18–20).
- More mature women in the church are to give encouragement through advice to younger women in the things of daily
  life as a means of strengthening the church and community
  (Titus 2:3–5).
- We're not only to teach but to share our very lives in relationships with others (1 Thess. 2:8).
- We're to be concerned about the spiritual well-being of the
  people around us, helping them grow toward maturity in
  Christ (Col. 1:28–29).

Discipleship cannot be done solely through preaching or programs.
It happens primarily in life-on-life relationships. So why don't we see
it happening more in our churches?

Because it's hard work. We'd much rather it happen in large-
group, low-commitment settings.

Because it's a process that is often messy and difficult.

Because most people don't feel capable of leading someone else
along in the process.

Because if we challenge someone to grow, we have to be living it
ourselves.

Because we worry we're disqualified because we weren't discipled
ourselves.

Because we know we don't have it all together.[1]

But none of those reasons should keep us from committing to God's great commission. Otherwise, we'll miss out on some of the most incredible blessings of our life!

A Picture of Discipleship

One such blessing in my life is my relationship with Emily. I knew I loved Emily the second I met her.

She first attended our church when it was a Sunday evening Bible study in our home. Not knowing anyone or what she might be getting into, she told me later that before she came in, she stood at the door of our home for several minutes, considering whether she should knock or run. As she debated, Kyle opened the door and invited her in, making the decision for her.

Now it's clear that God made the decision. He brought her to our church for me. And he brought her to our church for her. About six months after Emily came in our door that first time, I asked her if she would like to meet with me weekly in a discipleship relationship. Happily, she accepted. I was glad because the Lord had given me a special affection for her and had shown me how similar our stories were.

At first, however, Emily resisted going below the surface of her heart. She was afraid I would see her weaknesses, doubts, and resentments. I knew what she was doing, because I'm just like her. She and I are "good girls," exhausted from spinning plates and afraid that others will think less of us if we stop and receive God's grace.

Once each week we met up at a local bagel shop before she headed to her teaching job. We studied the book of Galatians together and, gradually, the walls came down between us, and we got into the nitty-gritty of spiritual growth. She told me how much she desired to be married and how she struggled to trust God in her singleness. I told her about the pressures I felt to keep it all together and how I struggled to trust God instead of fear, worry, and control. We looked to Scripture for direction and hope. Somewhere and somehow in the midst of those mornings, God grew and knit our hearts together.

After a time, we knew our discipleship relationship had come to an end. I commissioned her to take what she had learned and disciple a younger woman, which she did. And I asked someone else to join me in a discipleship relationship.

The following summer, I read Scripture in Emily's wedding. Oh, how I rejoiced when she met the man who would become her husband! At her bridal shower, I sat next to a college student from our church who was preparing to graduate and move into the adult world. She was ready, and I knew that because she'd been meeting with Emily in a discipleship relationship throughout her fourth year at the local university. I watched with joy as they interacted with each other, silently thanking God for how he had used discipleship in all three of our lives.

I'm convinced that investment in this kind of relationship is the most impactful ministry we can give ourselves: "an intentional relationship in which we walk alongside other disciples in order to encourage, equip, and challenge one another in love to grow toward maturity in Christ."[2]

Discipleship is intentional and includes regular meetings together, purposeful conversation, and commitment. It's relational, not something done in groups or classes. It's mutual and involves walking alongside another, not a teacher-student type of relationship but rather a reciprocal process of encouragement. It's spiritual: maturity in Christ is the goal, not merely instilling knowledge. And as we've already discovered, the nature of discipleship is not production but rather reproduction. We disciple one with the intention they'll be able to go and teach others also.

Qualifications for a Disciple-Maker

Titus 2:3–5 says,

> Similarly, teach the older women to live in a way that honors God. They must not slander others or be heavy drinkers. Instead, they should teach others what is good. These older women must train the younger

women to love their husbands and their children, to live wisely and be pure, to work in their homes, to do good, and to be submissive to their husbands. Then they will not bring shame on the word of God. (NLT)

No woman likes to think of herself as an *old* woman, but our "oldness" qualifies us for disciple-making. Every woman is an older woman to someone, whether it's a college student or a high school student or a mom of teenagers or a mom of young ones. The Bible calls each of us to teach a younger woman in the faith.

Most of us fit the description of an older woman, but there is a second implication of "oldness" in the Titus 2 verse: the older woman is not just chronologically old but *spiritually* old, or mature. Spiritual maturity doesn't imply that she is perfect, has life totally figured out, or has the Bible memorized from beginning to end. If that were so, none of us would qualify. But it does mean that she is F.A.T.:

Faithful. A discipler is a disciple herself, increasingly dependent upon the Lord (Matt. 4:19–20).

Available. She is available to the Holy Spirit and trusts him to work through her as she leads others. She knows growth and heart change don't happen because of her but rather because of the Holy Spirit (Titus 3:5–6).

Teachable. She is teachable, seeking to grow, responding to the Spirit's conviction, and willing to receive from the one she disciples (1 Pet. 5:5).

As a pastor's wife, you have countless opportunities to incorporate discipleship into your life. Perhaps as you're reading this chapter, you already have a neighbor, younger woman, or friend you met at the gym in mind for whom God has given you a special affection and with whom you'd like to share your faith or study the Bible.

Invite her to join you for coffee or lunch. Get to know her more and share more about yourself. At the end of your time together, invite her to a deeper, more intentional relationship, saying something like, "I have really enjoyed getting to know you. I wonder if you might be interested in meeting with me each week to study the Word, pray, and challenge each other in our walks with Christ." Ask her to consider and pray about it, and tell her that you will follow up with her by phone, text, or in person in a few days. Most women immediately recognize the value of being in deep relationship with a mentor and jump at the opportunity for discipleship.

And the blessing will be yours as well!

PART 7

You
AND
Your
Finish
Line

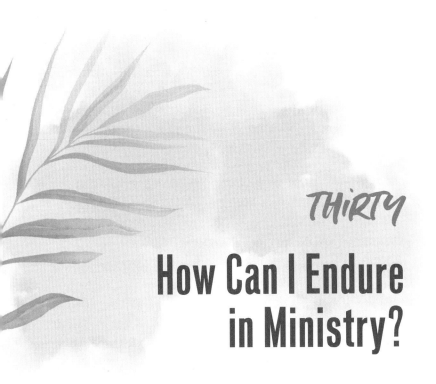

THIRTY

How Can I Endure in Ministry?

Recently Kyle and I went for a walk on a trail close to our home, and as it often does, our conversation turned toward ministry—not the minutiae of our tasks and meetings but rather the culmination of our years of serving the Lord side by side.

At one point, Kyle turned to me and asked, "Do you think what we've given our life to—this life of ministry—has been worth it?"

I hesitated, a telling reflection of the prior weeks and months, and tears sprang to my eyes. The uncertainty and difficulty we'd faced, so present and tangible in my mind, had caused me to shrink back. I wasn't sure I could see past the pain.

But then I thought about if, by God's grace, I could grow old and have a moment of clarity and hindsight on my deathbed. I imagined myself preparing to join my Savior in eternity and reflecting on a life lived, however imperfectly, for Jesus and others. With my finish line in sight, I knew if I were then asked, "Was everything you endured worth it?" I'd be able to confidently say, "Absolutely. There is no other life I'd rather have lived."

Walking with Kyle on the trail, I considered the gap between what is now and what could be then. Will we make it to the end? How do I endure until the finish line, and not just endure but flourish? How do I resist the siren song that offers me a way out of all that ministry requires? Will it always be this hard? Will I always be this tired?

Will it all be worth it?

The Mindset Needed to Endure in Ministry

Have you ever had a word spoken to you that changed the course of your life?

In high school I was in band, and at the end of each spring, we voted as students on who would be the next year's section leaders. Two or three students were chosen per instrument to guide their section, teach new students how to march, and communicate between our band directors and fellow students.

One afternoon of my freshman year, after the voting was done, I was sitting in the band hall after school, doing homework while I waited for my ride. My band director, Mr. Johnson, came up to me and said, "You were voted flute section sergeant by your peers."

I stared at him, dumbfounded. I was a freshman, our section could vote for anyone they wanted, and they'd chosen me? I think Mr. Johnson could tell I was somewhat overwhelmed and confused, because I hadn't even considered the possibility of this happening. Then he said words to me that I'll never forget: "Christine, you are a leader."

No one had ever called me a leader before, and I was an extremely shy kid, so I'd never considered myself one. But Mr. Johnson's words rang in my ears. He believed this vote was correct. He believed I could do it. Unwittingly, Mr. Johnson defined something for me that day that has continued to shape my life.

When I read 2 Timothy, I think of Mr. Johnson.

In his letter to Timothy, the apostle Paul did something similar for Timothy that Mr. Johnson did for me. He defined for Timothy what was true about him. He pointed out to Timothy how God had gifted him because, in a sense, Timothy was also a shy freshman, unsure he was in the right role as a pastor and uncertain he had what it took to endure. We know from Paul's words that Timothy had come to tears about it all and had expressed timidity, fear, and perhaps some anxiety about the calling God had placed on his life.

Paul exhorted Timothy to persevere, explaining to him what it would take to endure in his calling. Because it's not enough to know your calling; you must also think carefully about how you'll fulfill and complete it.

When Mr. Johnson said he thought I was a leader, he defined something about me. But at that time, I had no idea what being a leader entailed; I had never been tested in an actual leadership position. I hadn't faced the challenges and obstacles a leader faces. I hadn't honed my leadership skills. I hadn't learned to think and process difficult situations as a leader must. Learning to be a leader only comes from experience.

Paul, as a good mentor to Timothy, explained from his own experience what sort of mindset he'd need to endure in the ministry.

As pastors' wives, we aren't the ones standing in the pulpit, proclaiming the gospel like Timothy or like our husband. But we're each ministers of the gospel, and we're called by God to use our gifts to bring glory to him and to benefit others. Paul's words to Timothy, then, are applicable for us as we seek to be ministers of Christ in this world, whether it's at home with children or among our neighbors and coworkers or as a servant in the church. Paul tells us what it will take for us to faithfully serve others—all the way to the end.

Paul's exhortation of Timothy are the words in Scripture I return to over and over when I find myself unsure if I can continue, specifically 2 Timothy 2:1–7:

> You then, my child, be strengthened by the grace that is in Christ Jesus, and what you have heard from me in the presence of many witnesses entrust to faithful men, who will be able to teach others also. Share in suffering as a good soldier of Christ Jesus. No soldier gets entangled

in civilian pursuits, since his aim is to please the one who enlisted him. An athlete is not crowned unless he competes according to the rules. It is the hard-working farmer who ought to have the first share of the crops. Think over what I say, for the Lord will give you understanding in everything.

He begins with, "You then," which connects this passage to what he addressed in the first part of the letter: Timothy's tears and timidity. Timothy has suffered because of his calling.

Whether it's bearing the burden of a friend or faithfully loving and serving those who oppose us, any ministry, any outward service in the name of Jesus is going to involve tears and feelings of inadequacy. We often think it should be the opposite—that discovering who God has made us to be and doing what he's called us to do will result in an obstacle-free life. In fact, it's quite the opposite. Remember, Timothy was not tearful or timid because he hadn't yet started in his ministry. He'd experienced the difficulties of gospel-oriented work and was unsure if he had what it took to see it through to the end.

In light of Timothy's fears, Paul gave him three commands as to how Timothy should carry out his calling. Notably, they are all commands that involve the mind. In other words, Paul gave Timothy the perspective and mindset he needed to put on in order to serve Christ to the very end.

This must be our perspective and mindset too.

Be Strengthened by Grace

Paul told Timothy to think about "the grace that is in Christ Jesus" (v. 1) so that he would be strengthened for ministry. This is an imperative, which means it's a command, but it's also a passive imperative. Timothy's strength and confidence for ministry are not to be drummed up from within himself but rather found in grace, specifically the grace given to him in Christ.

How does grace strengthen us?

To answer that question, we can look for clues in what Paul told Timothy in 2 Timothy 1. He said that God had specifically gifted Timothy, and that this calling had been confirmed by others through the laying on of hands (2 Tim 1:6). *This gift came to him through grace.*

He said that Timothy had been saved by the power of God in order that God might fulfill his purposes through Timothy (vv. 8–9). *This salvation and purpose came to him through grace.*

And finally, Paul said that the Holy Spirit had made his home in Timothy. The same power that saved and called him was with him, helping him with what he'd been entrusted (v. 14). *The Holy Spirit came to him by grace.*

We often think of grace as the forgiveness of sins, and it most certainly is that, but grace is so much more than that. Grace is also about the riches of Christ we've been given. Something's been taken away by Christ's grace—our sin—while other things have been *added* to us in Christ's grace. We've been gifted with the presence of God dwelling in us—the Holy Spirit. We've been gifted with the righteousness of Christ, meaning we are forever right with God and cannot do anything to remove ourselves from righteous standing before God. And we've been gifted with supernatural gifts in order to serve others.

Thinking about what's been added to us in Christ's grace breeds confidence in us that is not based upon our own abilities but rather based on who God is and what he does in and through people.

That's why Paul exhorted Timothy to think about grace, because as he went about his daily ministry and came up against his own inabilities, he could then find his source of confidence and power in God's abilities.

What a beautiful truth for us all as we fulfill the calling God has placed on our life with the gifts he's given us, because often—always?—what God asks us to do is beyond our abilities.

Navigating life and church relationships as a pastor's wife at times feels impossible. When we experience discouragement or recognize we must obey a biblical command that seems too difficult given our circumstance—*love your enemies, pray for your enemies*—we often look first at ourselves: our abilities (we don't have enough), the logistics (where will the resources come from?), our kids (what will become of them?), and our circumstances (how will we get from Point A to

Point B?). Looking at ourselves doesn't make us bold. It only makes us feel weak.

But when we face a task or command that's beyond our abilities and instead look at God's ability and his willingness to share that strength with us, we become bold.

When I was a child, I was very shy, and when adults spoke to me, I'd hide behind my mom and peer out at them from a safe distance. I'd let her do all the talking for me. I felt protected and strong because of her presence.

This is what it means to be strengthened in grace. We go with the full power and protection of our Father. We can be bold in action and ministry when we know that the effectiveness of the ministry is not dependent on us.

Share in Suffering

Notice Paul exhorted Timothy to focus on making disciples and transmitting the faith to others. Because we've already touched on discipleship in the last chapter, I won't belabor the point, but the command is there, and it's notable that enduring in ministry involves discipleship. I personally have found that investing in discipleship relationships refreshes my soul for ministry, challenges me to grow in my own walk with Christ, and puts me in close proximity to the Spirit's work in others. In other words, though it's painstaking, we experience reward when we're in one-on-one relationships with others. God blesses his own plan, which is marked out for us in Matthew 28:19: "Go therefore and make disciples."

Immediately following his command to make disciples, Paul told Timothy that he should expect pastoral ministry to involve suffering.

No matter what we do, serving others entails suffering. We should never expect that it will be easy. Paul told Timothy that he was to carry his share of suffering, to "share in suffering as a good soldier of Christ Jesus" (2 Tim. 2:3). I find that to be interesting wording—that the suffering is a *shared* suffering. What kind of suffering did Paul prepare Timothy to encounter, and who would it be shared by?

Paul gave Timothy three pictures to help him understand what sort of suffering is entailed in ministry to others. Let's look at them one at a time.

First, Paul pointed to a good soldier. Timothy should, Paul said, think of himself as a good soldier whose commander is Jesus Christ.

What sort of suffering does a soldier endure in the midst of battle? Every battle and every war involve hardship. During the Civil War, soldiers withstood winter without proper clothing. In World War I, they slept in trenches and endured weather, rats, and sickness. During World War II, soldiers endured seemingly hopeless circumstances at Normandy Beach.

A soldier expects, prepares for, trains for, and endures hardship. What enables good soldiers to continually sacrifice themselves for others and withstand such hardship?

Most of them would name two things: their company of fellow soldiers and their commander. A soldier never goes into battle alone. They work together with others, and each one is trained not to think of self but to think and act according to a greater goal. Consider what we say to soldiers when they return from war or when we see them on Veterans Day: "Thank you for your service." We thank them because we know ultimately their service has been for something greater than themselves. It's been for us and for our country's good.

Similarly, the company's goal as stated by the commander becomes the individual's goal and purpose. A good soldier wants to please their commander, and they accomplish this by aligning their will with the commander's orders.

By using this picture, Paul communicated to Timothy that he was sharing in the sufferings of Christ for the sake of the greater good—for others. In other words, there's a mutual suffering among us so that the gospel can go forth among us. Elsewhere, Paul says that his suffering was for others, and theirs for him, so that they could all have the gospel and the comfort of Christ (2 Cor. 1:5–10).

But we also share in the sufferings of Christ *because of* and *for* Christ. Our "aim" in doing so "is to please the one who enlisted [us]" (2 Tim. 2:4). We're only willing to endure suffering as soldiers in order to please Christ when we know what Christ has suffered for our sake—that he is a commander who has already done what he's asking us to do.

There are many stories of great military leaders who were beloved because they were willing to endure what their soldiers were suffering, whether it was poor living conditions or difficult food rationing. Their soldiers would do anything for these commanders, even putting their lives on the line for their leader.

Paul told Timothy (and he tells us) that he should consider himself this type of soldier, one who has a commander who sacrificed and suffered for him and is worthy of any hardship he must face, for it brings God glory.

Second, Paul pointed to an athlete. Regarding what sort of suffering Timothy could expect in ministry, Paul said, "An athlete is not crowned unless he competes according to the rules" (v. 5).

Paul used a Greek word that indicates a professional athlete as opposed to an amateur. We could use this word today to describe someone like Serena Williams or any other well-known athlete competing at the top of their game in their particular sport.

What sort of suffering does someone like Serena Williams endure?

It's the suffering of self-discipline. If she wants to win, she must refrain from certain things and choose others that further her game. Are there times Serena Williams wants to sit on the couch and eat bonbons instead of training? I'm sure there are. But she trains so that she can keep her body in shape and her muscle memory in top form. She knows that if she eases up on her strict regimen, she won't win.

Paul uses this exact imagery in 1 Corinthians 9:24–27 to describe his own ministry:

> Do you not know that in a race all the runners run, but only one receives the prize? So run that you may obtain it. Every athlete exercises self-control in all things. They do it to receive a perishable wreath, but we an imperishable. So I do not run aimlessly; I do not box as one beating the air. But I discipline my body and keep it under control, lest after preaching to others I myself should be disqualified.

Paul says that ministry to others requires self-discipline. Without self-discipline, we disqualify ourselves. And if we're disqualified, we can't complete the race God has marked out for us. We can't cross the finish line or win the race.

The goal of all who serve Jesus is to cross the finish line and be crowned with an imperishable wreath of victory. The wreath is the crown of righteousness—God bestowing the same honor upon us that he has bestowed upon his Son. The highlight of the crowning ceremony will certainly be hearing God say to us, "Well done, good and faithful servant. . . . Enter into the joy of your master" (Matt. 25:23). What better goal could we have before us as we run the race God has marked out for us?

So we run. Today, tomorrow, and the next day. We're faithful in the small things. We "play by the rules," as Paul says, meaning we don't play by our own rules. We submit to God's rules, God's ways, just as a soccer player doesn't use their hands to move the ball down the pitch.

Our tendency as Christians is to think in terms of the "big game." We think, *When I finally get there* (wherever "there" is), *when I get such-and-such role or opportunity, when I magically become spiritually mature,* then *I'll be consistent in studying the Word,* then *I'll really give my life to serving the Lord,* then *finally I'll no longer struggle.*

But an athlete doesn't show up at the match and suddenly have muscle memory. In the Christian life and in vocational ministry, there are no magic formulas or shortcuts to faithfulness. That's why Paul says we must think like an athlete—because an athlete knows that the training is the most important part. The everyday, unseen, small things they do in order to be ready for the big game is what makes them an athlete. And that's why Paul told Timothy he should think like an athlete: he must be willing to suffer in the form of self-discipline in order to be found faithful and to endure to the end.

Finally, Paul pointed to the farmer. Paul told Timothy that he should be willing to suffer as a farmer suffers (2 Tim. 2:6).

My brother-in-law is a farmer, and I find it fascinating to talk to him about his work. Depending on the time of year, he may be tilling the soil, planting seeds, dealing with weeds, or even cleaning out the fertilizer tank. His work is backbreaking, messy, and most of all uncertain. He can do all the work he can do, but the weather plays a huge role in the fruitfulness of his crop. A few years ago, a hurricane came through just before harvest, dumping tons of water on his land and erasing his crop.

The suffering of the farmer is in the waiting and the uncertainty: Will all the work pay off? Will the crop come? The crop, remember, is their livelihood.

So when Paul told Timothy to take on the mindset of a hardworking farmer, he was telling him to faithfully serve with the end always in mind.

What is the end? Farmers will get the first share of the crops. They will eat the fruit of their labor. Think of that—they'll tangibly taste and see the results of their work!

So much of what Paul talked about with Timothy involves unseen labor. Soldiers serve in a distant land, fighting in battle. Athletes train in a private facility day in and day out. Farmers plant seeds hidden away in the ground and pray for rain in its proper time.

Do you see the common theme rising to the surface? Each of these types of people—the soldier, the athlete, the farmer—has a goal in mind: a commander pleased, a race won, a crop harvested and enjoyed. A soldier's pinning ceremony, a place on the podium at the stadium, tangible crops to see and taste and enjoy. At the end, all the invisible sacrifice becomes visible and seen. The people are rewarded, and I imagine every single one of them would, in that moment, do it all again.

Paul told Timothy, and he's telling us, that a life of faith and service is consistent, hard work over a long period of time. It requires sacrifice, because Christ sacrificed. It requires self-discipline. It requires us giving up trying to get quick results and immediate payoffs.

But Paul also draws our eyes to the finish line: all that we do in the name of Christ will be rewarded by Christ himself!

Look to the Finish Line

Do you need strength, dear pastor's wife? Do you wonder how you will endure? Are you weary and discouraged?

Be strengthened today by Christ's grace.

As we consider his grace toward us, we see that Christ fought for us as a soldier looks to please his commander. Christ suffered by denying himself and taking up his cross so we could be with God. And he did everything with a view of what was to come: "for the joy that was set before him [he] endured the cross, despising the shame" (Heb. 12:2).

Why must we consider this grace?

"Consider him who endured from sinners such hostility against himself, so that you may not grow weary or fainthearted" (v. 3).

This grace Christ so lavishly pours out on us shows us he is worthy of any hardship we must endure in ministry. And when we consider him, as we wonder, *Is this life of service, sacrifice, and obedience worth it?* we can affirm without hesitation, *Yes, because Jesus is our Finish Line.*

He is worth it all.

An Invitation

I pray this book has been a source of encouragement, empathy, and practical help that enables you to persevere for a lifetime in the ministry God has given you. I know, however, that while I've covered many topics relevant to our experiences as pastors' wives, there is so much more we could talk about together.

That's why I've created an online space meant to complement this book: HowtoThriveasaPastorsWife.com. I invite you to join me there to continue the conversation and enjoy additional resources that may help you navigate a specific situation, encourage you when you're feeling disheartened, and help you thrive rather than just survive in your role.

On this website, you'll find:

- Additional recommended resources I've found helpful in my own ministry.
- Questions to ponder as you reflect on what you've read in this book.
- Questions to guide a discussion about ministry for you and your husband.
- Podcast episodes in which I interview pastors and pastors' wives.

- Blog posts and articles about an array of subjects related to ministry.
- A reading guide for groups of pastors' wives or staff and elders' wives to discuss this book together.
- Free printables.

Join me at HowtoThriveasaPastorsWife.com today!

Acknowledgments

One of my greatest joys in life is encouraging and supporting other pastors' wives. Because of this passion, I've known for many years I wanted to write this book, so I'm thankful to my publisher, Baker Books, and especially Rebekah Guzman, for sensing a need for this type of resource and giving me the opportunity to write it.

Andrew Wolgemuth, I couldn't ask for a better agent. Thank you for your support, ideas, and help in navigating the publishing world.

Thank you, Jamie Chavez, for making my words shine.

Haley Roland, thank you for creating the architectural drawings. They are an essential (and beautiful) part of the book.

As I wrote this book, I thought often about the churches and pastors' wives that have formed my understanding of the Lord, Scripture, the church, and what it means to be a pastor's wife: First Baptist Church in Tyler, Texas, Gary and Alta Faye Fenton, John and Melinda Wheat, Central Church in College Station, Texas, Chris and Peggy Osborne, Kevin and Lynlee Ueckert, Tim and Jamie Skaggs, Jeremy and Niki Lewis, Mike and Terri Wilkinson, Oren and Cindy Martin, Matt and Shannon Blackwell, Ben and Shauna Pilgreen, Kathy Litton, Lori McDaniel, Adam and Lacy Nuckols, and Jenn Atwell.

I'm forever changed by the church we planted, Charlottesville Community Church, and her wonderful, godly people, especially those with whom we've served in leadership: Bill and Tara Bray, Louis and Claire DeLaura, Matt and Jessica Brumbelow, Tim and Karen Roland, Jack and Libby Taggart, Maegan Clark, John and Christina Bowman, and Joseph and Allison Holm.

As a pastor's wife, I don't take for granted that I have dear friends in our church, those who have helped me navigate my role, challenged me when I've needed it, loved me well, and helped me grow spiritually: Amy, Marylyn, Susan, Maegan, Jessica, Libby, Amanda, Ros, Valeri, and Tara.

To my parents, Larry and Dana Fleming, thank you for your support of Kyle and me and our calling from our seminary days on, even when it meant we moved the grandchildren far away.

My boys celebrate all my writing milestones with me and consistently ask how the writing is coming along. They also gave me ideas and feedback for the section on raising kids in ministry, for which I'm grateful. I couldn't ask for better young men to mother. Will, Reese, and Luke, I love you.

Kyle, you know more than anyone else what it's taken to write this book, not only the actual writing process but also the years and experiences we've walked through together to get where we are. If I've offered anything helpful or wise in this book, you alone know how hard-won it was. Knowing what I know now and what our shared calling would entail, I would not hesitate to go back and marry you all over again. I love our sacred space in the cabana.

To my Lord Jesus Christ, you are the reason for everything I do. May my life be a fragrant offering to you.

Notes

Chapter 2 You Are Anchored

1. Paul David Tripp, *Instruments in the Redeemer's Hands: People in Need of Change Helping People in Need of Change* (Phillipsburg, NJ: P&R Publishing, 2002), 138.

Chapter 3 You Are Called and Gifted

1. R. C. Sproul, *Who Is the Holy Spirit?* (Sanford, FL: Reformation Trust, 2012), 32.
2. Jeff Iorg, "Attributing Your Material," March 28, 2021, personal email to author.

Chapter 4 You Are Human

1. I think counseling for ministry couples can be very helpful. Kyle and I continue to occasionally see the counselor I mention here whenever we need a "checkup." Some churches help offset counseling costs for their ministry staff, and some denominations provide free, confidential counseling. In other words, don't let cost stop you from getting the help or perspective you need. It's worth the investment in your marriage and your well-being.

Chapter 5 Cultivating the Skill of Knowing When to Say Yes and When to Say No (Part 1)

1. Corrie ten Boom, *The Hiding Place* (Grand Rapids: Chosen Books, 2006), 206.

Chapter 8 What No One Else Sees, He Sees

1. Andy Crouch, *Strong and Weak: Embracing a Life of Love, Risk, and True Flourishing* (Downers Grove, IL: InterVarsity Press, 2016), 40, 35.
2. Crouch, *Strong and Weak*, 117.
3. Lifeway Research, "Pastor Spouse Research Study: Survey of 722 American Pastor Spouses," Lifeway Research, September 2017, http://lifewayresearch.com/wp-con tent/uploads/2017/09/Pastor-Spouse-Research-Report-Sept-2017.pdf.
4. Crouch, *Strong and Weak*, 138.
5. Crouch, *Strong and Weak*, 141.

Chapter 9 Cultivating the Skill of Lament

1. Mark Vroegop, *Dark Clouds, Deep Mercy: Discovering the Grace of Lament* (Wheaton, IL: Crossway, 2019), 26.

2. Stacey Gleddiesmith, "My God, My God, Why?: Understanding the Lament Psalms," *Reformed Worship*, June 2010, www.reformedworship.org/article/june-2010/my-god-my-god-why.

3. Vroegop, *Dark Clouds, Deep Mercy*, 43.

Chapter 10 What No One Else Knows, He Knows

1. I don't mean privately as in "speaking about it to no one." God gives gifts of grace in our life: people we can potentially share and process with, such as our spouse, companions who understand (as mentioned in the previous chapter), friends (discussed in future chapters), and godly counselors.

Chapter 13 Locating Your Marriage

1. Jani Ortlund, *Help! I'm Married to My Pastor* (Wheaton, IL: Crossway, 2021), 15.

Chapter 19 Seasons of Ministry with Younger Children

1. Interview with Barnabas Piper on June 17, 2014.

Chapter 20 Seasons of Ministry with Older Children

1. Interview with Barnabas Piper on June 17, 2014.

2. Interview with Barnabas Piper.

Chapter 23 Navigating Difficulties in Friendship

1. I'm passionate about the subject of adult friendship, so much so that I wrote an entire book about it: *Messy Beautiful Friendship: Finding and Nurturing Deep and Lasting Relationships* (Grand Rapids: Baker Books, 2017).

Chapter 25 Sunday Mornings (and Beyond)

1. Tim Keller, *Galatians for You* (Surrey, England: The Good Book Company, 2013), 143.

Chapter 28 Relating to Other Pastors' Wives at Your Church

1. Henri Nouwen, "From Solitude to Community to Ministry," *Leadership Journal*, April 1, 1995, https://www.christianitytoday.com/pastors/1995/spring/5l280.html.

2. Nouwen, "From Solitude to Community to Ministry."

Chapter 29 Cultivating the Skill of Making Disciples

1. These thoughts are based on Greg Ogden's book *Transforming Discipleship: Making Disciples a Few at a Time* (Downers Grove, IL: InterVarsity, 2003).

2. Ogden, *Transforming Discipleship*, 129.

CHRISTINE HOOVER has been a pastor's wife for over two decades, serving alongside her husband, Kyle, in various churches, sized small to large, and in church planting. In addition to serving in their church, Christine is a podcaster (*By Faith*), Bible teacher, and author of several books, including *The Church Planting Wife*, and a Bible study, *Seek First the Kingdom*. Christine and her family live in Charlottesville, Virginia. Find her at her home online, www.christinehoover.net.

Connect with Christine

www.christinehoover.net

⬜ ChristineHoover98
⬜ ChristineHoover
⬜ Author Christine Hoover

How do we live this life by faith? In her podcast *By Faith*, Christine Hoover asks this big picture question by getting into the details and daily lives of her guests: men and women who are walking forward by faith.

More Resources for Pastors' Wives

Head to www.howtothriveasapastorswife.com
for additional resources to help you thrive in ministry.
Listen to interviews, read articles, and check out
Christine's recommended resources
to help you run your ministry race.

More from Christine Hoover